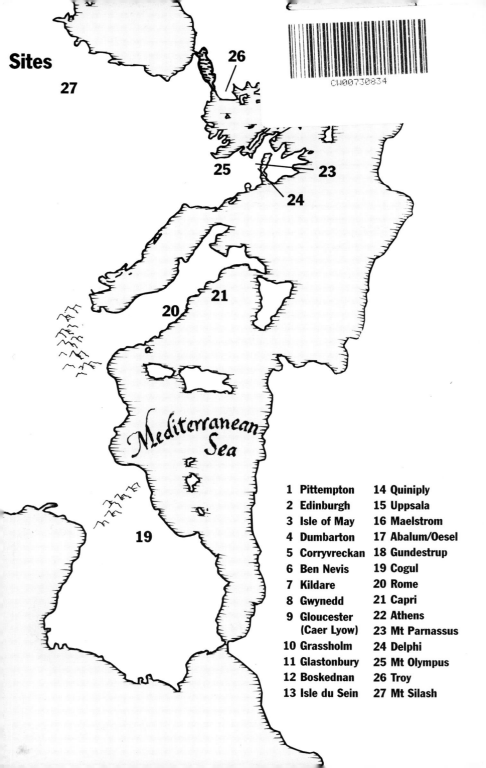

**Sites**

27

26

25    23

24

21

20

*Mediterranean Sea*

19

| | |
|---|---|
| 1 Pittempton | 14 Quiniply |
| 2 Edinburgh | 15 Uppsala |
| 3 Isle of May | 16 Maelstrom |
| 4 Dumbarton | 17 Abalum/Oesel |
| 5 Corryvreckan | 18 Gundestrup |
| 6 Ben Nevis | 19 Cogul |
| 7 Kildare | 20 Rome |
| 8 Gwynedd | 21 Capri |
| 9 Gloucester (Caer Lyow) | 22 Athens |
| 10 Grassholm | 23 Mt Parnassus |
| 11 Glastonbury | 24 Delphi |
| 12 Boskednan | 25 Mt Olympus |
| 13 Isle du Sein | 26 Troy |
| | 27 Mt Silash |

# The Quest for the Nine Maidens

# The Quest for the Nine Maidens

STUART McHARDY

**Luath** Press Limited

EDINBURGH

www.luath.co.uk

First Published 2003

The paper used in this book is recyclable. It is made from low chlorine pulps produced in a low energy, low emission manner from renewable forests.

Printed and bound by
Cromwell Press, Trowbridge

Typeset in Sabon 10.5 by Sarah Crozier, Nantes

This book is dedicated to my wife Sandra Davidson
in whom, for me, the Goddess walks.

# Acknowledgements

Thanks are due to Jennie Renton, Helen Rayner and Justin Crozier for their skills and tolerance. My friends and colleagues in the Pictish Arts Society deserve credit for tolerating my obsession with the Nine Maidens over many years and I would like to thank all the students at Edinburgh University's Centre for Continuing Education who have helped me clarify my thinking while teaching several courses on the subject.

# Contents

# NINE MAIDENS – APPROXIMATE TIME LINES

| | CELTIC | NORSE | GREEK | SHAMANIC | OTHER |
|---|---|---|---|---|---|
| **20th CENTURY** | Abernethy<br>St. Brides Well<br>Rites<br>Sanquhar<br>Closure of<br>Piltempton Well | | | 9 Daughters of<br>Solboni<br>9 Daughters of<br>Ulgan | Raratonga<br>'Nus Tarian' |
| **16th CENTURY**<br>**REFORMATION** | | | | | Kogi 9 Mamas<br>Venezuela |
| **1000 AD** | Corryvreckan<br>Tales<br>Cerridwen<br>Pictish 9s<br>Maidens of<br>Avalon | Thidrandi<br>Volva<br>Heimdall<br>Menglod<br>Valkyries | | | Kikuyu 9 Sisters |
| **BIRTH**<br>**OF CHRIST** | | | | | |
| **500 BC**<br>**GREEK**<br>**CIVILISATION** | | Mill Maidens | Apollo and<br>Muses | | |
| **3200 BC**<br>**EGYPTIAN**<br>**EMPIRE** | | | | | Ennead of<br>Heliopolis |
| **3500 BC**<br>**MEGALITHIC**<br>**PERIOD** | 9 Maidens<br>Stone Circles | | | | |
| **15000 BC** | | | | | Cogul Dancing<br>Maidens |

# Introduction

THE THEME OF THIS BOOK is the existence of groups of nine women who were involved in healing, prophecy, weather-working and shape-shifting over a remarkably wide geographical and chronological spread. Their activities suggest they are best understood as priestesses. Such groups of nine women exist in the mythologies of different cultures. Although I first came across them in my native Scotland, the search for the Nine Maidens has involved material from many countries, some of them well beyond Europe, and from many time periods. What is clear is that the Nine Maidens functioned as discrete sacred groups within many different societies, some of which have the Nine Maidens at the centre of their mythologies. Mythology can be understood as the process which gives rise to the earliest stories we have in which attempt to explain life in ways that are meaningful and understandable.

## Mother Goddess

Because so many of the different traditions of the Nine Maidens associate them with single goddess figures, I believe that the religion they followed was based on Mother Goddess worship. This is generally thought to have been the earliest form of human religion and the fact that we all have mothers is probably why humans developed the idea of a supreme Mother Goddess, giver of life and death. The material from Scotland, where our story starts, can be interpreted as showing the existence of an ancient dual Goddess figure portrayed in terms of light and dark, summer and winter, life and death. This duality is much more like the eastern concept of Yin and Yang than the Christian idea of the battle between good and evil. In Scottish tradition the goddess of Winter, the Hag, actually becomes the golden goddess of Summer, the Bride. Bride, the pagan precursor of St Bridget, was common

3: The author should, probably, cite Graves for this reference.

to both Britain and Ireland and is associated in different traditions with the Nine Maidens.

In other traditions we see the Nine Maidens associated with the Norse goddesses Menglod and Ran, the Welsh Cerridwen, in Siberian shamanic traditions, in a foundation legend from Kenya and of course in the case of the Muses we see them associated with a god, Apollo. While it is impossible to prove that the association with such male god figures came later than their link to the Goddess, we can be sure that their association with a single female figure is very ancient indeed. As we shall see, the earliest reference to the Nine Maidens is in a Magdelanian cave-painting from Catalonia which is perhaps as much as 17,000 years old. This painting clearly shows some sort of fertility rite. The association with the Mother Goddess might account for the existence of many Nine Maidens Wells in Scotland, water itself being the fount of all life. In one particular case, at Sanquhar in southern Scotland, nine white stones were still being placed in St Bride's Well in the 20th century, in memory of the Nine Maidens.

## Languages

The stories of the Nine Maidens survive in many lands in many tongues. I begin with a short place poem in Scots, still the first spoken language of at least a third of Scotland's population. Many of the versions of the tale in Scotland must have been told earlier in Celtic languages: Scottish Gaelic, Irish, Welsh and British (also known as Brythonic or Old Welsh; the language of the ancient Britons). Britain at the time the Romans left is generally thought to have been populated by a variety of tribes who spoke two basic different kinds of Celtic language. Early Roman sources tell us that some at least of these peoples were in regular, if sporadic, alliance with Germanic-speaking tribes and it is possible that some of these latter groups were also based in the British Isles. The Celtic-speaking peoples came to speak what we now know as Scottish and Irish Gaelic (Q-Celtic), and Welsh (P-Celtic). The tendency in the recent past has been to see these

1: More pertinently in Heimdal, who had nine mothers.

2: In Greek mythology, it is very clear that the link of the Nine with the Goddess came before a link with the God because the former clearly predates the latter and the Nine were her priestesses. (See Graves).

languages as defining people into separate ethnic groups but the fact that the British Nine Maidens stories survive language shifts – into Scots and English from originally Celtic roots – shows the danger of placing too much faith in language. The notion of ethnic purity is a racist concept and the fact that we know people were travelling the whole of the eastern Atlantic littoral on a regular basis as far back as 5,000 years ago shows that contact between widely-spread societies has been going on a long time. One example should illustrate this. Many scholars have noted the great flowering of Gaelic culture within the Lordship of the Isles in the mediaeval period. The culture of this society, which clearly saw itself as different from the emerging Scottish nation state, was in fact a combination of what is known as Gall-Gael traditions and learning. The Gall here is Norse, the Gael Celtic. Attempting to separate these two intertwined strands is an exercise in futility – like many human societies, the mixture of ideas, languages, social mores and skills emanating from different sources made the combination more vibrant and dynamic.

## Geographical Spread

We can be sure that Scotland and Ireland were still primarily inhabited by people living in tribes before and after the Romans controlled England. However, in other areas society was much more centralised and from the city states of Greece we have early written sources that tell us of the best known Nine Maidens group, the Muses. As I will show, there are grounds for seeing their god Apollo as originating in the north, but this is not of primary importance. What is important is that the extensive Greek sources show many Muse-like groups associated with mountain tops, springs and islands, just like many other Nine Maidens groups. Within the Celtic-speaking areas of Europe in Roman times we have references from Scotland, Ireland, Wales and a striking early literary reference to a group of druidesses in Brittany. These are not the only such groups in Breton tradition but the source gives them a definite historical provenance. It is

1: Thrace ?

striking that the Nine Maidens also play a considerable role in the
British Arthurian tales, which, though surviving in Welsh,
probably originated amongst the British-speaking tribes of south
and central Scotland.

Within the Germanic-speaking world, and we should
remember that contact between Britain and Scandinavia goes
back to megalithic times, we have various groups like the
Valkyries and the Nine Maidens of the Mill, who clearly belong
to the realm of mythology, while Icelandic traditions carry
memories of what appear to have been practising pagan
priestesses. I have also considered material from Eastern Europe,
Africa and South America which focuses on groups of nine
women. This remarkable spread is paralleled by the magic use of
nine which seems to have been almost universal. While the link
between the use of the number in ritual and the actual and
mythological groups of nine women is unclear, it seems more than
likely that there is some underlying concept common to both.

## Literature and Oral Transmission

Western education has for a long time been based almost
exclusively on literacy. Even in the modern world, literacy is not
universal and just a few hundred years ago only a tiny minority
of human beings were able to read. For the majority of our time
on this planet all knowledge was passed on by word of mouth
and example. Scholars have tended to be dismissive of oral
transmission and many historians consider a lack of written
sources an insuperable problem in understanding the past. This
attitude is now being severely challenged. There are examples
from Australian aboriginal tradition that show the capacity of
oral transmission to carry accurate data for period of tens of
thousands of years. If the indigenous peoples of Australia were
capable of this why should we think our own ancestors any
different? I believe that there is much we can learn from
traditional tales, particularly when used critically in conjunction
with other disciplines such as archaeology and place-name studies.

2: The Triunate Goddess of Girl, Woman and Hag X 3.
On the Matrd of Ireland, variously noted as 3 or 9.

Note: Much of what has been written up to now has been written by others,
and better.

The importance of oral tradition is that it arises from particular functions in tribal societies that mean it has to be treated conservatively. Ideas survive because of their relevance to society and in pre-literate societies ideas have to be transmitted from tongue to ear, or by practical example. The vast amounts of mythological and genealogical data that are common to most tribal societies were like the lore of healing, birthing, cooking, food-gathering, planting, hunting and all other activities – passed down from generation to generation by word of mouth. This meant that people passing on and receiving such information used their memories differently than we do. We write things down to remember them; oral societies with mnemonic skills have no need of that. Therefore, myth, legend and folklore may retain a great deal of knowledge from a very long stretch of the human story on this planet.

Most of what I have gathered about the Nine Maidens groups has of course been taken from written sources, but these sources vary in how close the original writers were to actual oral tradition. In Norway and Iceland the pagan religion lasted till circa 1000 AD and there we have clear representations of Nine Maidens as pagan priestesses. In Scotland we have early medieval sources presenting the Nine Maidens as a particular group of Pictish saints. In Greece the various nine-woman groups on islands and hilltops, though occurring in written sources, were also based on earlier oral traditions. What is also often forgotten is that most early European literature and thus history was created by monks who had a vested interest in obscuring, hiding or ignoring non-Christian traditions. In this light it is perhaps a testament to the tenacity of both pagan belief and the institution of the Nine Maidens that we have so many written sources for them. It is a fact that oral tradition continues after literacy is introduced, which may account for some of the survivals. What I hope I prove here beyond dispute is that groups of nine women, involved in some kind of sacral behaviour, and regularly associated with a single male figure, were known over a very wide geographical area for a remarkable length of time. What I hope I

1: And yet it was the same Irish Monks who wrote down the great Irish tales; although it is true that while keeping the tales they seemed to manage to excise any details of the old gods and their religion.

prove here beyond dispute is that groups of nine women, involved in some kind of sacral behaviour, and associated with both significant single male figures and a range of goddesses, were known over a very wide geographical area for a remarkable length of time. Although I have been investigating the Nine Maidens for a great many years, it is likely I have just scratched the surface. Further research into the Nine Maidens may lead to a new interpretation of the history of the human species. History has too long been written by men, for men and about men. The stories of the Nine Maidens tell us there is much more.

*Stuart McHardy*
Edinburgh
2003

# CHAPTER I

# Dragonslayer

THE STIMULUS for this book was a simple four-line poem, in Scots (a Germanic language distinct from English), which survived in oral tradition as the explanation of Martin's Stane, a Pictish symbol stone just to the north of Dundee. This is the poem as recorded in Andrew Jervise's *Epitaphs and Inscriptions*:

> It was tempit at Pittempton
> Draggelt at Badragon
> Stricken at Strikemartin
> An killt at Martin's Stane. (p206)

The story is of a group of nine sisters whose father farmed at Pittempton, and who were all killed by a dragon that appeared at the nearby well. The stone with which the tale is associated is known as Martin's Stane and stands in the shadow of the Sidlaw Hills, a few miles north of Dundee. Here is the story as told by Jervise in *The Land of the Lindsays*:

> Long, long ago, the farmer of Pittempton had nine pretty daughters. One day their father thirsted for a drink from his favourite well, which was in a marsh at a short distance from the house. The fairest of the nine eagerly obeyed her father's wish by running to the spring. Not returning within a reasonable time, a second went in quest of her sister. She too tarried so long that another volunteered, when the same result happened to her and to five other sisters in succession. At last the ninth sister went to the spring, and there, to her horror, beheld, among the bulrushes, the dead bodies of her sisters guarded by a dragon! Before she was able to escape, she too fell into the grasp of the monster, but not until her cries had brought people to the spot. Amongst these was her lover, named Martin who, after a long struggle with the

*I : I've seen the stone, it is inside a wrought iron fence and depicts a mounted man with, if I remember correctly, a lance.*

dragon which was carried on from Pittempton to Balkello, succeeded in conquering the monster. It is told that Martin's sweetheart died from injuries or fright; and the legend adds that in consequence of this tragedy, the spring at Pittempton was named the Nine Maidens' Well, and the sculptured stone at Strathmartine, also St Martin's Stane at Balkello, were erected by the inhabitants to commemorate the event. (p162)

Balkello is the name of a farm near where the stone stands. Local tradition has it that the original name of Kirkton of Strathmartine was Strikemartin, as in the poem, and the name has been reported as surviving in a medieval charter. There are also records attesting to the existence of a piece of another Pictish symbol stone with the figure of a man with a great club over his shoulder which used to be built into the wall of a nearby barn. It has been suggested that there were at one time around a dozen Pictish symbol stones in the immediate area but only three have survived. Such a collection of stones, like the collections elsewhere at Meigle and St Vigean's, both less than 20 miles from Dundee, suggests an important, probably religious, foundation in the area. It is a striking fact that many of the Pictish symbol stones have been found in conjunction with Christian church or burial sites. Given that it was common practice for the early Church to take over the temples of earlier worship, it is likely that somewhere around Strathmartine there was a major pagan religious centre.

Suggestions have been made that the story is merely an attempt to explain the meaning of the symbols on Martin's Stane. Until very recently the symbols on the Pictish stones were thought to be indecipherable, but modern research is now coming up with plausible, if not definitive, interpretations linking them with dynastic symbols or totems and with pagan worship. Some of the symbols – adder, deer, cauldron, lunate crescents – have strong associations with ancient Goddess figures, both within the myths and legends of the Celtic-speaking peoples and in other European mythologies. The representative and decorative styles of the Pictish symbol stones are now recognised to have had a seminal influence on what has become known as Late Insular Celtic art, perhaps best known in *The Book of Kells*. This great masterpiece of illuminated manuscript art was begun on the Scottish holy island of Iona, if not by Pictish artists, then by artists who had been trained by the Picts.

The place-names in the Martin's Stane rhyme suggest there is more to this story than the pursuit and killing of a maiden-eating dragon, fascinating as that might be. Pittempton, on the northern outskirts of the city of Dundee, appears to be a name combining the Pictish place name *Pit* with the Gaelic *tiompan* – a drum – giving 'the place of the drum'. Drums have been used in sacred rituals in societies all over the world for as far back as memory can tell and so the name supports the idea of some sort of cult or religious practice taking place in the immediate area. *Baldragon* is Gaelic for 'the township of the dragon', or 'hero', either of which meanings could be seen as deriving from the story.

Although the verse is in Scots, the place-names are in Celtic tongues – Pictish and Gaelic. Pictish was probably, like the ancestor of modern Welsh, a P-Celtic language, while Gaelic, like Irish, is a Q-Celtic language. The P-Celtic and Q-Celtic forms are thought to have developed separately from the same root. One of the most obvious differences is that where the Q-Celtic has a hard 'c' sound, the P-Celtic languages have a 'p' sound. Compare the Welsh Owen Map Owen with the Gaelic Ewen Mac Ewen – with *map* and *mac* both meaning 'son of'. Linguists believe that in the east of Scotland, Pictish was the native language before being superseded by Gaelic between the 9th and 12th centuries after which Gaelic was in turn replaced by Scots. Some scholars think that there were several languages spoken by the Picts and have even theorised that this might have included some form of Germanic language. It is possible that the story of Martin's Stane existed in both Pictish and Gaelic before being told in Scots, but as we have no written record of it before the 18th century it is impossible to confirm. Recent research in Australia suggests that the oral transmission of information, through storytelling, can preserve real events for as long as 20,000 years (McHardy, 1997,

*And what of the lowland Scots? Might they have spoken Brythonic Celtic? (The Britons)*

17

p107) so we cannot rule out the possibility of the story being as old as the carvings on the stone, if not older. The date of the stone is generally given as 8th century, but this depends on comparing Pictish material with art styles outside Scotland, and as yet we have no conclusive way of pinpointing the date.

The meaning of the story has been interpreted in various ways, one suggestion I was given being that it was told to mark the end of whatever 'power' was associated with the stone. In 1985 I saw the stone being dowsed to see if there was a ley line running under it. Ley lines are thought to be a kind of weak electro-magnetic current that link together ancient sites, many of the sites being of greatly differing ages. What ley lines signify is unclear. The dowser, American artist Marianna Lines, used a cut crystal ball on a revolving mount fixed to a silver chain which she held between the fingers of her right hand, palm upwards. As soon as she got close to the stone, the ball began to whirl furiously and the silver chain flew up to the horizontal. It was remarkable seeing the ball rotate at high speed on the end of this rigid chain. The conclusion of the people there that day was that there was certainly some kind of power in evidence. It is worth noting that the Chinese name for what we call ley lines is 'dragon lines'. In his *Hill of the Dragon*, P Newman makes the point that stories of dragons eating maidens are often references to the passing away of the old pagan religion in the face of Christianity.

The fame of the Nine Maidens Well at Pittempton lasted a long time. As late as the 1870s, according to Jervise, the farmer at Pittempton, fed up with people tramping across his fields to visit the well every first of May, the ancient feast day of Beltane, covered it over with a sheet of iron which he then buried. This survival of ritual activity at the well is remarkable testimony to the tenacity of the Nine Maidens story and the continuity of the ancient pilgrimage tradition to Scotland's holy wells. People had been visiting this site for over a thousand years. Jervise, in *Epitaphs and Inscriptions*, writes:

... people still alive in the parish recall of nine graves, near the east

I There was no well apparent when I visited the stone in the 1970's. But then I was not looking for one. Does the stone commemorate the place where the dragon died or the well? Where it died.

1: And what a dragon

end of the old kirk of Strathmartine, which were pointed out as those of the nine sisters; and it is uniformly added that the stone with two serpents carved upon it [now in Dundee Museum] stood at the head of one of these mounds. I am also told that no interments have been made in these graves during the recollection of the oldest inhabitants. (p206)

This last remark suggests a considerable degree of veneration by the locals for these nine graves. As interest grows in the beliefs and habits of our distant ancestors it is possible that the Nine Maidens Well might one day be re-opened. After all, the statue of a dragon, inspired by the story, now stands in the centre of Dundee.

When I first began to look into the Nine Maidens story I soon came across other material referring to them close to Martin's Stane. Just over Balluderon hill to the north lies the head of Glen Ogilvy, nestling in the Sidlaw Hills. It is said that in the 6th century St Donald lived here with his nine daughters, following a simple life of contemplation and prayer, eating one plain meal of barley bread and water a day. St Donald was widely respected for his holiness and when he died, his daughters carried on as before. Their reputation for holiness grew, and, in time came to the attention of the King at Abernethy. The story tells us that the king was called Garnard (a Garnard appears in the Pictish king list, virtually the only Pictish document to have survived down the centuries). We are told Garnard invited the nine maidens to come and live in his capital at Abernethy, which is about 20 miles to the south-south-west of Martin's Stane and on the south bank of the river Tay. There he built them an oratory and there they lived out their days in sanctity and prayer. It is said that they were buried at the foot of a large oak. This is how Bellenden translates Henry Boece's Latin *History and Chronicle of Scotland*:

> ... thir holy virginis, efter deceis of thair fader, come to Garnard, King of Pichtis, desiring sum place quhare thay micht leif ain solitar life, in the honour of God. Garnard condescendit to thair desiris and

gaif thaim ane hous in Abernethy, with certane rentis to be takin up
of the nixt landis, to thair sustentation quhare thay leiffit ane devote
life and war buryit at the rute of ane aik, quhilk is haldin yit in great
veneration amang the pepil. (ix ch xxxv)

Burial at the foot of a large oak has clear pagan connotations.
The story of this group of Nine Maidens was told in a series of
carved wood panels in an oratory on the north side of the
churchyard in Abernethy, which survived till they were destroyed
in the mindless vandalism that accompanied the Reformation in
Scotland in the 16th century. In a version of the story from early
sources quoted in the *Aberdeen Breviary* (1854) the Nine
Maidens are said to have come, at the request of the Pictish king,
to Abernethy from Ireland with St Brigid, a major figure in the
Celtic Church derived from the older goddess Bride, common to
Scotland, Ireland and certain parts of England. These Nine
Maidens crop up in a variety of early Scottish sources as a group
of Pictish saints. They are unusual within Christian tradition in
that they are known collectively. Forbes, in his *Kalendars of
Scottish Saints*, has this in the entry for 18 July:

> ... the nine virgine dochters to S. Donewalde under King Eugenius VII
> in Scotland... He spent a most holy life in the Glen of Ogilvy, and on
> his death his daughters entered the monastery at Abernethy... (p420)

The names of three of them survive, Mayota or Mazota, Fincana
and Fyndoca. All three are referred to as individual saints. In
Stewart's *Metrical Version of Boece*, written in the early 16th
century a few years after Boece's work appeared in Latin, he says
'The eldest hecht Mazota to her name /The secund sister callit
Fyncana;' (p329). St Mazota, sometimes also known as St
Mayoca, the eldest of the Nine Maidens, was commemorated on
22 December and had the parish of Drumoak, originally
Dalmaik, in Aberdeenshire, called after her. There was an old well
here called St Maik's Well and it is likely it too was a pilgrimage
well, visited at certain significant times of the pagan year.

Boece's history tells that one day in Glen Ogilvy, Mazota came to a field where geese were feeding on recently sown barley and charmed them into flying off and leaving the crop. This power over birds is reminiscent of the powers associated with goddesses and priestesses in many locations around the world and is told in Bellenden's translation of the *History and Chronicle of Scotland*:

> His [St Donald's] eldest daughter, Mayo, maid inhibition to the wild geese, to eat hir fader's corne, and thy obey hir holy monitions, and therefore, wild geese was never seen efftir on that ground... (p116)

This appears to be a reference to Mazota, and 22 December is the winter solstice, the shortest day of the year, a time of great importance in lands where the winter days are short and the weather is often severe. It has long been the time of great fire festivals which are believed to be the origin of the modern festivities of Christmas. The association with this date suggests not only antiquity but also that Mazota was a figure of some importance to the ancient peoples of Scotland. The Midwinter or Yule festivals of northern Europe celebrate the fact that from this time on the days grow longer, bringing the promise of the spring and summer to come. In countries where daylight lasts only a few hours at this time, midwinter has always been a time when people were in need of celebration. Within such festivities there was a strong undercurrent of supplication to the gods, or the Goddess, to carry on the turning of the seasons. The use of fire as a symbol of fertility and renewal continues to this day in Scotland, with the Burning of the Clavie at Burghhead, the whirling of fire-balls at Stonehaven and the Shetland festival of Up Helly Aa, when the festivities culminate in the burning of a replica of a viking longship. Other fertility rituals have survived with the decking of houses with boughs of evergreen trees and the hanging up of the once sacred mistletoe. Today's kisses under the mistletoe are probably a remnant of something much earthier in the distant past. Seasonal Affective Disorder Syndrome (SADS) is the modern term for depression due to the long periods of darkness in winter.

1: These fire-balls are reminiscent of the five wheels of fleece which were rolled down hills. Originally they contained the outgoing king and were part of an offering to the Sun, under the auspices of the Goddess's High Priestess.

Our ancestors seem to have realised that in the darkest months it is psychologically beneficial to have a major feast or festival celebrating the forthcoming return of the sun, and a pretty good excuse for a party.

St Fyncana had a church dedicated to her at Echt in Aberdeenshire and the parish of St Fink near Blairgowrie in Perthshire was supposedly named after her. Her name survives there in the place-name Chapelton of St Fink, where there are the remains of an ancient burial ground and a chapel. St Fyndoca is believed to have had a dedication at Dunblane and her name is also thought to have survived in the Perthshire parish of Findo Gask, where, according to the *Aberdeen Breviary*, she had founded a church. There are also references to a church dedicated to Fyndoca on the island of Innishail in Loch Awe in Argyll. F Marian McNeill in her marvellous exposition of Scottish folklore and folk belief, *The Silver Bough*, tells us:

> One of the Nine Maidens, St Fyndoca, erected a sanctuary on the lovely peaceful island of Innishail on Loch Awe, in the shadow of Ben Cruachan, and hither for centuries the clans of the adjoining territories – Campbells, MacArthurs, MacCalmans, MacCorkindales and others – brought their dead for burial. (1, p175)

JF Mackinlay stated, in his article 'Traces of the Cultus of the Nine Maidens' in the *Proceedings of the Society of Scottish Antiquaries* of 1905-6, that he believed all references and dedications to the Nine Maidens were in the east of Scotland, in the old counties of Perthshire, Forfarshire and Aberdeenshire, all within the ancient bounds of Pictland. In fact, Nine Maidens references are not limited to the Pictish area, or to Scotland, or even to the British Isles. Loch Awe itself is outside what is traditionally considered the Pictish area of Scotland. The MacArthur clan from this area claim descent from an ancestor who might have been the original of King Arthur. Arthurian legends contain a wealth of Nine Maidens connections. The generally accepted history of Scotland has Gaelic-speaking Scots coming into mainland Scotland not many miles from Loch Awe,

1. It was not just 'psychologically beneficial (although it no doubt was) it was a religious observance of great importance and integrally linked to the Calendar then in operation: a major Cardinal feast, as it were of the year. When the old year died in Greece the old King died

1: E. Sykes suggests that the Druids may have been pre-Celtic.

DRAGONSLAYER

around 500 AD. Whether or not this was the case, trading and cultural contacts over the Irish Sea were continuous from the Stone Age onwards – both ways. The motif of the Nine Maidens is very ancient and may date from the Stone Age, predating the arrival of the Celtic languages in the British Isles.

We have already travelled a fair distance from Martin's Stane and the association of the Nine Maidens with the oak tree at Abernethy suggests links with widespread pagan belief. The oak was widely venerated throughout the pagan societies of pre-Christian Europe and is often associated with that shadowy priesthood of the Celtic-speaking peoples, the druids. Oak groves were sites of ritual activity among both the Celtic- and Germanic-speaking tribal peoples of northern and western Europe. Place-name evidence has been utilised to locate a whole series of such sacred enclosures in ancient Scotland (Barrow, 1997). The association of the Nine Maidens in various tales with the oak, and the dragon, which, like the serpent, is associated with pagan worship, is highly significant, suggesting that the Nine Maidens are derived from pre-Christian times.

Several wells in Scotland were dedicated to the Nine Maidens, and some of these were the subject of particular rituals at specific times of the year. Even into the 20th century, young women were visiting Bride's Well at Sanquhar in south-west Scotland and placing nine white stones in it at Beltane, one of the great feast days of the tribal peoples of ancient Britain and beyond. The veneration of water is much older than the ritual of Christian baptism; within the old pagan religion it is conceivable that water could have been understood as the very life blood of the Mother Goddess – all life requires water, and she was the fount of all life.

In Scotland during the Reformation in the second half of the 16th century many of the new presbyteries are recorded as passing acts condemning a variety of rituals we now perceive as pagan, though then they were seen as 'Popish'. The village of Glamis, just a couple of miles from the foot of Glen Ogilvy and with its own Nine Maidens Well provides an example. Mackinlay, in *Ancient Church Dedications in Scotland*, says:

2. Dragon → Worm → Snake → Python worship (eg Athens and Erechtheous. Snakes were special to the Goddess. They were also used in Greek houses to predate on rodents.

23

he succeeded by historist or Twin (Graves: "The White Goddess")

> Even in the seventeenth century the fame of the oak at Abernethy was such that an enactment was passed by the Kirk Session of Glamis forbidding maidens to go to it on pilgrimage. (p16)

In parish after parish, acts or bye-laws were passed banning people from a whole range of activities including well and tree worship and the Beltane rites – and these acts had to be re-enforced for many years. The people hung on to the old ways, which have never been totally forgotten, and in the 1990s in Edinburgh, the annual Beltane fires were revived on Calton Hill. Calton is from Gaelic *calltunn*, 'hazel', which was a significant tree in traditional Scottish lore and the ceremonies on the hill now attract thousands of people every year. Perhaps this revival is symptomatic of people turning to the past to try and make sense of their lives in an increasingly impersonal and greed-dominated world where the pursuit of wealth has replaced spirituality for so many. Today's quest for spirituality and a sense of rootedness are perhaps all the stronger because we have for so long turned our backs on the past – telling ourselves that progress is an endless process – and thereby failing to realise that some human concepts and activities are themselves rooted in practices from the very dawn of time. Whatever the reason, Calton Hill, named for an ancient sacred tree and with strong links with the fairies, seems the perfect location for people to celebrate fertility just as their ancestors used to.

The dedications to the Nine Maidens at wells in such places as Cortachy, Finavon and Dundee in Angus, at Newburgh and Abernethy in Fife, at Tough and Pitsligo in Aberdeenshire and at Loch Tay and Murrayshall in Perthshire suggest that these collective saints were relatively popular in early Scotland. The name Ninewells, which crops up over a much wider area than ancient Pictland, could very well be a contraction of original Nine Maidens Wells. Some interpret the place-name Ninewells as meaning 'many wells'; others think the name derives from Ninian, the 5th century Christian cleric, who is said to have converted at least some of the Picts to the new religion. There is

1: In the case of Calton Hill, it could also be confused New Ageism and Tourism.

2: Nine Wells in Dundee at the 24 end of the H awkhill. There is also a pub in Dundee called the Nine Maidens.

strong case for at least some of the Ninewells having originally been Nine Maidens Wells. A further complication is that in Gaelic one word for maiden is *nighean*, pronounced 'nee-an'. If the motif of the Nine Maidens is as ancient as I suggest, it would be quite possible for the original meaning to become overlaid with similar sounding names, particularly if such names possessed their own associations with sanctity.

A well in Aberdeenshire has a story very similar to the story of Martin's Stane. A great Pictish warrior called Ochonochar, the ancestor of the modern family of Forbes, was called to the parish of Auchendoir in Aberdeenshire because a giant bear was terrorising the district. It had slaughtered Nine Maidens by the time he arrived and after a short, but bloody battle, Ochonochar killed the fearsome beast. The Nine Maidens Well here is at Logie on the river Don and at nearby Kildrummy there is the Nine Maidens' Green where tradition says the Nine Maidens are buried. There are reports that there was also a Pictish symbol stone there, but this has not survived. The name Forbes, in a piece of spurious local folk etymology, is said to have come from Ochonochar shouting 'For Bess', as he slew the bear, Bess having been his beloved among the slain Nine Maidens. This motif of the hero loving one of the Nine Maidens parallels the story of Martin's Stane.

Near Forfar, at Finavon (a Gaelic-derived name meaning 'the white water'), there was a chapel dedicated to the Nine Maidens. Jervise, in his *Lands of the Lindsays*, says that although some local people thought the Ninewell was a corruption of St Ninian's well:

> ... as the 'Nine virgin dochters of St Donewalde who lived as in a hermitage in the Glen of Ogilvy at Glamis' were canonised as the Nine Maidens, perhaps the fountain and the kirk had been inscribed to them. Like most of the primitive saints they were remarkable for industry and humility, and are said to have laboured the ground with their own hands and to have eaten only once a day, and then but barley bread and butter. (p162)

The common name for the church at Finavon among the locals was 'the kirk of Aikenhatt', a clear reference to the oak tree, and probably harking back to earlier pre-Christian traditions at the site. Nearby is Aberlemno, a site where there are several remarkable Pictish symbol stones, including one now thought to be a representation of the Battle of Dunnichen in AD 685, when the Picts destroyed an invading army of Angles from the northern English kingdom of Northumbria. A few miles west of Finavon at Cortachy, the Nine Maidens Well was renamed the Duchess Well by some local aristocrat indifferent to tradition. Mackinlay, in his *Ancient Church Dedications*, suggested that there was once a Nine Maidens altar in the kirk here.

Another Nine Maidens location exists at the far end of the Sidlaw range from Martin's Stane. Overlooking Strathmore just above Perth is Maidenwell on Parkside farm. This was previously the site of a 'wishing well', which usually is a reference to the sanctity of a particular well in the past; and it was named as Nynmaidenwell in a document from 1536. Even in the 20th century it was called Nynwell.

One particular story from Perthshire demonstrates a Nine Maidens theme we will return to, the location of Nine Maidens groups on an island. At the village of Kenmore at the east end of Loch Tay there was for many years a fair known as the Feill nam Bann Naomh – the Fair of the Holy Women, nuns who were said to have lived on the crannog or artificial island now known as Priory Island but formerly Eilean nam Bann Naohm – the Island of the Holy Women. The story has been interpreted as a Nine Maidens story, perhaps originally due to an early reference to the fair being held on the Nine Virgins' Day (see Chapter 5). However many aspects of this tradition fit precisely with recurring motifs in the Nine Maidens stories:

> The 'Holy Women's Fair' used to be opened with great state and ceremony. We have it from one who, in his youth, less than fifty years ago, was a delighted spectator of the scene, that the ground officer,

1: Again this suggestion that the Picts inhabited Scotland down to the borders of England / Northumberland. Historically the Picts were said to hold sway north of the Forth, while the area to the 26 south, ie the Lowlands and Borders were held by the Brythonic Celts. The Picts are not usually considered to be Celtic as very little is known of them.

carrying a drawn sword, walked in state, preceded by a piper, and followed by a dozen or so young men walking in regular order, each carrying a halbert. On the procession arriving at the cross or centre of the market the official proclaimed the 'Peace of the Fair'. Once this was cried there was perfect liberty. The debtor could not be taken up for his debt, or the reiver for his theft; even the fugitive bondman was free from arrest on that day, and though his owner met him in the fair he dared neither 'chase nor tak him', nor apprehend him on his way home. And besides there was unrestricted free trade, while at other times only those privileged to sell could do so. (Maclean p45)

This echoes what we know of ancient pagan festivals and some medieval fairs, during which the normal rules of society would be suspended. This was also a regular occurrence at the ancient feast days of Beltane and Samhain, midwinter and midsummer. The Holy Women of the island in Loch Tay are said to have been based at Inchadney, a mile or so down river, before moving to the island. This church was dedicated to the Nine Maidens. The nuns were said to have been driven off the island after a scandal involving a young man. In several cases folklore traditions of nunneries in Scotland cannot be substantiated through charters or other written documents; this suggests to me that such traditions might derive from pre-Christian female religious groups.

Other dedications to the Nine Maidens in Scotland support the contention that at the very least there was some sort of Nine Maidens cult. A grouping of nine women, often associated with a single male, is a motif that occurs over a wide geographic and chronological spread which suggests the saintly Nine Maidens of the Pictish Church were in fact a Christianised version of a grouping that stems from the very far past. Their connections with wells and other aspects of the Nine Maidens stories underline links with ancient traditions and worship of the past.

That the saintly Nine Maidens appear to be a Christianised idea of a much older concept is hardly surprising. At the dawn of the 7th century Bishop Mellitus was told by Pope Gregory to take over the temples of pagan worship and preach the word of God

Irish – Q Celtic - Goidelic
Welsh, Scottish Lowlands and Borders – P Celtic /Brythonic/
the Britons

therein. Many early Celtic saints seem to have developed from earlier pagan figures; even the much-vaunted St Columba seems to have been as much a druid as a Christian priest. The Nine Maidens of Glen Ogilvy and Abernethy fit this pattern. There are grounds for thinking that the concept of Nine Maidens, and associated cultic practices, came into Britain with the earliest settlers after the end of the last Ice Age. While some of the Scottish traditions concerning the Nine Maidens refer to groups of priestesses in specific locales, elsewhere they are often closely linked to important mythological figures. Some of these other groups are also closely associated with a single male figure. However, there are also extremely significant female figures with which these groups are linked in traditions from the British Isles.

As we shall see there are magic practices associated with the number nine that occur in societies all over the world just like the groups of Nine Maidens themselves. And at least one example of a group of nine women, involved in some sort of ritual, dates from the time when Scotland and the rest of the British Isles were under the ice.

# CHAPTER 2

# Bride and Monenna

IN BOWER'S SCOTOCHRONICON, a 13th century historical work,
the story is told of St Bridget coming over from Ireland at the
request of King Gartnait or Garnard:

> King Brude was succeeded by Garnard, son of Domnach... who
> founded and built the collegiate church of Abernethy, after blessed
> Patrick brought blessed Bridget into Scotland together with her nine
> virgins; just as we find in a certain chronicle of the church of
> Abernethy... Those nine virgins died within five years and were
> buried in the north part of the said church. (2 p303)

St Bridget has been commonly seen as the Irish precursor of the
Scottish Bride, handmaiden of Mary in Gaelic lore. There are
many Bride place-names in once-Pictish areas of Scotland, which
are accepted as having been Christianised by the Gaelic-speaking
Columban Church from the 6th century onwards. One would
therefore expect such place-names to contain the term 'St Bride'
or 'St Bridget'. However in many cases they are simply 'Bride'
names, suggesting that these names predate the arrival of the
Columban Church. It appears that Bride was one of the mother
goddesses of pre-Christian Scotland, as much at home in
Scotland, where Gaelic and Pictish and Welsh were spoken in the
6th century, as in Gaelic-speaking Ireland. In Ireland, St Bridget is
quite clearly a modernised version of a pre-Christian goddess
figure. Her central shrine was said to be at Kildare, meaning the
'cell of the oak tree', and there a perpetual flame was kept alive
within a fenced area into which no male might pass. Within the
enclosure, Bride's sacred flame was tended by Nine Maidens.
Some versions say the fire was tended by nineteen maidens – a

1 : The victor's history.

number with strong lunar, and therefore female, associations; the moon repeats its cycle of crossing the skies every 18.6 years. As we will see later, the lunar association with the number nine is also significant.

Bride is a figure common to both Scotland and Ireland; and remembering that there was a tribe called the Brigantes in what is now northern England, it would seem that any attempt to trace her to a single, locatable place of origin is an exercise in futility. The many commentators who have insisted on her originating in Ireland are implicitly expressing a prejudice in favour of the idea that if you have no records you have no history, thus ignoring what we can learn from oral tradition. In Britain the dominant model for interpreting the past arises from a militaristic, hierarchic and masculine perspective. Much of what we currently conceive of as history was written at the behest of kings and other powerful military or religious figures and it is thus their version of history. Oral history gives us some alternative to this history of winners. Another distorting bias in standard British history is that it is really little more than English history with a few sops to Scottish, Welsh and Irish sensibilities. Among these 'nations' this has led to a romanticised view of a glorious Celtic, rather than British past, but such ideas of 'Celticism' are no older than the 18th century.

Commentators tell us that the early literary material from Ireland is much more influenced by the written traditions of Christian literacy than by the mores of pagan society and thus all we can find in such old tales are museum pieces of dead paganism. This argument is extensively presented in Kim McCone's *Christian Past and Pagan Past and Christian Present in early Irish Literature*. There is some sense in this position – when the Christian monks began writing down the stories of Ireland (as they must have done in Scotland too, but due to the efforts of Edward 1, the Protestant Reformers and Oliver Cromwell, very few old Scottish texts have survived), they were almost the only ones who could read and write. Until the 19th century, most people throughout the world weren't literate and continued to pass on knowledge through the telling of the old tales, generation to generation. To this day previously unrecorded tales are still being gathered in Scotland and elsewhere. If the oral tradition can keep stories intact for millennia as seems clear from Australian experience, we should pay more attention to our indigenous oral traditions. In Australia the fossil remains of Diprotodons, giant extinct marsupials, were discovered in the 20th century in several locations. Until these fossilised remains were found, the educated approach to aboriginal stories which told of ancestor peoples hunting such animals was to consider them fantasy. These animals became extinct over 30,000 years ago, but the stories of them continued to be told by the aboriginal peoples into the 20th century. Other material too survived in such traditions. As Jennifer Isaacs tells us in *Australian Dreaming; 40,000 years of Aboriginal history*:

> From the Pleistocene era to as late as 5000 B.P. [before the present] the awe-inspiring sight of erupting volcanoes was witnessed by aboriginal people in the southern part of the content. A myth collected many years ago may well describe the eruption of Mount Wilson in the Blue Mountains near Sydney. (p29)

In Europe, in areas like the Balkans, stories are still being told that are over two thousand years old, and in tribal societies, in various parts of our planet, the oral tradition continues. Given the evidence from Australia, we have to at least consider the possibility that oral transmission in other parts of the world could contain material of the same antiquity.

A story that Loch Moan in south-west Scotland was where King Arthur returned his magic sword to the waters was told me by a student who first heard it over 30 years ago from an old uncle, who told her the story had been handed down through their family for generations. In this way such remnants of ancient lore survive where people still inhabit the lands of their ancestors. Additionally, stories would travel virtually intact with emigrants to new lands where they would be told as happening within the

1: Another story from Central Scotland claims it was the Lake of Menteith, the only lake in Scotland. Note that both bodies of water start with the letter 'M'; is this significant? What do the names mean?

31

new physical environment. There is a view that many such stories are a result of literacy – i.e. people originally reading them and then setting them in their own landscape in their retelling. What is now understood about storytelling traditions throughout the world suggests that this analysis is putting the cart before the horse, presenting as authoritative what is essentially supposition. Imparting knowledge from one generation to another is fundamental to human society, and in pre-literate societies all basic knowledge and ideas are passed on through stories, myth and legend. In order to have the maximum relevance and impact, such material is presented within the local landscape of the audience which makes it easier to learn or absorb. So wherever we find Bride or Nine Maidens stories being told, we can be pretty sure that they were part of the lore of the people who inhabited that environment. Such lore can encompass memories of actual events, individuals and groups, as well as the more fundamental and essentially sacred concepts that underpin mythology, the basis of religion. The Nine Maidens seem to belong to both these strata of orally transmitted tradition.

Whatever their origin, Bride and her Nine Maidens are placed securely in the Pictish capital of Abernethy by early Scottish historians such as Boece and Wyntoun. Abernethy seems for a time to have been the most important Christian centre in Dark Age Scotland, till perhaps as late as the 11th century. However, as noted by JG Mackay, there were numerous dedications to these Nine Maidens elsewhere in eastern Scotland. Small, in *Interesting Roman Antiquities*, mentions Bride and her maidens as coming not from Ireland but from Glenesk, which lies in the mountainous parts of Angus on the north side of the river Tay. A mountain location is something that occurs again and again with both the Nine Maidens and the Mother Goddess.

The association of Bride names with prehistoric sites in areas once inhabited by the Picts further suggests that this version of the Goddess was common to both Picts and Scots. In the Pictish area of Angus alone, there are Bride's Bed, Bride's Coggie and Bride's Ring and several wells dedicated to her, though wells dedicated to

Bride are found all over Scotland. It has been accepted till recently by Scottish historians that Gaelic did not come into Scotland till around AD 500, and spread over the rest of the land as the power and influence of Dalriada increased. This is despite several Roman sources referring to attacks from the north by 'Picts and Scots' prior to this date. As the Picts and Scots were not totally united before the middle of the 9th century under the kingship of Kenneth Macalpin, it is fair to assume on this model that the farthest parts of Pictland would be the last to be Gaelicised. In that case, we would expect the Pictish province of Circinn, corresponding to the area of Angus and the Mearns, to be influenced late, by which time the Scots of Dalriada were thoroughly Christianised. It would therefore seem unlikely that Gaelic-speaking Christian Scots would give the name of a pagan goddess to sites in Pictland and as it has been noted, many of these place-names are not St Bride names but Bride names. This would suggest that Bride is not an imported figure but is indigenous to Scotland, a view shared by the historian Henry Chadwick according to his wife in her Introduction to his *Early Scotland*:

> [He] certainly suspected that St Brigit had her origin in Scotland or northern Britain, and was originally connected with a heathen Goddess Brigantia. For this of course he was not, originally responsible. (xii)

This is not to say that Bride did not exist in Ireland, but the idea that she must have come to Scotland from Ireland is due to the aforementioned tendency of Scottish historians to be blinded by the romantic notion that all truly indigenous Scottish culture stems from Gaelic tradition, simply because we have written sources in Gaelic from Ireland earlier than any from Scotland. The references we have that Bride brought the Nine Maidens over from Ireland are from sources written long after the Christianising of the Picts by the Columban Church based on Iona. The languages of the Columban Church were Latin and

Gaelic. St Columba and his original followers were Irish and the combination of Dalriadic power and the new Church has led to the notion that Ireland is the original homeland of Scottish culture. This is an assumption that flies directly in the face of the evidence. The Picts did not disappear from the face of Scotland because dynastic rule passed into the hands of a Dalriadic family who appear to have traced their roots back to Ireland There are even theories that suggest the name 'Scots' originated in Scotland and that this people, or perhaps tribe, subsequently went to Ireland in the prehistoric period. Given that Northern Ireland and several parts of western Scotland are within sight of each other, that we know the earliest peoples of Britain had boats, and that the archaeological record shows no great variation between these areas, the idea that this people came from Ireland to Scotland for the first time in the 6th century is unsustainable. We would be better thinking of the people on both sides of the water here as being in regular contact from the Stone Age onwards. Whatever the case, we can be sure that the traditions and beliefs of the various tribes who made up the population of the new kingdom of Scotland in the 9th century did not all become subsumed in those of the new Dalriadic dynasty.

Given the importance of Bride/St Bridget to the search for the Nine Maidens, we must now look at certain aspects of Scottish tradition concerning her. The fact that some of this material stems from Gaelic sources does not mean that these ideas must have originated in Ireland, merely that these are the earliest written records we have. Ideas, myths and stories can survive language shifts. The preponderance of Nine Maidens locations in east Scotland, away from the Gaelic west, reinforces the idea that they did not come in to Scotland from Ireland, either as a mythological or actual group.

Two important motifs concerning Bride are her portrayal as the goddess of summer and the tale of the Cailleach changing into Bride after drinking from a sacred well on Imbolc (1 February), the day dedicated to Bride and St Bridget. This is how McNeill gives the first story in *The Silver Bough*:

Bride is kept prisoner all winter in Ben Nevis, where she awaits her rescuer, Aengus of the White Steed, Aengus the Ever-Young, who has his home in that green island of perpetual summer that drifts about on the silver tide of the Atlantic. Aengus beholds Bride in a dream, and sets out to succour her, riding on his milk-white steed with flowing mane over the Isles and over the Minch. The Cailleach strives in vain to keep them apart, and the Day of Bride celebrates their union. (2 p21)

A similar duality is expressed in the traditional Gaelic concept of the sun as having two seasons – the time of the Big Sun and the time of the Little Sun. These seasons were separated by the great feast days of Beltane and Samhain, which today we know as Mayday and Halloween. Given the virtually universal human experience of having early foundation mythology explaining the creation of the seasons, the weather, and the formation of the land in terms of a goddess, here we appear to be dealing with a very ancient motif, a motif which long predates the supposed arrival of Gaelic-speaking warrior tribes into Scotland c. AD 500. The supposed 6th century invaders from Ireland would have found similar warrior societies to their own with roughly equivalent economic patterns, speaking Celtic languages – the Picts and the Britons. Similar societies and related languages suggest similar mythologies and traditions.

Mackenzie mentions a Romanian tale, in which a hag called Malvinia, based on a mountain top, had eight witch companions (1935, p173). This is a clear example of the Nine Maidens motif, in that we have the nine women as witches, situated on a mountain called Silash, and actively involved in spreading winter. In a further echo of Scottish traditions, these nine witches were turned to stone on the mountain top, echoing the widespread British tales of standing stones and stone circles being witches, or sometimes Sabbath revellers, who were turned to stone.

In *The Silver Bough*, McNeill gives a tale that shows the concept of Bride and the Cailleach as being two aspects of the same Goddess figure:

At foot, the Britons. They were the people of Lowland Scotland and the Borders who spoke P Celtic, ie Brythonic Celtic, they are traditionally called the Scots, not to be confused with the 'Scots' who come from Ireland.

35

> On the Eve of Bride, the Cailleach repairs to the Isle of Youth, in whose woods lies the miraculous Well of Youth. There, at the first glimmer of dawn, before any bird has sung or any dog barked, she drinks of the water that bubbles in a crevice of a rock, and having renewed her youth, emerges as Bride, the fair young Goddess at the touch of whose wand the dun grass turns to vivid green, starred with the white and yellow flowers of Spring. (2, p21)

Over millennia, ideas evolve as societies change and we should therefore not be surprised to see some variation in even the most ancient and fundamental of ideas. This does not diminish the capacity for the oral tradition to preserve remnants of a wide range of ancient belief and practice over remarkable time scales, but does show the necessity for maintaining a critical approach. Mackenzie gives us another version of the same story:

> Another conception was that the Cailleach changed from a fierce old hag to a beautiful maiden. In a folk-story which was connected with the Fians, she appears one night as a creature of uncouth appearance who claims hospitality. Fionn and Oisean [Ossian] refuse to let her under their coverings. Diarmaid pleads that she should be allowed to come to the warmth of the fire. Soon afterwards she sought to be under the warmth of the blanket together with himself. Diarmaid turned a fold of the blanket between them. Before long he gave a start, for the hag had transformed herself into the most beauteous woman that men ever saw. (p138)

Here a clear duality is expressed, with the Cailleach changing into a desirable young woman, akin to story of the Cailleach going to the well at Imbolc and becoming Bride. This duality is clearly differentiated from the more usually noticed triple aspect of so many motifs in early European societies which has been treated extensively by many commentators. I suggest this dual motif is the older. In a lecture to the Pictish Arts Society in 1999, Dr Emily Lyle of the School of Scottish Studies at Edinburgh University presented a model for potential matrilineal succession among the

Picts, in which one female line provided direct succession for the queen while another gave a line of mothers of kings who attained sovereignty by marrying the queen. Such a structure could ultimately have derived from precisely such a duality. The story of the Cailleach turning into Bride would appear to be a remnant of this that has passed into Gaelic from a source of great antiquity. This duality would appear to be more like the well-known eastern philosophical concept of Yin and Yang, than the Christian idea of black versus white, good versus evil.

The Cailleach is closely associated with mountains. Before the growth of major cities, people were more aware of their natural environment. They would have observed mountains as the points around which changes in the weather originated. An early meaning of *Cailleach* is 'the veiled one'. This meaning led to the term becoming the word for a nun in modern Gaelic. If you watch the clouds gather around Scottish mountains at almost any time of the year you will see this idea made remarkably explicit in the landscape. And not just Scottish mountains. Just as the Cailleach is veiled, so is the mountain she inhabits. The Cailleach is strongly associated with Ben Nevis, the highest mountain in the British Isles and notable for its dramatic and ever-changing weather patterns. The Corryvreckan, the remarkable whirlpool on the west coast of Scotland between the islands of Scarba and Jura, is said to be where the Cailleach washed her plaid (the one-piece traditional garment of the Highlands, generally tartan) in late autumn and then spread it out over the mountains to dry. As she was the oldest creature, her plaid was pure white: so the story explains both the period of heaviest activity of the whirlpool and the first serious snowfall of the year. The Cailleach is also said to have created Scotland by dropping a creel full of peat and rocks. McNeill tells us in *The Silver Bough*:

> The Cailleach is the genius of winter and the enemy of growth. Her chief seat is Ben Nevis. She ushers in winter by washing her great plaid in the whirlpool of Corryvreckan (Coire Bhreacain – the Cauldron of the Plaid) Before the washing, it is said, the roar of a

37

coming tempest is heard by people on the coast for a distance of twenty miles, for a period of three days until the cauldron boils. When the washing is over, the plaid of old Scotland is virgin white. (2 p20)

Here the Cailleach's cauldron is the whirlpool of the Corryvreckan. The cauldron is associated with other Nine Maidens groups in other areas. Surviving folklore also refers to this whirlpool as being the breath of the Goddess beneath the waves. Only since humans have achieved space flight has it become known that the oceans contain eddies, up to 20 kilometres across, which circulate warm surface water into the depths thus releasing life-sustaining nutrients. This gives the motif of the whirlpool as the cauldron of the Mother Goddess a whole new level of meaning. Mythology explains the physical universe and its attributes in human terms. Such material can often contain sophisticated observations and insights. In order to give lore and tradition the strongest possibility of being remembered, and to ensure that the moral lessons as well as its practical applications would be appreciated, tradition-bearers would present their material within the environment familiar to their listeners. This accounts for the widespread instances of names in the Scottish landscape like Allt na Cailleach (Stream of the Old Woman), a name that can be interpreted as originally meaning the stream of the Goddess. The Cailleach's relation to the physical world, to seasonal change and to weather, shows we are dealing with a fundamental mythological statement.

The figure of the Cailleach in Gaelic tradition is paralleled in Scots tradition by the Gyre Carlin, also often portrayed as a winter hag and linked to the traditions of the witches which survive in many areas. Donald Mackenzie in *Egyptian Myth and Legend* writes:

One of the many versions of the Scottish Hag story makes her the chief of eight big old women or witches. This group of nine suggests Ptah and his eight earth gnomes, the nine mothers of Heimdal the Norse god and the Ennead of Heliopolis. (p xxxviii)

In this association of the Cailleach with a group of nine, she is one of the nine whereas most of our Bride references are to Bride and nine others. Mackenzie goes further and compares this group to the nine mothers of Heimdall in Norse myth and the Ennead of Heliopolis in Egypt. He makes the point, 'A people seldom remember their early history, but they rarely forget their tribal beliefs...'. This is a particularly relevant statement for Scotland where Celtic-speaking warrior tribes were in existence till 250 years ago and had in many ways retained the characteristics of Iron Age society.

More support for the Scottish provenance of Bride in Scotland comes from Jhone Leslie who writes in his 16th century *Historie of Scotland*:

> The Scottis, Peychtes, Britanis, Inglismen & Irishmen with sik veneratione in ilk place have honoured S Brigida, that innumerable kirkes erected to God, amang them ale, to her, ye sal se; yie and mae to her than to ony of the rest: the Irland men contendes that her haly body thay have with thame in that toune quhilke thay cal Dun, in quhilke place the body of thair Apostle S. Patrik is keipet. our cuntrey men ascrynes the same Glore unto thame, quha thinkes, that hitherto thay have honouret it in the Chanrie of Abernethie, & richtlie have done thay think. (1 p229)
>
> The Scots, Picts, Britons, Englishmen and Irishmen with such veneration in every place have honoured St Brigid, that innumerable churches erected to God, among them all, to her, you shall see; yes and more to her than to any of the rest. The Irish people contend that her holy body they have with them in that town which they call Dun, in which place the body of their Apostle St Patrick is kept. Our countrymen ascribe the same Glory unto themselves, who think, that hitherto they have honoured it in the Chancery of Abernethy and have done so rightly to their own thinking. (translation)

In referring to the different tribal confederations/kingdoms of Dark Age northern Britain, Leslie is clearly differentiating between Britons and Englishmen. By Britons he appears to mean the P-Celtic people of Strathclyde, and possibly the people of Manaw Gododdin, known to the Romans as the Votadini and inhabiting the lands from East Lothian to possibly as far as the headwaters of the Forth, and perhaps as far south as the Tyne at some point. He is making it clear that St Brigid was known to both the P- and Q-Celtic tribes and to the Germanic-speaking peoples in what we now call Scotland. This supports of the idea of Bride being indigenous to Scotland and clearly points to a cult of St Bridget among Christians in Scotland in the pre-Reformation period. The belief that Brigid is buried at Abernethy in no way precludes her Irish provenance, but, taken together with the other evidence, this appears to be part of a continuum of belief which was indigenous to Scotland.

McNeill describes the following ritual in *The Silver Bough*:

> The parish church at Sanquhar in Dumfries-shire, stands on the site of a chapel dedicated to the saint, and not far off is St Bride's Well, where the young girls of the district used to repair on Beltane morning, each bringing an offering of nine white stones, symbolic of the traditional nine virgin attendants of the saint. (2 p29)

The use of white stones here is perhaps a variation on the ancient practice of including white pebbles in burials – a practice that started in pagan times and carried on into the early Christian period in Scotland; the use of the nine stones here was in honour of the Nine Maidens.

McNeill gives several examples of rituals performed in honour of Bride and St Bridget, whose importance in the Gaelic tradition is emphasised in her title as Handmaiden to Mary, or Birthmaiden to Christ. This would seem to be a transference of an established Goddess figure into the pantheon of a new religion – it was always the practice for the early Church to absorb some elements of previous belief when it moved into a new area. Even today, many of the fiestas of Mediterranean Europe appear to contain ideas that are closer to pagan religion than conventional

Christianity. The Scottish Hebrides have been interpreted as the Eilean-Bride – the Islands of Bride – and were said to have been created by the Cailleach, though the etymological derivation from Bride has been considered unlikely. Within Gaelic tradition one association with Bride that stands out as a strong echo of pre-Christian thought is her association with the serpent. The serpent in Christian terms is of course a symbol of evil but it is cast in a different light in several rhymes. In Scottish tradition Bride's association is specifically with the adder, Scotland's only indigenous snake. The adder is also linked with various druidic traditions. McNeill gives this version of a hymn to the adder emerging from its hibernation on Imbolc, St Bride's Day, 1 February:

> Today is the day of Bride
> the serpent shall come from the hole
> I will not molest the serpent
> Nor will the serpent molest me. (2 p27)

This hymn to the adder has been regarded as a relic of serpent worship by several commentators, but it is probably more accurate to say that the serpent/adder is a symbol associated with the Mother Goddess. In many cultures the serpent has been seen as symbol of knowledge. It is particularly fitting as a symbol of fertility, more specifically regeneration, as it seems to disappear into the earth through the winter, like seeds that are planted in autumn, lies dormant and comes up in the spring. The annual replacement of its skin is also symbolic of rebirth and regeneration. The worship of the dead, in rituals associated with ancient chambered cairns and other prehistoric sites, can be interpreted as prayers to the departed spirits – who have returned to the earth – to work their magic on the planted seeds to ensure next year's harvest grows. This idea is discussed in Hutton's *The Pagan Religions of Prehistoric British Isles*. A variety of serpent/adder representations on many Pictish symbol stones suggests that the Picts too saw the snake as a powerful religious symbol and it is at least possible that they associated it with Bride herself.

McNeill tells us of other rites associated with Bride. It seems that in Rutherglen on the Eve of Bride's Day, groups of women (we are not told how many) would gather together and make an oblong basket they called *leaba Bride*, the bed of Bride, which they would decorate. Then, taking a selected sheaf of corn, they would fashion it into the shape of a woman and then they would, '... deck this ikon with gay ribbons from the loom, sparkling shells from the sea, and bright stones from the hill.' The figure was called Bride:

> When it is dressed and decorated, one woman goes to the door of the house and, standing on the step with her hands on the jambs, calls softly into the darkness, 'Bride's bed is ready.' To this a ready woman behind replies, 'Let Bride come in. Bride is welcome.' The woman at the door again addresses Bride, 'Bride come thou in, thy bed is made. Preserve the house for the Trinity.' The women then place the ikon of Bride with great ceremony in the bed. They place a small straight white wand (the bark being peeled off) beside the figure. The wand is generally of birch, broom, bramble, white willow or other sacred wood, 'crossed' or banned wood being carefully avoided. The women then level the ashes on the hearth, smoothing them carefully. In the early morning, the family closely scan the ashes. If they find the mark of the wand of Bride they rejoice, but if they find lorg Bride, the footprint of Bride, their joy is very great, for this is a sign that Bride was present with them during the night, and is favourable to them, and that there is increase in family, in flock, and in field in the coming year. Should there be no marks on the ashes, the family are dejected. It is a sign that she is offended and will not hear their call. To propitiate her and gain her ear the family offer oblations, and burn incense on the hearth. (2 p26)

It should be remembered that these practices are recorded as happening in communities that had been ostensibly Christian for over a thousand years. They underline the hold that the idea of Bride, an aspect of the Mother Goddess, continued to have on both community and individual until relatively recently.

Just as Bride is associated with the serpent, the Cailleach is associated with the cauldron, another symbol often found on the Pictish symbol stones. There are literally dozens of Bride and St Bride place-names not only in the Western Isles but all over Scotland and a good exposition of these can be found in Mackinlay's *Ancient Church Dedications in Scotland*. If the suggestion here, that Bride was common to Scottish and Irish societies, is correct, the influence of Gaelic culture in the period subsequent to the 9th century would simply strengthen her centrality. Further, as works on Scottish folklore, such as Dalyell's *The Darker Superstitions of Scotland* and Gregor's *Folklore of North-East Scotland*, show, pagan belief has never been totally eradicated in Scotland. Bride and the Nine Maidens maintained a strong hold on the imagination of people in those communities where the oral tradition continued to play a strong role. The attendance at the Nine Maidens Well at Pittempton until the 1870s, mentioned in Chapter 1, and the survival of the rite at Bride's Well in Sanquhar are cases in point.

The early history of the British Isles is full of individuals portrayed as saints who, like Bridget, are based on earlier pagan figures. The Nine Maidens themselves, after all, are entered in the *Aberdeen Breviary* as being Pictish saints and there are other figures who seem to be part of similar traditions. One of these is St Monenna, who appears under a variety of names including Darerca, Modwenna and Moninne, and the same figure seems to be behind the saints Edana and Medana. Like the Nine Maidens, she does not appear in the official Roman Catholic lists and therefore must be seen as indigenous to the British Isles. Monenna is said to have been a friend of St Bridget's, who came to Scotland from Ireland with eight virgins, a widow and the widow's son. / Forbes' *Kalendars of Scottish Saints* has the following:

When St Patrick came to her neighbourhood she presented herself

1: The widow and the widow's son is interesting, this is a masonic motif.

43

before him, and received from him the virgin habit near the pool of Brigius, the translation of which means abundance. She proceeded to associate herself with eight virgins and one widow, with her baby named Luger, whom Darerca adopted, and who afterwards became a bishop. (p404)

Here Monenna, like Bridget, is associated with a group of Nine Maidens and as is often the case, there is mention of a single male, as in the stories of Martin's Stane and of Ochonochar. This association of the Nine Maidens with a single male figure crop ups again and again. Stories which have it that this male figure is born to one, or all, of the Nine Maidens occur mainly in Norse tradition. Modwenna was baptised in a pool of abundance, echoing the pagan traditions of fertility, specifically of cauldrons of abundance. In his *The Early Christianizing of Scotland,* Knight gives the following story from Galloway where there are several place-names associated with Modwenna:

> The legend states that the maiden and her companions took to a rock in the sea, which by her prayers, became a boat and carried them over the thirty miles to Farnes, now a part of Glasserton parish on the east side of Luce Bay. Still her admirer followed her and tracked her down. Climbing into a tree, she asked, 'What is it that you see in me that excites your passion?', 'Your face and eyes,' he said. Instantly she tore out her eyes and flung them at his feet! Horror-struck and filled with remorse, the soldier departed, and Modwenna, descending from the tree, washed her face in a spring that had miraculously gushed up. (p250)

The same story is told of Triduana whose well at Restalrig in Edinburgh was known far and wide for its efficacy in curing disease of the eyes! There is an ancient motif concerned with eyes and healing behind these tales, but the Christianised versions have left us with little more than a bloody horror story. OGS Crawford in *The Eye Goddess* has written extensively on the link between the Goddess and the eye symbol. The great Australian scholar and poet Alexander Hope in his delightful *A Midsummer Eve's Dream* makes the point that Triduana was in fact the name of a three-day fast in the Celtic Church and was associated with three female figures, the others being Potencia and Emeria. He sees them as deriving from the tripartite protective goddess of a sacred well.

The list of churches Monenna is said to have founded in what we now call Scotland is given in Skene's *Celtic Scotland*:

> ... she is said to have founded seven churches in Scotland: one at Chilnecase in Galloway, a second on the hill of Dundonald in Ayrshire, a third on Dumbarton rock, a fourth in the castle of Strivelyn or Stirling, a fifth at Dunedene which in Anglic is called Edinburgh, a sixth on the hill of Dunpelder in East Lothian, and the seventh at Lanfortin or Longforgund in Gowrie, where she is said to have died. (1 p37)

Edinburgh, the capital of Scotland, was a tribal capital in the Dark Ages as were: Dumbarton, the fort of the Britons, associated with the legendary Arthur; Stirling Rock, a capital of the Gododdin or Votadini, who are the subject of Britain's oldest extant heroic poem *The Gododdin*; and Traprain Law, a hill-top settlement of the Votadini in Roman times and home of the legendary King Lot, brother in law to Arthur and grandfather of St Kentigern. Dundonald was also a hill-fort and could have been a local capital, while Chilnecase is interpreted as being Candida Casa, the site of the foundation of Scotland's earliest Christian saint St Ninian, who lived in the 5th century and with whom Monenna was said to have been in contact. These are all important political and possibly religious/ritual centres except Longforgan (Longforgund) on the north bank of the Tay, which has no great place in history. However, this is not to say that it was not important, merely that we have no record of the fact, nor any particular traditions to fall back on.

Such locations suggest the intriguing possibility that there were groups of Nine Maidens at several tribal capitals of Dark Age Scotland, just as the Pictish capital of Abernethy had its Nine

Note: Is there an association with the Nine and Dunkeld?

45

Maidens, who were pagan priestesses involved in augury and healing. In support of this contention a name for Edinburgh Castle from 12th century written sources is *Castella Puellarum* – the Castle of the Maidens – and a local tradition said it was where the Picts kept their daughters. The term 'Picts' was for a long time a generic or catch-all word for 'the ancestors' throughout Scotland. The term 'Castle of Maidens' is used for Edinburgh, or Holyrood Abbey, in several 12th and 13th century chronicles (Anderson 1990 II pp 224, 297, 303, 304, 498, 581, 690). Monenna is mentioned in the Annals of Ulster as having died in 516 or 517 and this is supportive of the reference being to a Maidens group. It is particularly noticeable that the term 'Castle of Maidens' is the most common one used for Edinburgh in this period. 'Castle of Maidens' was used extensively by the writers of European Arthurian romances in the Middle Ages. As we shall see the Nine Maidens motif occurs extensively within Arthurian tradition. JS Glennie in his *Arthurian Localities in Scotland* gives well-argued locations for all of King Arthur's supposed battles in Scotland. Skene gives an 8th century P-Celtic name for Edinburgh Castle as Mynyd Agned (p76), translated as the Mount or Castle of Maidens. If, as has been suggested elsewhere, Arthur was common to the mythology and legendary traditions of all the P-Celtic speakers, the tales would also have been known amongst the Picts, accounting for the survival of the story of Arthur and Vanora (Guinevere) at Meigle in Perthshire. The first datable reference to Arthur is in the 6th century epic poem *The Gododdin*, detailing a disastrous battle expedition to northern England by a group of warriors from near the Forth.

The location of these Nine Maidens groups on fortified hilltops is reminiscent of the Vestal Virgins on Capitol Hill in Rome, and there are many references to groups of priestesses similarly located on hilltops in classical sources. This corresponds to the association of the Cailleach with mountain tops in Scotland. We can also see some correlation in such groups being close to seats of temporal power like the Vestals, and the above sites were all certainly important political and military sites in

1: Would this be the Battle of Cathroath ?

Dark Age Scotland. It might even be that such sacral functions predate any military use of these sites. Most European hilltop excavations to date have concentrated on the sites' military usage. James Grant, in his *Old and New Edinburgh* tells us of St Monenna:

> The site of her edifice is supposed to be that now occupied by the Chapel of St Margaret, the most ancient piece of masonry in the Scottish capital; and it is a curious circumstance, with special reference to the fable of the Pictish princesses that close by it, as recorded in the Caledonian Mercury of 20 September 1853, when some excavations were made, a number of human bones, apparently all females, together with some coffins, were found. (1 p15)

He also tells us that according to the 16th century English historian Camden:

> The Britons called it Mynydh Agnedh – the maidens' or virgins' castle – because certain young maidens of royal blood were kept there in olden times. (ibid)

Wilson, in his *Memorials of Edinburgh in the Olden Time* has the following:

> According to Father Hay's apocryphal account, certain nuns attached to the royal chapel, and from whom the castle derived the name Castrum Puellarum, were thrust out by St David, and in their place canons introduced by the Pope's dispense, as fitter to live among soldiers. (2 p4)

The discovery of female bodies and the name Mynydh Agnedh both support the idea that Edinburgh Castle was a Nine Maidens site and it is possible to see the story of the expulsion of the nuns from Edinburgh Castle as being akin to other stories of other Nine Maidens being expelled or punished for sexual misbehaviour. There are traditions in several parts of Scotland where nunneries were said to have been established but for which there is no historical evidence. These may be Christianised versions of tales about earlier priestess groups. One example is Inchnacailloch in Loch Lomond which tradition says housed a nunnery. A tale was told here of a priest killing a nun who planned to escape the island with her lover. The idea of the nunnery perhaps arises from the use of the term Cailleach, the hooded one, for nuns. Sites of priestess groups worshipping a Mother Goddess figure might easily retain the name of the Goddess. It is also possible that such groups of pagan priestesses could be interpreted as nuns by later, Christianised society.

The motif of Nine Maiden groups living in communities on hill-top sites or on islands occurs repeatedly and not only in Scotland. That there were specific groups of Nine Maidens associated with Dark Age capitals in Scotland is clear, and it is tempting to see such groups as being part of a common religious structure that existed across tribal and religious boundaries in contemporary Scotland and beyond.

The term 'Maiden Castle' is relatively common and it is strikingly obvious that these 'castles' are not all defensive structures. Hope makes an interesting connection:

> The shapes of certain hills may by themselves suggest such names as the Maiden-pap in Perthshire or the Hill with the Paps (Bennachie) in Aberdeenshire. But the Paps of Anu in Kerry remind us that not only were such hills sometimes named for their likeness to breasts but because they were thought to be the breasts of a Goddess. (p37)

While Edinburgh Castle Rock is not one of this particular type of site, the association with St Monenna, the discovery of female bodies, and the name 'Castle of the Maidens' all strengthen the likelihood of it as a Nine Maidens site. Given the suggested link from earlier Goddess worship, it is interesting that the castle has become so closely associated with St Margaret, one of the, if not *the*, foremost of Scottish female saints. The links between the Cailleach figure and so many different mountain locations in Scotland suggests that the choice of hill-top locations for priestess groups is not just fortuitous, the concept of mountain tops being sacred places is commonplace throughout human societies.

# CHAPTER 3

# The Nine Maidens in Welsh Tradition

THE GREATEST SURVIVING COLLECTION of early mythological material from Wales is *The Mabinogion*, which, along with the works of the semi-mythical bard Taliesin, contain much of what we know regarding the beliefs and ideas of the P-Celtic speaking tribes of Britain. These included not only the Welsh and Cornish peoples but the Picts and the tribal confederations in most of the west of Britain south of the Clyde. Many historians think that the whole population of what is now England, Scotland and Wales spoke variants of P-Celtic languages when the Romans first arrived in Britain in 55 BC. It is quite likely however that the picture was considerably more complicated than that. With the relative ease of travel by sea at certain times of the year, there was trade in such commodities as amber and gold between Ireland and Scandinavia in prehistoric times and there was ongoing contact between the peoples adjoining the Irish and North Seas and along the Atlantic coasts from Megalithic times on. There seems no reason to doubt that the people of these islands were the direct descendants of the people who had raised the Megalithic monuments from Stonehenge to Calanais and from New Grange to Maes Howe in Orkney which show a cultural continuity over most of the north-eastern Atlantic littoral. Trading links between the east coast of Scotland and the Baltic have survived till the present day. Strong similarities between certain aspects of legendary and mythological material in Britain, Scandinavia, Gaul and Greece suggest either a common origin or strong ongoing cultural contacts, or indeed both.

The oldest surviving poem in Welsh is *The Gododdin*, originating in 6th century Scotland amongst the contemporary P-Celtic speaking peoples. It describes a tragic raid by a group of

*1: There seems to have been a mass migration/invasion from lowland Scotland to Wales in the 5th Century A.E.C A.D.*

warriors from near Edinburgh to the south – a raid which saw virtually the entire force wiped out. The poem would appear to have gone south to Wales with those tribes who, at different times in the Dark Ages, left Scotland. There is an understandable temptation to project known realities back into periods of which we have little knowledge. Thus Dark Age Britain is presented as being formed of a number of petty kingdoms. I suggest a more appropriate picture would be to look at them as tribal areas or tribal confederations. The reaction against the Roman invasion in both north and south shows a capacity among the various tribes to unite in the face of a common adversary. In the south there was the revolt under Boudicca and in the north the Caledonian confederacy opposed the Roman general Julius Agricola at the battle of Mons Graupius. This pattern of behaviour is therefore not uncommon. Once any immediate threat was over, gathered clans or tribes would return to their own area and people. War leaders, chosen for their ability not their lineage, would revert to their former status after such events. This pattern of behaviour survived into 17th century Scotland amongst the Highland clans, Celtic-speaking warrior tribes whose life seems to have changed little for hundreds of years, perhaps even since the Dark Ages. The notion that there was some kind of feudal tie between a leader and his followers in this period is unsustainable – which has not stopped historians analysing them as if they were exactly like later kingship-based societies. The relationship between the warriors of a tribe and their chief is totally unlike that of feudal subjects and their king. This is borne out by what we know of late Scottish Highland Celtic society. An example of the relationship between tribesman and chief comes from Burt's *Letters of a Gentleman*, a collection of letters from the 1730s. He is telling us about the Highlanders' relationship with their chief:

> ... and as the meanest among them pretend to be his Relations by Consanguinity, they insist upon the Privilege of taking him by the Hand whenever they meet him. Concerning this last, I once saw a Number of very discontented Countenances when a certain Lord, one

of the Chiefs, endeavoured to evade this Ceremony. It was in Presence of an English Gentleman in high station, from whom he would have willingly have concealed the Knowledge of such seeming Familiarity with slaves of so wretched Appearance, and thinking it, I suppose, as a kind of contradiction to what he had often boasted at other Times, viz., his despotic Power over his Clan. (2 p109)

It was a clansman's right to shake his chief's hand. While this does not mean that the two were absolute equals it does show that the tribal/clan system was totally unlike that of post-feudal, hierarchic societies elsewhere in Britain and Europe with aristocracy, gentry, and those who were effectively serfs, or as Burt puts it 'slaves'. There is in clan societies a level of egalitarianism that not only contradicts but has no precursors in feudalism. Burt's eyewitness account bears this out. We also know that the Highland warriors were usually led into battle by the most able of their number, rather than the chief, and that chiefs could be, and sometimes were, replaced. This, allied with the well-attested elective aspect of chieftainship, and even kingship in tribal societies, in early Irish and Welsh sources, suggests strong levels of continuity within the social structure of the indigenous tribes.

The importance of kings and aristocrats in earlier societies has been consistently exaggerated. This can be explained to some extent because what we now of Dark Age British society comes from sources which were not written down till later in the medieval period, at a time when the role of the king was much more important. Early Dark Age peoples seem to have been living in societies which were kinship- rather than kingship-based. This however does not diminish the centrality of warrior traditions in such societies.

Alfred P Smyth in his *Warlords and Holy Men*, dealing with Dark Age movements from Scotland to Wales, writes:

Welsh tradition asserted that Cuneda and eight of his sons migrated from Manaw to north Wales where they drove out Irish invaders who had settled there and founded in their turn various Welsh kingdoms and sub-kingdoms in Gwynedd. (p16)

This shows the links between different Celtic-speaking areas of Britain at this period. We are dealing here with an ancient link between tribes whose descendants ended up speaking different languages, but who inherited some common traditions from when they were speaking the same, or closely related, tongues. Such survivals are not surprising given similarities in economy, lifestyle and belief. To concentrate on linguistic differences as if they defined everything about these tribal peoples is to forget that language has never been a badge of ethnicity.

For most people, for much of human history, travel of more than a few miles from home was probably a rare event even though there were ongoing links between geographically diverse groups. My grandmother, for instance, lived in Dundee and her single trip to London, travelling by train, was a notable event in her life. However though most people in the Dark Ages might travel rarely and for no great distance, there can be no doubt that communication between different societies in Britain and the Continent had been constant for millennia. Traders and fishermen were capable of travelling great distances. Travel by water had been the norm from Megalithic times and provided a much easier alternative to overland travel, which involved passing through dense forests and vast areas of bog and marsh, particularly in the river valleys. In addition to river travel, the very existence of the Megaliths along the Atlantic littoral of Europe shows that the capacity for crossing the sea passages had been around for a very long time before the Dark Ages. Travelling by sea from central Scotland, or further north to Ulster or Wales at certain times of the year would be eminently practicable.

Up until the early Middle Ages, much of Britain and Europe consisted of self-sufficient, arable farming based economies which had developed from tribal structures. Tribes are aggregates of family groups bound together within a shared environment, with a shared culture, beliefs and ancestry. Much scholarship has concentrated on the warrior and leadership aspects of such societies, reflecting the obsession with militarism and aristocratic dynastic structures. Such structures although arising from tribal societies do not define them. In the Highlands of Scotland the basic cattle-economy warrior society survived at the very least from the Iron Age c. 500 BC to the 18th century. What existed before the Iron Age was probably also kinship-based. The term 'clan' means 'children', that is the children of the tribe. This concept is in no way feudal – it represents a fundamental attitude of communality among the Highland peoples, who were descended from both tribal Picts and tribal Scots. And between the Picts on the east and the Scots on the west, lay the lands of the Gododdin.

Manaw Gododdin, the land of the Gododdin, appears to have stretched from modern Stirling to Dunbar along the south side of the River Forth and included Edinburgh and all of East Lothian, perhaps going considerably further south. On the north-east, it adjoined Pictland and the Pictish tribespeople spoke a P-Celtic language closely related to that of the Brythonic tribes of Manaw. The beliefs and oral traditions of these peoples would be similar – they lived in contiguous environments, had similar economies and technologies and spoke closely related if not identical languages. While we cannot definitely state that they shared precise religious practices, surviving evidence would suggest similar belief patterns. The tribes from Manaw, or at least some of them, are referred to in Welsh tradition as the Gwyr Y Gogledd, the Men of the North, which indicates the shared heritage of much of early British tribal life. One intriguing possibility is that the tales of Arthur, like those of Cu Chulainn or Finn Mac Cuill in Gaelic-speaking areas, might have in turn derived from some older mythology in a language predating any of the Celtic tongues. The 19th century Scottish scholar WF Skene went as far as to suggest that the tales of both Arthur and Cu Chulainn originated in the lands around Loch Lomond, possibly the western limit of Manaw Gododdin.

In Welsh tradition we meet the Goddess figure Cerridwen. Just as Bride's flame was tended by Nine Maidens at Kildare, so

Cerridwen's Cauldron of Poetry and Inspiration is said, in the poem *The Spoils of the Abyss*, to be attended by Nine Maidens. The poem is attributed to Taliesin and this translation is from Lewis Spence's *The Mysteries of Britain*:

> By the breath of nine damsels it is gently warmed.
> Is it not the cauldron of the chief of Annwn in its fashion
> With a ridge round its edge of pearls. (p122)

In this poem, King Arthur has gone into the Otherworld (Annwn) on a quest for a magical cauldron. As with so much mythological and legendary material, the story would be told in many places and in each would be an integral part of the traditions and beliefs of local society. Cerridwen's cauldron is, like many others in the various Celtic traditions, a singularly magic vessel. F Marian McNeill pointed out in *The Silver Bough* that such cauldrons have influenced later ideas:

> The legend of the Holy Grail is one of the most striking instances of the fusion of Druidical and Christian beliefs, for it derives in part from the Magic Cauldron of Celtic paganism and in part from the Sacred Chalice of Christianity... (2 p164)

In one particular tale Cerridwen prepares a magic potion in her cauldron to give knowledge to her fearsomely ugly son Avagddu, as compensation for his looks. A serving boy, Gwion Bach, is set to watch over the brew. Cerridwen gives him explicit instructions not to touch the liquid, which has to brew for a full year when it will yield three drops of divine fluid which Cerridwen intends giving to her son. As the end of the year approaches, the three drops of the potion jump from the cauldron and land on Gwion Bach's finger which he immediately sticks in his mouth, thus becoming divinely inspired instead of Avagddu. Cerridwen immediately knows what is going on and rushes to the cauldron. In an endeavour to escape from her, Gwion becomes first a hare, then a fish and finally a grain of

1: Cerridwen also intends to kill little Gwion when his task is completed. It is this knowledge which inclines him to flee

corn. Cerridwen chases him as a greyhound, then as an otter and finally, in the shape of a hen she pecks up the grain of corn. Nine months later she gives birth to the bard Taliesin, Shining Brow, whom she casts on a river in a small basket. He is rescued by Gwuiddno Garanhir and grows to be the greatest bard of all time. MacCulloch in his *The Religion of the Ancient Celts* says of Cerridwen's Cauldron:

> ... Cerridwen was a deity of inspiration, like Brigit, though, like other Celtic Goddesses, her primary function may have been with fertility, of which the cauldron, supplying plenty and giving life, is a symbol. (p112)

The similarity with Bride, given here as Brigit, is striking, but the point here is that we have a clearly portrayed group of nine females who can be interpreted as priestesses of the Goddess. They tend Cerridwen's Cauldron which is used for both inspiration and prophecy and this would appear to make their role as priestesses explicit. Divination, like the shape-shifting in the chase sequence of this story, is a common attribute of many Nine Maidens groups. Inspiration and divination are part of a complex layer of ideas associated with the Nine Maidens and the shape-shifting stresses possible links to shamanism. Many societies have seen poetry and music as being divinely inspired. It seems that in both Bride and Cerridwen we are seeing two different cultural manifestations of a Mother Goddess figure common to the Celtic-speaking peoples, perhaps a figure from what was remote antiquity even to the people of Dark Age Britain. MacCulloch suggests that Cerridwen had been a corn-goddess at an earlier stage and the association of the cauldron symbol with fertility would tend to support this.

Loomis in *Celtic Myth and Arthurian Romance* talks of the Caldron of Tyrnog (could this be the fabled Q-Celtic Tir-nan-Og, the land of perpetual youth, sometimes associated with Avalon?) which was one of the fabled Thirteen Treasures of Britain in Welsh tradition:

Of this caldron it is said that 'if meat were put in it to boil for a coward, it would never be boiled, but if meat were put in it for a brave man, it would be boiled forthwith'. It is obviously the same as the pearl-rimmed cauldron of the Head of Annwn, which would not boil the food of a coward or a perjurer. (p233)

Both Welsh and Irish traditions have magical cauldrons which are in some ways similar. The Cauldron of the Dagda, a primeval father god figure in Irish tradition, is undoubtedly also a symbol of fertility. This cauldron could feed a host, significantly nine at a time, and also could bring warriors back from the dead, though they could not speak. This is like the cauldron Arthur brings from Annwn, the Welsh Otherworld or Hades, and as we have seen this concept of the magical cauldron is believed by commentators to have been part of the original inspiration for the idea of the Holy Grail. As McCulloch writes:

The three properties of the cauldron – inexhaustibility, inspiration and regeneration – may be summed up in one word, fertility; and it is significant that the god with whom such a cauldron was associated, Dagda, was a god of fertility. But we have seen [the cauldron] associated with Goddesses – Cerridwen, Branwen, the woman from the lake – and perhaps this may point to an earlier cult of Goddesses of fertility, later transferred to gods. In this light the cauldron's power of restoring life is significant, since in early belief life is associated with what is feminine. Woman as the fruitful mother suggested the Earth, which produced and nourished, was also female. The cult of fertility was usually associated with orgiastic and indiscriminate lovemaking, and it is not impossible that the cauldron, like the Hindu yoni, was a symbol of fertility... (p382)

McCulloch goes on to compare the concept of human food being interpreted as the food of the gods, (perhaps a bit like the wafer and wine in Christian communion?), with the idea of the actual family cauldron representing the cauldron of the gods. He suggests that myths then arose about the acquisition of magical cauldrons such as the Cauldron of Annwn sought by Arthur. Loomis makes the point that, in Arthurian Romance, the Grail has many aspects in common with such magical cauldrons, saying:

> ... in the Grail there was a fusion of the magic cauldron of Celtic paganism and the Sacred Chalice of Christianity, with the product made mystic and glorious in a most wonderful manner. (ibid)

In *The Mabinogion* there are references to the same or similar cauldrons. In the story *Branwen, Daughter of Llyr*, King Bendigeidfran says to Matholwch:

> I will give thee a cauldron and the virtue of the cauldron is this: a man of thine slain today, cast him into the cauldron, and by tomorrow he will be as well as he was at the best, save that he will not have the power of speech. (p124)

This is an exact match for the cauldron of the Dagda in Irish tradition. Also in the *Mabinogion* story *Peredur, Son of Efrawg*, there is reference to a similar vessel of healing:

> Peredur set out on his way thence, and he came to the court of the sons of the King of Suffering. And when he came to the court, he could see none but women. And the women rose before him and made him welcome. And at the beginning of their converse he could see a horse coming, and a saddle on him, and a corpse in the saddle. And one of the women rose up and took the corpse from the saddle, and bathed it in a tub that was below the door with warm water therein, and applied precious ointment to it. And the man rose up alive, and came to where Peredur was seated and saluted him and made him welcome. And two other men came in inside in their saddles, and the woman gave these two the same treatment as the one before... (p174)

There is also the Welsh tradition of Gwyddneu Long-shank's hamper which has some of the same attributes as the cauldron of

1: Bendigeidfran = Bran.
The 9 treasures visible in all Celtic realms to a greater or lesser extent are 58 the sword of light, the lance, the cauldron and the stone.

*'/ ʃ yddᵣₑₐₑ caᵤ le eₑᵤₐₜₑₗ ᵤᵢₜₕ Meᵣₗᵢₙ*

the Dagda. In the *Tale of Culhwch and Olwen*, the giant
Yspadden sets Culhwch a series of tests before he will give him
his daughter's hand in marriage. One of the tasks is to get
this hamper:

> ... there is that thou will not get. The hamper of Gwyddneu Long-
> shank: if the whole world should come around it, thrice nine men
> at a time, the meat that every one wished for he would find therein,
> to his liking. I must eat therefrom the night my daughter sleeps
> with thee. (p96)

This, incidentally, is the same Gwyddneu who found the baby
Taliesin and raised him. This hamper, like the cauldron, is a
deeply significant symbol. Cooking food in a cauldron suspended
over a fire, which was generally at the centre of the house below
a smoke hole, was widespread in much of the world. Not only did
this put the cauldron at the centre of all family and social life but
symbolically at the heart of the universe. In cultures where
shamanism has survived there are references to the shaman going
on his spirit journey by climbing a tree. Such trees have been
represented as linking the hearth to the centre of the sky through
the smokehole. Such symbolism is at one level quite mundane and
at another remarkably intricate. It is a mistake to underestimate
the potential for complex thought and communication in pre-
literate societies. The cauldron is the cooking pot of the family
and also a central mythic object at the same time. In votive
deposits, materials deliberately cast into wells, lakes or rivers,
cauldrons sometimes appear and there is a particularly striking
one from Carlingwark Loch at Castle Douglas near Dumfries in
Scotland, which can be seen in the Museum of Scotland. The
name of the loch, Carlingwark, has the term Carlin, the Scots
version of the Gaelic Cailleach, a term used until very late to
signify the Queen of the Witches in Scotland.

Among the Picts we have direct evidence of the importance of
the cauldron. Cauldrons are shown in a variety of forms on both
Class 1 Pictish symbol stones, which only have pagan symbols,

and on Class II stones, where Christian crosses appear with pagan symbols – generally on opposite sides of the symbol stone. The stone at Glamis Manse (there is a Nine Maidens Well nearby) has a particularly striking example of the cauldron with two pairs of legs protruding from it. This has been interpreted as showing some form of ritual execution. However, when we think of the respective cauldrons of the Dagda and Bendigeidfran in Irish and Welsh traditions there is a much more obvious explanation. This is a cauldron in which dead warriors are being brought back to life. The stated policy of the Christian church was to include pagan or pre-Christian ideas in their procedures and this seems to be is exactly what we see on the Pictish Class II stones – the combination of both sets of symbols. Perhaps the most famous ancient cauldron, the Gundestrup Cauldron, found in Denmark, but believed to have originated in a Celtic-speaking area, shows in its motifs and symbols what seems to be an intricate and complex mythological series of scenes. It is made of silver, showing how important this artefact was. The powers associated with these cauldrons, fertility, regeneration and abundance, are fundamentally feminine and associated with Mother Goddess figures. The link to Cerridwen's cauldron is significant in that we can see here the Nine Maidens as the tenders of the sacred symbol of the cauldron. Later we will look at another group directly referred to as druidesses, a rather vague term, but one which underlines this aspect of Nine Maidens groups as officiating priestesses in pagan ritual.

The Christian use of pagan temples to preach in was meant to ensure a smooth transition to the new religion; the continuing use of known symbols would have been reassuring for people coming to terms with the new religion. This perhaps explains how so many remnants of paganism survived into Christian times. It might also suggest why so many Pictish symbol stones have pagan symbols on one aside and Christian symbols on the other. The example of the Nine Maidens Well at Pittempton, where people came on the first Sunday after 1 May, suggests that traditional practices which stemmed from pre-Christian times were deep-

*r', Cei Later become Sir Kay.*

rooted in the minds of the people until surprisingly recently. It seems likely that this well would initially have been visited at Beltane, and that the day was moved to the first Sunday in May under the influence of the Christian church. There are several locations in Scotland where wells are still being visited.

The number nine crops up time and again in folklore and mythology in many parts of the world. We will look at this in greater detail in a later chapter but meantime a couple of examples from *The Mabinogion* itself will serve to illustrate this. In the story of Culhwch and Olwen we have the following:

> Cei had this peculiarity, nine nights and nine days his breath lasted under water, nine nights and nine days would he be without sleep. (p90)

Cei is of course one of the Arthurian warriors who later become Knights of the Round Table in popular romance. Another example from the same tale:

> She went to her chamber. They then arose to go after her to the fort, and slew nine gatemen who were at nine gates without a man crying out and nine mastiffs without one squealing. (pp93-4)

In the poem *Cad Godeu*, Taliesin himself says he was created 'of nine-form faculties' (Skene 1988 p137). It is clearly feasible to interpret the Nine Maidens associated with the Cauldron of Cerridwen as pagan priestesses but there is another group who show up in *The Mabinogion* with a different aspect. Peredur in the story *Peredur, Son of Efrawg* is generally accepted to be the basis for the later Perceval in Arthurian literature. He is a hero on a quest who meets with many adventures. As Lewis Spence said of this material:

> ... the Peredur story was derived from a number of older British tales dealing with the figures of British myth, and it reveals 'the peculiarly weird and fantastic impress of Celtic mythic tradition'. (1995, p171)

In time we will see that the motif of the Nine Maidens is indeed 'older' – but much, much older than any British tradition could possibly be.

In *The Mabinogion* story, Peredur comes to a castle. He hammers on the door of the castle with the butt of his spear and the door is opened by a powerfully-built, handsome, red-haired lad who leads Peredur into a hall. There a large handsome woman is sitting in a chair surrounded by her handmaidens. She welcomes him and offers him hospitality. The story continues:

> And when it was time to go to meat they went. And after meat, 'Twere well for thee chieftain,' said the woman,' to go elsewhere to sleep.' 'May I not sleep here?' 'Nine witches, friend,' said she, 'are there here, and their father and mother with them. They are the witches of Caer Lyow. And by daybreak we shall be no nearer to escaping than to being slain. And they have overrun and laid waste the dominion save for this house.'
>
> 'Aye,' said Peredur, 'here would I be tonight. And if trouble comes, if I can do good, that I will. Harm, however, I will not do.' They went to sleep. (p164)

The following morning just after dawn Peredur is awakened by a dreadful screaming. Picking up his sword he rushes outside, still half-dressed, to see the castle watchman being chased by a witch. The watchman is screaming. Before the witch can harm the watchman Peredur catches up with them and strikes the witch on her head with his sword, crushing her helmet. The witch then pleads for mercy:

> Thy mercy, fair Peredur, son of Efrawg, and the mercy of God.' 'How knowest thou, hag, that I am Peredur?' 'It was fated and foreseen that I should suffer affliction from thee, and that thou shouldst take horse and arms from me. And thou shalt be with me awhile being taught to ride thy horse and handle thy weapons.' 'On these terms,' he replied, 'shalt thou have mercy: thy pledge that thou should never do hurt to this countess's dominion.' Peredur took assurance thereof, and by

leave of the countess he set off with the witch to the Witches' Court. And he was there three weeks on end. And then Peredur took his choice of horse and arms, and set out on his way.' (ibid)

This episode with Peredur being trained and given arms by the witches is strikingly reminiscent of the Irish hero Cu Chulainn and his journey to receive training in arms from the female warrior Scathach. Although some writers have tended to associate Scathach with the Isle of Skye, off Scotland's west coast, Rees and Rees in their *Celtic Heritage* have the following:

Then Domnall, king of Scotland, told Cu Chulainn that he would not be fully trained until he came to Scathach [Shadow], at this [he] set out to the abode of this female champion in the East of Alba [Scotland]. (p254)

The east and north of Scotland were, of course, the areas where the Picts lived; areas where we have seen there are many remnants of Nine Maidens traditions. Like Peredur, Cu Chulainn has to face many perils but like Peredur also, he is trained in arms under female supervision. As Ross points out in *Pagan Celtic Britain*, Cu Chulainn is in fact trained by two warrior women:

The warrior Goddess, who is also a mother figure, clearly underlies the two powerful women whom Cu Chulainn trains under in Britain. They are called Scathach 'The Shadowy One' and Buananna 'The Lasting One'... (p291)

This motif is also present in the story of the arming of the Norse god Thor. Donald A Mackenzie writes in *Scottish Folklore and Folklife*:

Heroes who fight against them [giants] are invariably assisted by dogs... and they are instructed by indispensable wise women who possess magic wands. What appears to be the oldest Thor story belongs to this class. When Thor sets out to visit Geirrod he has neither hammer nor belt of strength. The Hag Grid, like the Scottish 'wise woman', warns and instructs him, and gives him her belt and magic wand. (pxxxiii)

The wand/hammer is reminiscent of the great Scottish Mother Goddess in her winter aspect of the Cailleach who hammers frost into the ground with her hammer and might suggest that Thor is being made divine by the Goddess herself. Are we seeing something of this same idea in the tuition and bestowing of arms on both Cu Chulainn and Peredur? If so, this would strengthen the link that appears to exist between Nine Maidens groups and the Mother Goddess herself.

The Isle of Skye has been associated not only with Scathach but in ancient tradition with a fearsome nine-headed, half serpent, half-human giant who is killed by a local hero after kidnapping Nine Maidens in order to eat them. It is from the body of this slain monster that the Long Island of the Hebrides – Lewis, Harris, North and South Uist and their associated islands are said to have been formed (see Chapter 6). Here again we have the motif of a monster and Nine Maidens though in this case the hero is successful in rescuing the group. Also we have a repetition of the lover-hero motif found in the Nine Maidens tales associated with Pittempton and Pitsligo.

However in the Peredur story, the nine witches – *gwiddonod* – of Caer Lyow are ambivalent in their nature – on the one hand they are devastating the land and on the other they give training and arms to the hero Peredur. Another group of Nine Maidens from Welsh tradition are also clearly malevolent, as recounted by Lewis Spence:

> In the life of the Welsh St Samson of Dol we are told that when he and a companion were passing through south Wales they had to traverse a vast forest. Suddenly they heard a series of shrieks so appalling that St Samson's companion took to his heels. The clamour arose from a forest-spirit which appeared in the shape of a very aged woman, with shaggy grey hair and wearing blood-red garments, who

bore a large trident dripping with gore. She swiftly came up with the flying man and plunged her three-headed lance into his body. She addressed the saint abusively when he asked her to desist from attacking his comrade and seemed to revel in her wickedness. But she informed him that it was impossible for her to leave the wood, while in a more distant part of it there dwelt others of her species, her mother and her eight sisters. (1948, p97)

Mont Dol is in Brittany, and this story continues the link to mountains and hills already noted. A Nine Maidens group there was associated with Belenus, generally seen as an early God among the Celtic-speaking peoples (Darrah, p218). Robert Graves in *The Greek Myths* states that St Samson's acolyte was killed and eaten by this group of Nine Maidens, but this is possibly because Graves was thinking of his own interpretation of the nine dancing maidens at Cogul, whom we will presently consider. I have found no other reference to cannibalism in this context.

The reference to her mother and eight sisters by this wild woman of the woods is possibly more reminiscent of the witches of Caer Lyow than either Bride or Cerridwen and their particular maidens. However, the tale seems to be a possible reference to sacrifice and recalls other tales in which the Nine Maidens are associated with a single male, though here a second male, St Samson himself, is spared to give us the tale. Just as Martin and Ochonochar are each associated with groups of nine women, so too are Arthur, the Norse god Heimdall, and the classical Apollo.

The oldest language spoken in Brittany is Breton, another P-Celtic tongue, related to Welsh. Breton traditions have references to yet another Nine Maidens group. Spence in his *Legends and Romances of Brittany* compares this being, the Korrigan, to the Welsh Cerridwen, telling us:

Like Cerridwen, the Korrigan is associated with water, with the element which makes for vegetable growth. Christian belief would, of course, transform this discredited Goddess into an evil being whose

1: The folk tale of Hansel and Gretel from Grimm? Echoes at least, but which way?

one function was the destruction of souls. May we see a relation of the Korrigan and Cerridwen in Triduana, or St Triduana of Restalrig, near Edinburgh who presided over a certain well there, and at whose well-shrine offerings were made by sightless pilgrims for many centuries? (p59)

He goes on to tell us about the traditions of the Korrigan abducting children and her habit of luring unwary travellers. She had the power, using her magic wand, to change the deep forest where she lived, into a magnificent castle, filled with delights, into which she would invite her chosen victim. There, seeing her surrounded by her nine attendant maidens he would fall deeply in love with her and abandon all that he had previously held dear, home, hearth, family, wife or lover. Then, as the sun rose:

> ... the charm was dissolved as the Korrigan became a hideous hag, as repulsive as before she had been lovely; the walls of her palace and the magnificence which had furnished it became once more tree and thicket, its carpets, moss, its tapestries, leaves, its silver cups wild roses and its dazzling mirrors, stagnant pools. (ibid)

Spence then recounts a specific tale concerning the mediaeval hero-knight Roland and his encounter with the Korrigan, from which he was lucky to escape. There are several remarkable features in this story. We have a clear representation of what was once the Goddess accompanied by Nine Maidens, but the switching from the beautiful, Bride-like figure to the Cailleach-like Hag is the opposite of many folktales in which the hero has the courage to kiss a loathly hag who then turns into a beautiful young woman. This is probably a sanitised version of an earlier tale where the hero would have made love to the loathly hag. The underlying pagan motif would seem to be that behind the duality of the Goddess lies the oldest duality of all, life and death. There is another similarity between the Korrigan and the Scottish Cailleach. The Cailleach has a hammer with which she pounds winter into the ground whereas the Korrigan has a wand that instantly changes her surroundings. The great French folklorist Paul Sebillot saw clear similarities between the Korrigan and her maidens and an earlier Breton group of Nine Maidens – the Gallicenae, mentioned in classical sources, who are considered later. The vision of the Korrigan, surrounded by her beautiful maidens is also similar to a tale from Norse mythology where the central figure is the goddess Menglod.

The generally accepted history of Brittany, at least in the British Isles, presents Celtic-speaking people migrating there from Cornwall in or around the 6th century, bringing with them mythology and legends which were originally British. If so this would strengthen the similarity Spence sees between Korrigan and Cerridwen. The suggestion of a link with St Triduana is not so clear but there are strong similarities in the stories of Triduana and Monenna, who also had nine female companions. Both are presented as having torn out their eyes to dissuade ardent suitors and both are associated with healing wells.

The association of Nine Maidens with Cerridwen, and also with the wild women of the wood that St Samson is said to have encountered, supports my contention that what we are dealing with in these cases are stories about what were, at one time, actual groups of pagan priestesses.

To return to Peredur: at the close of his story in *The Mabinogion* he is informed that the witches of Caer Lyow have killed his cousin and crippled his uncle:

And Peredur and Gwalchmei [Gawain] resolved to send to Arthur and his war-band, to ask him to come against the witches. And they began to fight with the witches. And one of the witches slew a man of Arthur's before Peredur's eyes, and Peredur bade her desist. And a second time the witch slew a man before Peredur's eyes, and Peredur drew his sword and smote the witch on the crest of her helm, so that the helm and all the armour and the head were split in two. And she raised a shout, and bade the other witches flee and said that it was Peredur, the man who had been with them learning knighthood and who was destined to slay them. And then Arthur and his war-

*1: The witches are armed and militant.*

band fell upon the witches and the witches of Caer Lyow were all
slain. (pp187-8)

Just before this section there is a statement which directly links
the Gloucester witches to traditions of the Grail Quest. A yellow-
haired youth tells Peredur he had appeared to him earlier as a
black maiden at Arthur's court and then says:

> ... I came with the head all bloody on the salver, and with the spear
> that had the stream of blood from its tip to the hand grip of the spear.
> And the head was thy cousin's, and it was the witches of Caer Lyow
> that had slain him. And 'twas they that lamed thy uncle. And thy
> cousin am I, and it is prophesied that thou will avenge that. (p187)

Here we are deep in mysticism. The head on the salver is reminiscent
of the Grail itself, often carried on a silver tray; the blood-tipped
spear is a recurring motif in Grail Romances and the lamed king is
another version of the Fisher King who is central to later Grail
legends. Additionally Peredur's cousin has already appeared to him
as a maiden – a strong suggestion of shape-shifting. The colours
yellow and black are also the colours associated individually with
Bride and the Cailleach in Scottish tradition.

A similar situation to Peredur's occurs in Early Welsh
literature. Loomis in his *Arthurian Literature in the Middle Ages*
quotes a poem from *The Black Book of Carmarthen*, 'In the
heights of Ystafngwn Cai pierced nine witches...' (p14). Although
we do not know where Ystafngwn was located, it is notable here
that the reference is to 'heights'. This suggests that, as with the
Dark Age sites associated with St Monenna, we are dealing with
a hill-top location. The witches with whom Peredur is involved
are based at Caer Lyow and Caer generally refers to hill-top sites.
Whether all hill-top structures are forts is debatable. The
standard military and aristocratic interpretation which promotes
this idea ignores the fact that many hill-top sites were used for the
great tribal fire festivals of Beltane and Samhain, and that hill and
mountain tops are widely associated with Mother Goddess

figures. Such sites were also likely to have been used in tribal society for a range of socio-political functions such as law-giving and land allocation.

The motif of the Caer Lyow witches, like that of the wild women of the wood, seems likely to have come about through the necessity for a Christian explanation of these female groups who are so unlike the predominantly masculine Christian idea, in which women are at best presented as meek and obedient and, at the worst, as the bearers of all sin. The wild women St Samson meets, like the nine witches of Caer Lyow, could hardly be further from the standard Christian ideal of womanhood. The Mother Goddess figure central to the old pagan religion was herself subsumed to a certain extent in the person of the Virgin Mary (or in the case of Bride through extremely close association with Mary) but these groups of nine pagan priestesses presented a different problem.

Whenever possible the Christian missionaries of the early Middle Ages substituted Christ, Mary and a host of saints as figures to be worshipped in the place of pagan gods and goddesses. Bede's *Ecclesiastical History* quotes the letter, originally in Latin, from Pope Gregory to Bishop Mellitus in AD 605:

> I have come to the conclusion that the temples of the idols in England should not on any account be destroyed. Augustine must smash the idols, but the temples themselves should be sprinkled with holy water and altars set up in them in which relics are to be enclosed. For we ought to take advantage of well-built temples by purifying them from devil-worship and dedicating them to the service of the true God. In this way, I hope that the people (seeing their temples are not destroyed) will leave their idolatry and yet continue to frequent the places as formerly, so coming to know and revere the true God. And since the sacrifice of many oxen to devils is their custom, some other rite ought to be solemnised in its place such as a Day of Dedication or Festivals for the holy martyrs whose relics are there enshrined. On such high days the people might well build themselves shelters of boughs round about the churches that were once temples and

1: Pope Gregory had specifically identified the Celtic church then existing in Scotland and Ireland as in need of swift and direct Romanisation. He perceived it as a great threat and rival to the Roman doctrine. He feared the pagan concepts which it had interwoven with the doctrine of Christianity to such an extent that

I amounted almost to a rival religion.

celebrate the occasion with pious feasting. They must no more sacrifice animals to the Devil, but they may kill them for food to the glory of God while giving thanks for his bounty to the provider of all gifts. (1, p30)

So killing animals as a sacrifice to pagan gods was not allowed but killing them for food and giving thanks for them to the Christian god was perfectly acceptable. For a religion that claims to be monotheistic it was very handy that the Christian missionaries had not only a supreme feminine figure but also a plethora of saints through whom to present their new ideas. It would have been difficult to deal with the Nine Maidens in this way as they had no direct similarity within the Christian pantheon of saints. Within Pictland, however, this is what seems to have happened. In other instances we have seen them portrayed as dark and malignant pagan figures. One Nine Maidens group was seen as druidesses, in Brittany, and some Scandinavian sources portray them as brutal and sadistic. It is hard to avoid the comparison with the propaganda spread about witches – who seem in the main to have been women notable for their knowledge of traditional lore and healing skills. A reading of trial transcripts from Scotland or England soon shows that 'witches' were tortured into repeating the exact formulae that their torturers, good Christians all, wanted to hear. Whether the witches were intending to work good or evil was deemed irrelevant.

In discussing both the witches and the Nine Maidens groups, we are largely reliant on early written sources that as far as we can tell were created exclusively by men – usually monks whose primary agenda was the propagation of their religion. I have noted elsewhere (McHardy, 1997) that ideas can survive for millennia through oral transmission before being written down, and suggest that what is seen as folklore has much to teach us. At the very least such oral traditions can give us material to compare with literary sources.

Another striking point about the witches of Caer Lyow is that they are fully armed and armoured. In this they resemble the

1. It was said that there were women warriors in the Celtic tradition. Also, women could hold land in the Celtic realms and were the full equals of men. Compare and contrast this with the Romanised role allotted to women.

Amazons, those shadowy female warriors of classical lore. There are also scattered references to women warriors in Celtic sources and in Scandinavian legend we have the Valkyries who are clearly warrior women of some kind. We should be aware that the training of the hero and the granting of arms to him are clearly some sort of initiation and that this is not necessarily just military. We know that sexual activity at sacred sites was not unusual in pagan times, and, given the references to sexual activity among different Nine Maidens groups, this may have been a component in such initiations. Most of what we know as history over the past few centuries, particularly in the dominant western culture, has excluded the social importance of the feminine aspects of human existence, preferring to deal with military and masculine areas of human activity. Such an approach is not designed to recognise the situation in which the hero figure only reaches his potential because of feminine influence, whether directly from a goddess or through some sort of priestess, which may be the most significant point of such tales.

Another striking similarity among the different language groups of Dark Age Britain is the figure of the Sow which is associated with Cerridwen. In one Arthurian poem, the *Spoils of Annwn*, Arthur goes to the Underworld to seek out Tyrch Twylth, the sacred boar who has a comb and scissors between his ears. This boar is reminiscent of the magical boar of Ben Gulbain which brings about the death of the hero Diarmaid in an Irish tale of Finn Mac Cuill. There are of course Ben Gulbains in various parts of Ireland and Scotland given as the locale of the story. MacCulloch in writes of this Goddess/boar association thus:

> A bronze statuette represents the Goddess riding a wild boar, her symbol and, like herself, a creature of the forest, but at an earlier time itself a divinity of whom the Goddess became an anthropomorphic form. (1992, p42)

Further to this the boar turns up on several Pictish symbol stones and the name *Orc*, meaning 'pig', is thought to have been the

The boar and abherence of matriarchy held by the Greeks would seem to have been transferred to the Romanised Church and the rest of Christianised Europe over time.

71

1'. The spiral is also prominent on the ring and cup carvings to be found in Scotland, Ireland and much of Western Europe. I first saw them in the Tayside region in Scotland. ‡

tribal name of the people from whom the Orkneys got their name. There is also the story of the sow which swam out from the Corryvreckan and then gave birth to nine piglets near Loch Craignish who were the progenitors of all the wild boars in Scotland. It is of direct interest that one of the islands in that loch is Eilean na Nighean, the Island of the Maidens, on which there is ancient structure, given on the Ordnance Survey map as a dun, or fort.

The association of the sow with the 'pot', or cauldron, of the Corryvreckan is reminiscent of Cerridwen. Perhaps what we have here is a veiled reference to a group of nine priestesses associated with the Corryvreckan. It might also be of some relevance that the shape Corryvreckan whirlpool makes on the surface of the sea is the spiral that occurs on carved rocks at the prehistoric chambered cairn of New Grange in Ireland and in prehistoric locations in several parts of Scotland, including some in the mainland area adjacent to the Corryvreckan itself. Here we have a cluster of ideas linking various prominent symbols and mythological motifs within an area that includes an Island of Maidens.

Before looking closer at the concept of Islands of Maidens or Islands of Women we should return briefly to the idea of the Grail. Many scholars have noted that the Grail seems to have developed from an earlier concept in the mythology of the Celtic-speaking peoples of Britain, and that the idea of the magic cauldron is the original of the Grail. It certainly seems to be a prime candidate. The Nine Maidens stories and other material point to the pre-Christian pagan tradition of the British Isles having the idea of the Mother Goddess at its core. Later ideas of gods cannot be ignored, but are not relevant here. The point of mythology is to give an explanation of life and death and the physical world in human terms which are easily understood by all. The Corryvreckan itself could be interpreted as the original idea from which the Grail eventually developed. It appears as a physical cauldron at certain times of the year, is strongly associated with the Goddess, and its whirlpool creates a spiral

Both the sow and the spiral have long associations with the Goddess

effect on the surface of the sea whenever the tide runs. This spiral is sent out into the full force of the Atlantic tide due to a particular alignment of local tides caused by the geography of the islands. It is a truly awe-inspiring sight even in relatively calm weather and it is not difficult to imagine how such a remarkable permanent geophysical event could affect people whose idea of the Mother Goddess encompassed all existence. In Norse tradition there is the motif of the roaring cauldron Hvergelmer, which is at the centre of the creation of the physical universe itself. There is also the Norse tale of the world being ground out on a giant mill, tended by Nine Maidens. Several scholars have drawn attention to the close links between deer and the Mother Goddess in several parts of Europe, including Scotland. Jura, the island on the south of the Gulf of Corryvreckan, means 'Deer Isle'. The wild boar has also been seen as a symbol of several Goddess figures in the British Isles. Here at the Corryvreckan there is the Goddess herself, associations with animals and symbols linked to her and foundation mythology explaining the onset of winter. It is a rich mythological mix indeed. And in nearby Loch Craignish there is that ancient structure, interpreted as a dun, or fort, on Eilean na Nighean, the Island of Maidens.

In Cerridwen we have a figure that is more like Bride than the Cailleach but it is within Welsh tradition we have the clearest and most explicit ideas of the Grail as they developed in a Christian context. As we have seen, here are explicit continuities between Scottish and Welsh traditions and it is conceivable that these continuities result from the central importance of the Mother Goddess figure in pre-Christian religion. And, time and again, with the Goddess we find the Nine Maidens.

1: There is also a cauldron or maelstrom in the somewhere in the Scandinavian countries.

Note: The goddess and her attendants are a concept which probably stretches back to the middle East, at least; it being brought West by the migrating peoples over the millennia. It would change in response to time and circumstance but the kernal or germ would remain to develop wherever it finally lodged. This would account for the strong similarities between many of the religions from China to South America, Palestine to Scotland.

Were witches covens not composed of 12 women and 1 man (ie the Dean)?
nine maidens and one man?

# CHAPTER 4

# Sisters of Avalon

IN HIS VITA MERLINI, the *Life of Merlin*, written in the 12th century, Geoffrey of Monmouth relates that after the final, fateful battle of Camlaan, the mortally-wounded King Arthur is taken away to the mystic isle of Avalon by Morgan, a mysterious and magical figure, similar to other mythological figures in the Celtic-speaking world. As Loomis puts it in his *Celtic Myth and Arthurian Romance*:

> [Geoffrey] tells of the nine sisters who dwell there, of whom Morgan is the fairest. She teaches them how to use healing herbs, and herself knows how to change her form and how to fly through the air. (p191)

These attributes of healing and shape-shifting link the sisters of Avalon to other groups of nine women and also to the later traditions associated with witchcraft. Healing and shape-shifting are also associated with shamanism and we should bear in mind that shamans are not always male, even today. Shape-shifting, taking the shape of various animals, is found in many traditions.

The Isle of Avalon is in many ways like that other mythical Celtic Otherworld – Tir nan Og, the land of eternal youth – and is itself a form of Paradise. Jean Markale tells us in *Women of the Celts*:

> ... it was also called the Fortunate Isle, because all the vegetation there grew naturally with no need of cultivation. The harvests were rich and the forests thick with apples and grapes, nine sisters ruled over it... It is the island of the apple trees, as Eden was the apple orchard and the Garden of the Hesperides contained the golden

In West Russia there were Islands of the Dead, which were local cemeteries approx 8,000 BCE.

Islands of the Dead is a concept which stretches from the Middle East to the Atlantic. They seem to have been ? funerary islands cited next to larger land-masses.

apples. The name Avalon became the Celtic word for apples (Breton and Welsh aval, English apple and Latin malum). In Irish legend, the Island of Women, towards which the hero Bran sailed, was known as Emain Ablach, and poets praised the apple trees that grew there and the beauty of their fruit. (p79f)

Here we are dealing with an ancient and widespread motif indeed. Rolleston in his *Celtic Myths and Legends* says that Caliburn (Excalibur) was made on the island, telling us:

Avalon, a word which seems to imply some kind of fairyland, a Land of the Dead, and may be related to the Norse Valhall. It was not until later times that Avalon came to be identified with an actual site in Britain (Glastonbury). (p138)

There are several important points here. The connection with the idea of the Land of the Dead links us back to the ideas of ancestor worship which is central to so much pagan religion. The suggestion of a similarity to Valhalla is striking in that, as we shall see, the Valkyries of Norse tradition can be interpreted as a Nine Maidens group. The suggestion that it is only in later times that Avalon became identified with a particular locale however goes against the idea I have put forward that such mythological material would be naturally sited in many different locales.

Avalon is an idealised concept and would thus be located in more than one place. In *Paganism in Arthurian Romance* Darrah makes this point when he writes, 'There were several cult sites of the same type, of which Avalon is merely a well-publicised example' (p217). Such cult sites, however far apart in space or time, share common characteristics suggesting that there is continuity in their being the focus of worship. Such worship I believe is the Old Religion, the worship of the Mother Goddess, the unifying symbol of all life itself. Behind this concept is the physical reality that we all come from our mothers. This gives the idea of the Mother Goddess a very strong psychological resonance. The significance of the Nine Maidens accompanying

1. If it comes from the Stone Age, then it is pre-Celtic. Perhaps the Celts merely continued on earlier concept of persuasive power.

Arthur on Avalon has been diminished because of models for interpreting the past which emphasise the masculine, military and hierarchic aspects of human existence. This is perhaps why so many commentators have not realised how widespread the motif of the Nine Maidens is. Their role as healers would appear to be central to the notion of Avalon, just as they are at the heart of so much other mythological and legendary material in other areas.

It is arguable that the motif of nine women involved in ritual activity, and therefore priestesses, comes from the Stone Age as we shall see. It is therefore possible that the sanctity of Avalon and other similar locations originates from the presence there of these women. It is worth considering the possibility that Arthur also inherited his original mythological significance from being associated with them. This could also apply to the other male figures associated with the Nine Maidens groups. The putative historical Arthur is a somewhat different case and, as with the Nine Maidens, he seems be just as at home in Scotland as in Wales or England, perhaps even more so. It is quite common in societies dependent on oral transmission that heroes can be given the names of gods and can perhaps become gods themselves. The key point would be whether such developments gave the resultant stories more benefit for contemporary society, by making the tales themselves work better.

In *The Celts*, Professor Jean Markale gives us the following:

> Morgan's kingdom is the Isle of Avalon, the mythical isle somewhere in the sea, the island in the middle of the world, a kind of navel but also a matrix, an inexhaustible store of energy. There Arthur stays until he can be reborn and return to the world. There Queen Morgan reigns... (p285)

The 'inexhaustible store' is reminiscent of the magical cauldrons of Celtic tradition, and at a more fundamental level signifies fertility and perhaps the womb, hence the recurrence of sexual motifs in this material. Despite the inability of the Christian and other male-dominated religions to come to terms with human

2. It is also worth noting that the Nine are always identified as having one who is fairer or wiser, in fact a leader.

This may mean a college of priestesses led by a Chief Priestess, one who stands in for the Mother. So it may be interpreted as the One –

sexuality such ideas will not go away. This perhaps also explains why so much originally pagan material has had to be disguised, while being assimilated, and why we get such divergent interpretations of the Nine Maidens – saints in Abernethy, witches in Gloucester, and so on. Markale goes on to make a similar point:

> As mistress of Avalon, Morgan must be the Mother of the Gods, or at least a transposition of a Mother Goddess myth into medieval times. Psychoanalytically speaking, the journey to Avalon is the regressus ad uterum, which appears to motivate most human activity and which finds its most poetical expression in Celtic legends. (ibid)

Without accepting this Freudian view of mythological and legendary material, it is clear that we are dealing with material with a strong hold on human thought. It is also interesting that Markale suggests Morgan may represent the Mother Goddess. This seems somewhat different from other Nine Maidens groups associated with figures like Cerridwen, Bride and perhaps Monnena where there is a clear Goddess figure to whom the nine are attached. Female fertility figures in mythology and folklore are often interpreted as direct representations of the Mother Goddess herself. However in situations where the Nine are presented as a priestess group then perhaps their chief priestess could herself be seen as a direct representative of the Mother Goddess. There has been a widespread assumption that Mother Goddess worship, which many scholars now accept played a significant part in early human development, disappeared completely with the rise of patriarchal religions like Judaism, Christianity and Islam. The widespread and late existence of so many variants of the Nine Maidens motif suggests the Old Religion never totally disappeared. Many magical or 'superstitious' rituals in folklore have long been considered as possible remnants of actual earlier worship.

In the *Vita Merlini*, Morgan is clearly the leader and teacher of the rest of the group, being the most skilled in the healing and

2: It was seen as such with the Queens of pre-Achaen Greece.
3: It just went 'sideways to the Sun', like the Tuatha De Danann. It/they are still there if one looks.
d the Eight. But where, dart from reproduction, does the male figure fit in?

1: Yet the Picts were not held to rule south of the South,
it was the Brythons/ Goddodins/ Votadini .

THE QUEST FOR THE NINE MAIDENS

magical arts. In the development of Arthurian traditions she takes
on a variety of roles. Some Arthurian romance tales like the
French *Estoire de Merlin* have her as Arthur's sister, others like
the Latin *Vulgate Merlin* and the French *Huth-Merlin* have her as
his niece and daughter of Lot, King of the Lothians, in Scotland.
Lot's supposed capital was Traprain Law, historically manned by
the British tribe the Gododdin, known to Ptolemy in the 2nd
century AD as the Votadini, and the site of one of St Monenna's
chapels. Traprain Law is some twenty miles east of Edinburgh. As
we have seen the first recorded mention of Arthur is in the Early
British poem, *The Gododdin*, written in Scotland in the 6th
century AD and describing a warrior raid into England by the
Votadini or Gododdin. The late Matthew MacDiarmaid
suggested in a literary periodical that *The Gododdin* was actually
written amongst the Picts, and Arthurian tales have survived
within areas we know were Pictish. Traprain Law, like Edinburgh
Castle, can be interpreted as a Castle of the Maidens, through the
association with St Monenna. The importance of this motif, and
of Lot and his sons Modred and Gawain, within the Arthurian
material is quite obvious. Arthur, as a mythological figure, or as
a figure derived from a particular heroic character, had an
important role in the traditions of the Gododdin, next-door
neighbours to the Picts on one side and the Scots of Dalriada on
the other. Arthur's association with the Nine Maidens is echoed
by other heroic and god figures in other traditions and appears to
suggest a stratum of belief underpinning such material, which
harks back to the notion of the Mother Goddess material
previously discussed.

In Arthurian literature as it developed in Europe, particularly
in France, Morgan became known as Morgan le Fay. Markale, in
*Women of the Celts*, gives us a description of Morgan:

> She was the sister of King Arthur, very gay and playful; she sang most
> agreeably; though dark in the face, very well made, neither too fat
> nor too thin, with beautiful hands, perfect shoulders, skin softer than
> silk, engaging of manner, long and straight in the body: altogether

*[handwritten margin note: Yet strife of the governments put almost all statues of the Virgin too present a beautiful beautiful, physically attractive women.]*

wonderfully seductive and, beside all that, the warmest and most sensual woman in Britain. Merlin had taught her astronomy and many other things, and she studied them so well that she became an excellent scholar and was later called Morgan la Fée because of the marvels she wrought. (p137)

This idealised female figure is perhaps a specific representation of the original Mother Goddess. The reference to her overt sexuality makes her the complete opposite of the idealised Virgin Mother of the Christian Church. There is an the ongoing awareness and appreciation of such female sexuality within the oral and song traditions of most European rural populations, harking back to pre-Christian times and recognising the importance of sexuality in human existence. In Malory's 15th century *Morte D'Arthur* this perfect Goddess figure has transmogrified into a devious plotter set on usurping Arthur by stealing Excalibur to give to her lovers, most notably Accolon of Gaul whom Arthur eventually kills in combat. This suggests that the magical sword itself was symbolic of power. The opposite portrayals of Morgan sit very well with the idea of the Mother Goddess as both giver of life and bringer of death.

Loomis draws attention to the possible link between Morgan and Modron, a goddess who was known in ancient Gaul. He tells us in *Celtic Myth and Arthurian Romance*:

> Celtic scholars are agreed that Modron is the old Gallo-Roman Goddess Matrona, who gave her name to the river Marne and to that extent at east was associated with the waters. But of course she [Morgan] was originally entirely distinct from the nine island priestesses, of whom she later became the chief. (p193)

*[handwritten margin note: as ?]*

The reference to the association with the waters is significant, reminding us of the sanctity of wells in particular. The suggestion that Modron derives from Matrona seems to be made on the usual grounds that because the Romans were writing things down before the rest of Europe (except Greece), their ideas must take precedence over all others, but Loomis here reinforces the possibility that a chief priestess could be seen as the direct representation of the goddess herself. And as we shall see Morgan and her sisters are not the only Nine Maidens to inhabit an island.

Many scholars have commented upon the similarity between Morgan and the Irish goddess, the Morrigan. The Morrigan and her sisters Badb and Mach, sinister and destructive beings said to haunt battlefields, are like the tripartite Goddess figures which occur all over Europe. The sisters often appeared as crows or ravens, carrion birds traditionally associated with the dead in battle and, in the portrayal of the three sisters as Furies, there is some similarity with the Norse concept of the Valkyries. They in turn are closely associated with the Norse god Odin who had two ravens, Hugin and Munin, representing Thought and Memory. In the late medieval Scottish ballad, *The Twa Corbies*, two ravens talk over the corpse of a dead knight, intriguingly linking these themes and reflecting how the Germanic and Celtic traditions, far from being separate, are interwoven at many levels. The appearance of Morgan, with or without her sisters, on the battlefield of Camlaan where Arthur lies mortally wounded would appear to derive from the same idea as the Irish battle-goddesses and the Norse battle-maidens and there are clear parallels between the taking of Arthur to the Paradise Island of Avalon and the Valkyries convoying the dead warriors to the Norse warrior heaven of Valhalla. This reinforces the point made by Rolleston that there are similarities between Avalon and Valhalla.

In the Irish saga the *Tain Bo Cualnge*, the Cattle Raid of Cooley, the Morrigan gives direct assistance to the great hero Cu Chulainn who, like the later Finn Mac Cuill, is very similar to the figure of Arthur in P-Celtic tradition. Initially Morrigan offers Cu Chulainn counsel which he is glad to take but later when she offers him love, he spurns her, always a dangerous course of action, and later they actually fight each other. In this light it is interesting that when Cu Chulainn dies, having tied himself to a standing stone so he would die on his feet facing his enemies, a crow comes and settles on his shoulder. This can be construed as the Morrigan coming to claim him, either from revenge or in her role a battle-goddess carrying off the dead hero. Again in this classic Irish saga we see two sides to the goddess.

Darrah mentions that:

> Avalon has already been mentioned in this book in the story of the dying raven which changed into a beautiful young woman and was carried off through the air by her raven companions to recover in Avalon. (p216)

Here we have a strong similarity to both the Morrigan and possibly the Valkyries, though here the crow figure is injured after a battle. The crow is a maiden who has shape-shifted and is one of a group from Avalon. This motif of groups of women living on islands and capable of shape-shifting is known elsewhere and it is not stretching a point to see this raven-woman as one of a group of Nine Maidens.

Morgan has been interpreted, then, as the leader and teacher of the sisters of Avalon and also as a version of the Mother Goddess herself. It seems feasible to see Morgan then as a High-priestess and as such, a living representation of the divinity worshipped. This idea survives in Christianity with the notion of the Pope being God's representative on earth and, as such, infallible. Whatever her dominant role, as Goddess or priestess, the figure of Morgan has continued to fascinate. Ideas and motifs, like myths and legends, survive because they continue to have relevance to the societies in which they function.

In the *Vita Merlini* Geoffrey of Monmouth gives the names of seven of the other maidens who inhabited Avalon with Morgan. Most scholars have seen these as a hotchpotch of references from classical sources. However there are possible links to other Celtic and Germanic sources. The names as given by Geoffrey are Moronoe, Mazoe, Gliten, Glitonea, Gliton, Tyronoe, Thiten, though the latter is given as 'Thiten, cithara notissima Thiten'. Geoffrey speaks of nine sisters so we must accept the possibility that two of these women were called Thiten, one of them being

Note! 2 names + morgan begin with M
3 names begin with G
2 names, possibly 3 begin with T
Could this in fact be a reference to a trinity X 3.
Some sources cite the Morrigan as 3, some as 9; as

the noted exponent of the lyre. Parry in his notes on the *Vita Merlini* says:

> The personal element in Geoffrey's names may here frustrate permanently a conventional solution about sources. Allowing for this, some suitable classical allusions may after all be present. Otherwise there is only a tenuous hint of acquaintance with Irish names. This added to the more likely link in the case of Morgan may mean that Geoffrey possibly saw some Irish material or was shown it by visitors or returned travellers and had it explained. Assuming Geoffrey was based at Llandaff at a suitable period of his life, contacts between that part of south Wales and Ireland were old, and sea access, by the evidence of the Llantwit Major breakwater, was still easier in the twelfth century than later. (p208)

Sea transport was of major importance in communications from the earliest times till relatively recently and can be seen as the medium by which the commonalties we have noticed within separate language-based traditions were developed and maintained. Trade alone, if continuous over generations, will foster extended cultural contact and communication.

The names of Morgan's sisters on Avalon are perhaps somewhat less obscure than Parry suggests:

**Moronoe:** other than its slight similarity to Morgan, or to Morrigan, this seems to convey little else. However if one takes note of how many names of goddesses or supernatural females have names beginning with Ma or Mo, we perhaps here have a reference to something other than the Q-Celtic *mor* meaning 'great' or 'big'. This, however, is purely speculative. Some scholars have suggested that the *mor-* prefix could have derived in names from a word like *muir* meaning 'sea'. As we will see, the idea of a great sea goddess is not obscure.

**Mazoe:** This name is very like Mazota, the eldest of the nine daughters of St Donevald (Donald) and a saint in her own right according to the *Aberdeen Breviary* and Forbes' *Kalendar of*

*Scottish Saints.* Mazota or Mayota is given as the original dedication of Drumoak on Deeside and it is an intriguing thought that she might be behind the name Portmoak at Loch Leven, given the plethora of antiquities in the area which include place-names referring to St Serf, tutor of St Mungo (Kentigern), the now collapsed natural stone tower known as Carlin Maggie and Gruoch's Well on Benartney, a name taken by some to be Arthurian. There is also the place-name Navitie Hill, at the east end of Benartney, which derives originally from *nemeton* meaning a sacred enclosure or area. Mazota is said to have talked to geese eating corn and convinced them to desist suggesting a possible remnant of a belief that the Goddess, or her priestesses, had power of animals. It is also notable that her saint's day, according to the Aberdeen Breviary is 22 December – the Midwinter solstice. Mazota is the most clearly distinguished of the Nine Maidens from Glen Ogilvy and seems to stand in the same sort of relationship to her sisters as Morgan does to the other eight inhabitants of Avalon.

**Gliten, Glitonea, Gliton:** these three are clearly linked and a possible comparison exists with Cliodhna's wave, mentioned in the early Irish text *Acallamh na Senorach*. It was a term given to every ninth wave, supposedly the strongest.¹ The references there are in the forms Clidna, Cliodhna and Cliodna within a few lines. Both of these are possibly examples of the common motif of three linked goddesses so common in the ancient world. The reference to waves brings to mind the daughters of the Norse sea-goddess Ran, who are often portrayed in Norse material as the waves themselves. One old Irish text refers to 'the seven daughters of the sea who fashion the threads of long life' which could be taken to be a degraded reference to the Nine Maidens of the Mill, another Norse group of Nine Maidens. It is worth also thinking here of the tale of Ruad, Son of Rigdonn, who is stopped at sea by nine sea-maidens. His journey seems to have been from Ireland to Scandinavia, linking the Irish and Norse material. Parry also tells of Kleite who appears as the wife of King Cyzicus, one of the

1: It is most usually held that there are 7 waves.

Argonauts seeking the Golden Fleece (Graves 1958, 1 p796), and who had a fountain of nymph's tears named after her following her suicide. This at least continues the link with water.

**Tyronoe**: Parry tells us this is like the Tyro who Odysseus meets in Hades (*Odyssey* II 235) and who is said to be the daughter of Ocean. This is explicit and very similar to the notion of the daughters of Ran mentioned above. It is tempting to see a link with the Irish place-name Tyrone and WJ Watson in his *Celtic Place-Names of Scotland* mentions a female name Turanais occurring in an Ogham inscription. Ogham, line or notch writing, primarily surviving on standing stones, occurs both in Ireland and in the Pictish areas, although in highly differentiated forms and apparently in different languages. Oghams in Scotland mainly occur on Pictish symbol stones.

**Thiten**: this name has been seen as deriving from Thetis, herself an ocean nymph and mother of Achilles. However another similar name with an equally marine connection is Tethys who in Ovid's *Fasti* was the wife of Ocean and herself a mother of sea-nymphs and river gods. Parry tells us that Teite's wave was, like Cliodhna's wave, a common expression in Cork on Ireland's west coast. He quotes the story of Teite, daughter of Ragamain, who was drowned along with many girl friends while out surf-riding! One interesting similarity, though not really close enough to suggest an identification with Thiten is Thenew, the legendary daughter of King Lot of the Lothians who had his capital on Traprain Law in East Lothian, already mentioned as a Nine Maidens site. Lot is also father of Modred and Gawain in Arthurian legend. Thenew converted to Christianity, was cruelly seduced and made pregnant, then, on refusing to marry, was first thrown off the citadel in a chariot which floated to the earth, then set adrift in the Forth estuary in an oarless boat. She drifted to the Isle of May, an important pagan and early Christian site, the name of which means the Island of the Maiden. It is perhaps not stretching a point to see that this could have been seen as Avalon within local tradition in the Forth valley. From here, accompanied by a shoal of fishes, she went upstream where she landed at Culross on the north shore and gave birth to St Kentigern. Here Kentigern was raised by St Serf, a character associated with dragon lore and that long-surviving remnant of the Celtic Church, the Culdees. Kentigern went on to fame himself at the court of the King of Strathclyde. He later became the patron saint of Glasgow under the name given him by St Serf – Mungo. In some Arthurian material Morgan herself is given as the wife of King Lot. Again there are strong marine references in Thenew's story as well as links to pagan and Christian sites. JS Glennie in *Arthurian Localities in Scotland*, suggested that Thenew was one of the maidens accompanying Monenna, who were nine in number.

Because of the truly ancient provenance of our earliest source, a Magdelanian cave-painting in Catalonia, it seems highly probable that the classical, Celtic and Germanic sources are waters from the same well. By the time Geoffrey of Monmouth was alive there were probably some literary sources, as Parry noted – and he may even have had access to oral material regarding the priestesses on the Isle of Sena. Oral tradition also preserved some of the relevant material within the islands of Britain. Given the ongoing survival of such traditions as those at the Nine Maidens Well at Pittempton and the ritual at Bride's Well at Sanquhar, more than half a millennium after Geoffrey was writing, it would appear folly to argue against such a possibility.

In Malory's *Morte D'Arthur* the hero is spirited away after his final battle to the Isle of Avalon having ensured the return of his magic sword Excalibur to the Otherworld. The story of the return of the sword to a lake, or loch, has survived in folklore in out of the way places such as Loch Moan in Galloway in south-west Scotland, an area long inhabited by people speaking a P-Celtic language. Similarly, in Dorset, Loe Pool is said to be the location for the return of Excalibur. In this case a further connection is the source of the river Loe which feeds the Loe Pool basin. This rises to the north on the Nine Maidens' Downs. We are close to Cornwall here and Cornish like Welsh, Breton and Pictish is a P-Celtic language, currently undergoing a revival. As we have seen, similar societies, with closely related languages are likely to have closely linked sets of beliefs, myths and legends. Such beliefs are the psychological glue of any given society. Striking similarities in mythology and folklore, originally passed down through storytelling, exist in significantly different human societies. One such motif closely linked to the Nine Maidens themselves is the notion of the Island of Women.

Much of this material seem to refer back to Pre-Celtic times. It is a pity that we do not know more about the inhabitants of these islands and their religious beliefs before the Celts arrived.
What we do know of religious belief seems to have an affinity with that of pre-Achaean Greece, eg Mother Goddess, Solar temples and Titans / Giants
References to dwarves can associated with the Norse Gods.

# CHAPTER 5

# Islands of Women

WE HAVE ALREADY SEEN that Avalon was inhabited by Nine Maidens. The concept of Islands of Women is quite widespread in early Irish and other European sources. The concept of men, or in a number of instances, a single man, visiting an island to make love to the isolated women there, is also widespread. Talking of the motif within the Celtic-speaking world, Rees and Rees tell us that, 'The Island of Women is... the quintessence of femininity and erotic pleasure' (ibid p323). This is quite explicit and we should remember the importance of fertility within what we know of pagan religions. In Arthurian legend, Avalon is the home of healers. It is linked to the concept of Emhain Ablach, the Island of Apples which has often been interpreted as a Celtic Paradise. Markale identifies Emhain Ablach as an Island of Women and compares it to Abalum in the Baltic, an important prehistoric centre of the amber trade. Amber was sometimes described as the tears of the Goddess. He suggests that the Celtic Paradise island was non-patriarchal and suggests that such manifestations might be relics from an earlier time. To support this idea of older origins Markale then gives two classical sources which are of fundamental importance to the search for the Nine Maidens.

The first he quotes is Pomponius Mela, a Romanised Iberian geographer writing in the 1st century AD, and giving an account Markale sees as tallying very closely with Geoffrey of Monmouth's account of Avalon:

> Facing the Celtic coast lie a group of islands which takes the collective name Cassiterides because they are very rich in tin. [Britain] Sena in the British Sea [English Channel], facing the coast of Osimi

1: In ancient Greece the apple was frequently associated with Hera, the Queen of the gods, and taken to be her fruit. It was also a symbol of death.

87

[North Finistere] was renowned for its Gallic oracle, whose priestesses, sacred for their everlasting virginity, were said to be nine in number. They were called 'gallicias' [Gallicenae] and were reputed to have the power to unleash the winds and storms by their spells, to metamorphose into any animal according to their whim, to cure all disease said to be incurable, and finally, to know and predict the future.

But they reserved their remedies and predictions exclusively for those who had travelled over the sea expressly to consult them. (1986, p81).

These Breton druidesses, as they are referred to elsewhere, are in many ways similar to Morgan and her sisters. Shape-shifting, weather working and divination also link these women to that much later, and much maligned group, the witches. Markale draws attention to a similar account from the Roman geographer Strabo:

In the ocean, not right out in the open sea, but just facing the mouth of the Loire, Posidonius pointed out to us a rather narrow island inhabited by the so-called Namnete women, who were possessed by Bacchic passion. They tried by means of mysteries and other religious ceremonies to appease and disarm the god who tormented them. No man ever set foot on their island: it was they who crossed to the mainland every time they wished to do business with their husbands. (ibid)

He informs us that Mela seems to have perceived these island groups of women as being like the Roman Vestal Virgins who were priestesses and goes on to differentiate Morgan and her sisters from this idea:

Judging from the various accounts of King Arthur's sister, 'the hottest and most lustful woman in all Great Britain', as the author of the Lancelot en prose described her, Morgan and her sisters were more like bacchantes. (ibid)

Bacchantes were the female followers of the god Bacchus and were known for drunken orgiastic behaviour. Markale notes that ancient writers interpreted the term virgin differently from today. The term could be used of a woman with a child or a married woman without a child, that is, a female who is not a matron. They did not use the term to mean *virgo intacta*, a female who has not had sexual intercourse. This is a later meaning.

Several earlier writers made the connection between Morgan of Avalon and the Gallicenae of Sena, and it is surprising they did not see further connections. Darrah mentions the similarities between the Isle de Sein and Avalon and raises another interesting link:

> There is a close parallel to Sein in the ancient Welsh epic Preiddeu Annwfn which describes Arthur's raid on an Otherworld Island surmised to have been Grassholm, off the east of Pembrokeshire where there was a cauldron tended by nine virgins. The cauldron evidently had an oracular function for it was warmed by their breaths to provide inspired utterances. Nine priestesses on an island is a feature common to Avalon, Sein and Grassholm, and there is a remarkable similarity in the situation of two of them, Sein and Grassholm. Both are some miles off extreme west-pointing peninsulas, and both are off shore from megalithic holy places, in the case of Sein, from the south of Brittany leading to Carnac in the east; and of Grassholm, not far from the source of the bluestones [of Stonehenge] at nearby Prescelli. (p216)

He comes very close to anticipating the proposition presented here, which is that an ancient religion, possibly rooted in the Stone Age, survived through an institution of nine priestly women existing over a wide geographical area. He goes on to say:

> To have several recollections of this cult, again in three entirely different literatures, Latin, Welsh and French, gives some idea of its original power, but it does not lead directly to the location of Avalon. Glastonbury certainly fits, but at this stage only because it was once surrounded by water. On the other hand, the three recollections, of

three different places of similar characteristics, two of them identifiable and far apart indicate that Avalon was not unique. There were several cult sites of the same type, of which Avalon is merely a well publicised example. (ibid)

Although these locations are distant from each other, the journey from Grassholm to Sena is practicable by sea through much of the year and similarly Glastonbury would have been accessible while it retained its island form, an annual occurrence till the area was extensively drained. Glastonbury has often been suggested as the site of Avalon and is certainly a very important sacred site. However, so far, I am unaware of any direct association there with Nine Maidens.

JF Campbell in his great work *Popular Tales of the West Highlands*, written in 1860, mentions the maidens of Sena when discussing the Gaelic term *gruagach* which he said generally meant a maiden and that:

> ... this may be the same word as Groac'h or Grac'h, a name given to the Druidesses, who had colleges in an island near the coasts of Brittany. (p10)

The Isle of Sena, a few miles of the north-west coast of Brittany is now deserted. It is known today as the Isle of the Druidesses and is something of a tourist attraction. Campbell also mentions a 'Greogaca' that had druidic connections and haunted the island of Insch near Easdale (p61). Lewis Spence in his speculative and entertaining *History of Druidism*, commented on the widespread occurrence of Islands of Women. A section of his book is devoted to 'Insular Communities of Women'. Here Spence talks of the Gallicenae and tells the story of the contemporary Namnete Women with their annual rebuilding of their temple, which was originally reported by Strabo in the 2nd century AD:

> Each woman brought a bundle of building material to the work, but should any of them permit her burden to fall to the ground, she was

instantly torn to pieces by her companions. It is noteworthy that later Norse lays retain memories of such cults in the Channel Islands, allusions being made in the Helgi lays to the existence of sibyls or hags such as Mela mentions in Guernsey and other adjoining insular localities. (p63)

Both the description of the killing of one of the women and the choice of the word 'hag' are significant here. This passage seems to be a memory of some sacrificial rite. Spence goes on to mention similarities to Circe in the *Odyssey*, suggesting a link with the lost account of the travels of Pytheas to north-western Europe and then mentions Campbell's reference to *gruagach* and *grac'h*. He continues:

> We find a parallel to the priestesses of Sein, perhaps in the legend of the sorceresses or fairies of Gloucester, who guarded the thermal waters of that city. One of them indeed appears in the legend of Peredur, who, it was prophesied, should overcome her and her sisters. (p63)

Somehow he does not make the connection to Morgan and the sisterhood of Avalon. The Breton term *grac'h*, whether or not related to *gruagach*, undoubtedly has the something of the same meaning as the Welsh *gwrach*, meaning 'hag', or 'witch' – Breton and Welsh are after all related P-Celtic languages. The Welsh term survived at least into the nineteenth century in Pembrokeshire where the last sheaf of the harvest was called *gwrach*, exactly as the last sheaf in Scotland was called the Cailleach in Gaelic-speaking areas. The association with the harvest and the exact match of the words leads to the conclusion that this was initially in the far distant past a term for the Mother Goddess herself which had perhaps been transposed to her devotees by Celtic-speaking times.

Some similar ideas from Breton lore are mentioned in Anson's *Fisher Folk Lore*:

> On the intensely Catholic Isle-de-Sein there used to be the conviction that certain women had what was known as 'le don de vouer', i.e. the

power of communicating with the Devil or his emissaries, in other words that they were witches. Fishermen alleged that they had seen these women on dark nights launching mysterious boats (bag-sorcérs) to enable them to take part in a witches' Sabbath or coven known as groach'hed. (p30)

These women are clearly witches but their location and the name of their meeting is a tantalising link with previous inhabitants. In fisher communities around the coast of Britain many witches were reputed to be able to raise the wind – an attribute of the Gallicenae, according to the early accounts.

In the late 17th century, church leaders on the Castennec peninsula in southern Brittany were worried by an upsurge of what appeared to be pagan worship of a Goddess figure. The idol was called *Groa-hourn*, Breton for 'old woman' or 'sorceress', a title that is like *grac'h* and *gwrach* with the same sense as Cailleach in Gaelic or Carlin in Scots. It seems that the figure was possibly something like a sheila-na-gig, the naked females found carved on churches in England, Ireland and Scotland, holding their labia open to display their sex. The statue was thrown in the River Blavet by outraged priests but thirty years later was rescued by a local aristocrat. The local people were disappointed to hear he was to keep her locked up on his estate and eventually he commissioned a mason to clean her up. In trying to do this the statue was destroyed and the count ordered a new, more respectable one which he considered fit to be seen by the general public. This still exists, known as the Venus of Quiniply. Although it was possibly nothing like the original *Grou-hoaurn*, the locals took the new 'Venus' to their hearts and began to pray to her. This suggests a transference of belief that is hardly to be wondered at, if we are indeed dealing with a pattern of belief originating thousands of years ago.

Another author who noticed links between Arthurian tradition and the Gallicenae of Sena was Robert Sherman Loomis. In his *Celtic Myth and Arthurian Romance*, he says:

1: Groa was the name of a giantess in Norse mythology, she had connections with thor.

This name, according to some medieval writers was either due to the many apples to be found there or to a certain Avalloc, who is said to have lived there with his daughters because of the secrecy of the place. Rhys also quotes an anonymous Latin description which mentions not only the eternal spring, the abundance of flowers, the absence of age or disease, but also a royal virgin, most beautiful, surrounded by her maids. She bears the wounded Arthur to the hall of King Avallo, and heals him. It goes without saying that the relation of this regia virgo to rex Avallo is that of daughter to father. Geoffrey of Monmouth in his Vita Merlini gives another description of the fairy isle under the name Isle of Apples. He tells of the nine sisters who dwell there, of whom Morgan is the fairest. She teaches them how to use healing herbs, and herself knows how to change her form and how to fly through the air, so that when she will, she is at Bristol, Chartres or Pavia. After the battle of Camlaan, the wounded Arthur is brought across the seas by Telegesinus and Barinthus (in whom have been recognised the mythical bard Taliesin and a sea-god) to Morgan, who undertakes to cure him if he is left with her long enough. De la Rue has justly pointed out how strikingly this story of nine women, skilled in healing and shape-shifting, who live on an island, ministering to those who come, bears to the account which Pomponius Mela gives of an island, Sena off the coast of Brittany, the modern Sein, which modern tradition connects with Merlin. (p191)

Loomis did not think that Geoffrey had access to Pomponius Mela's *de Geographia* in which the Gallicenae were described. Nor does he notice the widespread occurrence of the Nine Maidens motif. The presence of a King Avallo is an example of how the past has been interpreted through masculine and hierarchic models – such an important island would simply have to be ruled by a king! He does mention that several medieval texts refer to Morgan as a goddess and that she was called Modron in an early Welsh source. This he connects to the old Romano-Gallo goddess Matrona as others have done. It is also significant that he has Morgan as the teacher of the other sisters on the Isle of Avalon, underlining her possible original function as the Goddess, or at least her role as chief priestess directly representing the Goddess. Discussing the fundamental role of Mother Goddess in providing fertility, Loomis says:

> According to the vulgar traditions of the Bretons Arthur was borne away to the Isle of Avalon in order that his wounds, annually reopening, may be cured by the Fay Morgan with her healing applications. Now I venture to say that the immortal hero, whose wounds break out afresh every year, must be like the Maimed King, in sympathetic tune with the vital forces of the earth, with the ripening and rotting grain, with the greening and withering trees, with the waxing and waning solar heat. (p194)

One of several possible instances of the Islands of Women motif within Scotland is Innishail in Loch Awe. In Mackinlay's *Ancient Church Dedications in Scotland* it is described thus:

> Its church, of which some remains are still to be seen in an ancient burying-ground, was under the invocation of St, Fyndoca, whose name appears in a shortened form in that of Findo-Gask... in the Strathearn district of Perthshire, where the church is believed to have had the saint as its titular. (p488)

This St Fyndoca is one of the Pictish Nine Maidens referred to in Chapter One as being at Glen Ogilvy and Abernethy. Nigel Tranter in *Argyll and Bute* refers to a tradition of there being a nunnery on Innishail. He further says that, '... it was renowned as being tainted by the evils which were apt to beset such places' (p168). This is a reference to widespread tales of illicit sexual activities.

Priory Island in Loch Tay is a crannog or artificial island which was also supposedly the site of a nunnery. We have already seen that the memory of these women survived in the Feill nam Ban Naomh – the Fair of the Holy Women – which they began and which took place on 26 July at Kenmore till the turn of the 20th century, having moved there from its original site at nearby Inchadney where there was an early Christian site.

Heather Wheater in *Kenmore and Loch Tay*, tells us:

> It is said too, that they did emerge once a year to go to the market,
> but not to sell their wares. To have, instead a rollicking good time one
> day of the year and then return to their celibate cloister for the next
> 364 days. (p3)

Tradition tells us that they were eventually expelled and crossed
by the ferry at Kingharry to Portbane on the south side of the
loch. Above nearby Acharn is a hillock called Faire nam Ban, the
Nun's Watch, where it is said they looked for the last time on their
former home before tramping away across the hills forever.
Strictly speaking we might translate Faire nam Ban as the
Woman's, rather than the Nun's, Watch and the name of the Holy
Women, Ban Naomha, crops up in many locations across
Scotland. John Christie in his *The Lairds and Lands of Tayside*
gives a reason for the expulsion of the nuns from the community:

> According to local tradition, the Priory... [was] occupied by nuns
> who, breaking their vows of celibacy, were summarily expelled from
> the island, which was never again templed by a religious body. (p32)

A charter known as the Chronicle of Fothergill, long kept in
nearby Taymouth Castle, and published in *The Black Book of
Taymouth*, tells us:

> The year of God 1615 on the Nine Virgin's day the procession and
> market was held and begun at Kenmore on Loch Tay, and there was
> no market nor fair held at Inchadin where it was wont to be held.
> (trans p324)

The Chronicle does not mention the presence of any nuns.
Perhaps the nuns are themselves a late development in this story
of Nine Maidens or virgins. These local traditions present a
picture of what appears to be a Nine Maidens group living on an
island late into the Christian era and taking an active part in the

social life of the community by organising an annual fair. We also have a tradition that stresses the disruption of the 'nunnery' because of sexual activity. It is an intriguing aspect of the Nine Maidens that in their role as priestesses of some kind, several of their stories have such strong erotic overtones. A society which worshipped the Mother Goddess might well have been free of coyness and repression when dealing with female sexuality. However, the possibility cannot be totally discounted that the story of the banished nuns was Protestant propaganda after the Reformation. Even so it would still leave us with what appears to be a Nine Maidens group on an Island of Women.

Innishail and Priory Island are not the only possible Islands of Women in Scotland. Eilean Nighean (Island of Maidens) in Loch Craignish has already been mentioned but there are others, suggesting the Nine Maidens' link with islands is very strong and very ancient. Tradition has it that Inchcailleoch, the Island of the Cailleach in Loch Lomond, had a nunnery though there is no other evidence available for this. A similar tradition exists concerning Nuntown on the Hebridean island of Benbecula. This story intriguingly involves a woman called Cailleach nam Mogan or the Old Woman of the Footless Stocking! Whether this is a misreading of an original reference to Morgan is impossible to say, but as the founder of this nunnery was said to have been an Irish princess, there may be a connection with the Morrigan. The idea of Islands of Women is particularly strong in Hebridean tradition as are associations with Bride.

In her book *The Inner Hebrides and their Legends* Otta Swire tells of the island of Eigg being called Eilean nam Ban More, the Island of the Big Women. JG Mackay mentions that there is a loch on the island known as the Loch nam Ban Mora and that it contains a crannog. He says that the women of the place were '... of such unique proportions that the stepping stones by which they gained their home were set so far apart as to be useless to anyone else.'

This finds an echo in the tale of Mac Iain Direach in which the hero works for the Seven Big Women of Jura in order to gain their Glave [sword] of Light to help in his quest to find a particular blue falcon. These women are clearly magical and may represent another ancient grouping of pagan priestesses. Whether the women were giantesses or not, they clearly fit into this motif of Islands of Women. Just as there is an Eilean Ban (Island of Women) off the isle of Iona, sacred before Christian times, there is mention of something similar in Ireland. Borthwick in his interesting *Irish Druids and Old Irish Religions* says:

> ... in the Bog of Monaincha are two islands. On one was a monastery for men, their wives occupying the neighbouring Woman's Isle. Giraldus Cambrensis, who wrote of the Community of Monaincha in the twelfth century, called it the church of the old religion, and politely designated as Demons all who belonged to that former church. (p285)

It is also interesting that another well-known group of forceful women – the Amazons were said to live on a lake in Libya. Graves in *The Greek Myths* writes that they 'once inhabited Hespera, an island in Lake Tritonis which was so rich in fruit-bearing trees, sheep and goats, that they found no need to grow corn' (1 p147). This fertility is very much like the idea of Avalon and the name Hespera seems linked to the Hesperides, the female guardians of the golden apples of the goddess Hera on Mount Atlas. Another similar Greek idea is mentioned by Graves. Elysium is a Paradise island where it is perpetual day, always pleasantly warm, and where there are constant games and revels. Graves also points out that 'Elysium seems to mean apple land – as does the Arthurian Avalon.' (1 p123)

We have already seen that Avalon was inhabited by Nine Maidens and that the concept of Islands of Women existed in early Irish and European experience, the best known possibly being the Island of Women in the *Odyssey*. Odysseus manages to pass the notorious island of the Sirens without his crew being lured to their deaths by the Sirens' singing. This is because he had been advised to fill his crew's ears with wax by Circe, an enchantress who also lived on an island.

In the Gaelic story type known as *Imrama*, journey tales, there is one strikingly relevant example. This is in the *Imrama Mael Duin*, generally thought to have originated in 8th century Ireland and surviving in a text from the 10th century. Mael Duin sets off on a journey to locate the slayer of his father. On the advice of a druid he takes 17 companions who with himself comprise 18 souls. Rees and Rees, in their *Celtic Heritage*, tell us:

> An Island of Women. Here Mael Duin and his seventeen men are received by a queen and her seventeen daughters [two groups of Nine Maidens?] The women feast them, consort with them and try to induce them to remain there to live a life of perpetual pleasure and eternal youth. (p321)

A later, more generally known version of the tale is the Voyage of Bran or Brendan. St Brendan is considered as being specifically Irish. However it is interesting that one of the wells above Abernethy was dedicated to the saint as mentioned by Butler, in *The Ancient Church and Parish of Abernethy*:

> A well in this parish, adjacent to the Gattaway stream, was known to the old inhabitants as Brendan's Well, and the name still survives in the corrupted form Brendi Well... Tradition states that St Brendan died and was buried at Glamis in Forfarshire, and an ancient cairn there was known as Brendi's cairn. ... it seems beyond doubt that he did visit this district, it is more than likely that he must have been at the early Abernethy church. (p102)

As we have seen, Glamis was very strongly associated with the Nine Maidens and perhaps in this association with Brendan, who also visited an Island of Women, we may be seeing some remnant of belief linking him directly with the Nine Maidens. The motif of a single man, or a group of men visiting an island to make love to the socially isolated women there frequently recurs, raising the possibility that Brendan's voyage is a Christianised, sanitised, version of this motif.

Folklorist and storyteller Dr. Sheila Douglas gives a tale collected from storyteller John Stewart of Blairgowrie in her book *King of the Black Art and other folk tales*. John Stewart was illiterate and all his stories came to him through oral transmission. It is likely that none of his direct ancestors had been literate. It is only fairly recently that the children of the travelling people in Scotland generally learned to read and write. Remembering that the Australian material earlier referred to showed how long data can survive within the oral tradition, perhaps the similarities in the following with the Imram of Mael Duin are not so surprising. In the tale Jack and his companions are setting off in pursuit of pirates who killed his father eighteen years before. After preparing for all of two months they are just about to set off when Jack is asked by an old man if he has the right number of men. He tells the old man, who happens to be a druid, that he has six companions making a total of seven. They set off and were rowing past a castle when two young princes came out and asked to accompany them. Jack tells them that the druid said it would be unlucky to take more than seven. Despite this the two young princes threaten to jump in the sea and swim out to the boat until Jack agrees to take them along. The company now numbers nine. After about a week they come to an island with a big castle. They go ashore and approach the castle but seeing a big crowd of people gathered there, they decide to bide their time and sit down. Soon a splendid lady on horseback approaches, but she rides straight past them without a word, and on up to the castle. Soon a woman comes down from the castle and says the queen wants them to visit her.

The story goes on:

> So Jack an his men were ushered into this great big hall, an there were seven cups a sittin down this long table an decanters o wine, an bread an fruit, an a long sofa. So Jack counts the seats an says, Seven seats. She must hae known we were comin! But she doesnae know there's two extra. But we'll try an roll them in an they'll maybe no notice... So they stayed and they wandered about the island, hunting an havin fun wi the girls till they'd been there a month. (p56)

The last comment clearly hints at sexual escapades. In the end, despite the tricks and remonstrations of the queen and her daughters, Jack and his companions escape. There are no specific mentions of a woman for each of the sailors but this does seem to be an Island of Women: the erotic motif is not explicit, but there are nine sailors so we can perhaps assume there were originally Nine Maidens in this tale. The story continued to be told within traveller tradition well into the 20th century having survived the social upheavals resulting from the major industrial and urbanising developments of western society.

The tale of the Hebrides being created by the Cailleach dropping an apron full of material she had intended using to help build Scotland was mentioned earlier. Here is an ancient tale from the Skye also mentioned by Otta Swire in her *The Legends of the Outer Hebrides*.

Long ago, before the Outer Hebrides had come into being, before the druids or their ancestors had raised the stone circles of Scotland, a fierce giant lived in a great castle on the only island beyond the Inner Hebrides, Stack Rock. This giant was half human, half serpent and had nine heads with appetites to match. He favoured the flesh of young girls and was constantly raiding the Inner Hebridean islands like Skye, Eigg and Rum, taking nine maidens at a time. One day he raided Skye and made off with his nine captives. One of these lasses was betrothed to a local lad who on hearing the news, refused to mourn for her. He decided to try and rescue her. He headed off for a remote mountain loch he knew of. There he spoke to the kelpie, or water-horse, of the loch, and enlisted his help. Together they headed off for Stack Rock and went straight into battle with the giant. After a long, fierce struggle the young man and his kelpie assistant overcame the giant and killed him, cutting off eight of his nine heads. He then freed his betrothed and her friends. His assistant, back in the shape of a horse, wanted to return to Skye immediately. But the young hero wanted to bury the giant. There was no land big enough. They tried to sink his great body in the sea with rocks, but this proved fruitless. So they gave up and returned to Skye, all ten of them fitting on the horse's back. Swire finishes the tale:

Mighty is the sea, able to cope even with a monster. The birds of the air came in their flocks, called by the murmuring of the sea waves, the fishes came in their shoals and soon all that remained were bare bones, but even the skeleton was too large to be sunk completely below the water, so it lay, buffeted by the wind and waves, a shelter for birds and fish, until at last its bones turned to rocks and cliffs, earth formed from the flotsam and jetsam of the sea and the sea-wrack [seaweed], and the Long Island [Harris and Lewis], the two Uists, Benbecula and Barra grew from the skeleton. If you look at it from above you can still see a vague outline of his bones, with his one remaining head the Butt of Lewis and his soles the cliffs of South Bernera rising some 600 feet above the sea. The monster's other eight heads which had been cut off, floated round him like marker buoys and soon they too grew into islands. Bernera, Eriskay, Mingualay, Vallay, Gramsay, Taransay, Pabbay and Killegray though they do seem to have varied rather in size. Thus came the Outer Isles into being. (p2)

This account of the creation of the Outer Hebrides recalls a Norse legend of the formation of the world. There the original world is formed from the bodies of the Frost Giants, led by Ymir, who were defeated and killed by the Norse gods. It also bears some similarity with the story of Martin and the Nine Maidens at Pittempton, though here the hero is successful in saving his bride and her companions. The tale carries the recurring motif of the nine females, the single man and a fearsome beast preying on women. There are other traditions of nunneries on the Hebridean islands of South Bernera and Benbecula and far out in the Atlantic on Heisgeir near St Kilda. None of these can be substantiated through early church records. It would be ironic if the liking of Columban monks for islands and out of the way places was preceded by a tradition of isolated pagan female communities when learned opinion sees this Christian tradition as undoubtedly having been inspired by the isolation in the desert of Middle Eastern monks in the early centuries of Christianity.

That the Hebridean tradition of insular communities of Women was widespread is reflected in place-names such as Sgurr nam Ban Naomha on Eigg, Rubha Sgor nam Ban-naomha on Canna, Eilean nam Ban off Colonsay, Eilean ban-leac off Insh near Easdale, Eilean Ban at the Kyle of Lochalsh and Eilean nam Ban between Iona and Mull. *Ban* can mean 'woman' or 'women' and *Ban-naohma*, 'holy woman' or 'women'. If Eilean nam Ban off Iona refers to an actual island of pagan priestesses, it would shed a different kind of light on the pre-Christian history of that island. Stories of women shape-changing into deer occur in Scottish tradition. There possibly were groups of such deer priestesses, since the deer has been a particular symbol of the Goddess in Europe for millennia; it may also signify a link to shamanistic practice and belief. This possibility was investigated by JG Mackay in an article on the Scottish deer-goddess cult in which we will consider below.

Within the widespread traditions of Islands of Women, one worth looking at is the island off the Dutch coast called Walcheren. A shrine there in the 3rd century AD was dedicated to the goddess Nehalennia, a fertility goddess related to the common European goddess grouping, the Mothers, of whom there were usually three. There is some similarity here with the Danish goddess Nerthus who travelled among her people in a sealed wagon, into which only her priest was allowed to look or enter. HRE Davidson describes the practice in *Gods and Myths of Northern Europe*:

> When the wagon was not in use, it was kept in a grove on an island. When the Goddess returned to her sanctuary, the wagon, the cloth that covered it, and some symbol which it contained were all cleansed in a sacred lake by slaves who were drowned when their task was over. (p95)

A further link can be seen when she writes:

*1: Sounds similar to Iduun in Norse mythology*
*Iduun's apples bestowed immortality.*

> ... in the Roman period, the Goddess Nehalennia, whose shrine stood
> on the island of Walcheren, was depicted as a woman, sitting in a
> chair with a bowl of what appears to be apples beside her... (p166)

Here the symbol of the apples as a symbol of fertility leads us
back to the idea of Avalon as Emain Ablach and as Davidson
points out, the apple as a symbol of youth and regeneration is
common to Celtic and Scandinavian traditions. The link between
female sanctity and islands is also present in both of these
instances. McCulloch made a telling point about such islands
within Celtic tradition in *The Mythology of All Races*:

> The tradition of the Isle of Women still exists in Celtic folklore. Such
> an island was only part of the divine land and may have originated
> in myth from actual custom – women living upon or going at certain
> periods to small islands to perform rites generally tabu to men...
> (3 p117)

It seems to be the case that the Nine Maidens entered tradition
from actual practice, and that the practice continued in some
areas even after they had been assumed into myth. However
or wherever the cult of the Nine Maidens originated, it has at
some point in the pagan past been closely linked to islands,
healing and divination. The significance of the island motif – land
surrounded by water – might spring from a reverence for water
among pagan people, water representing, or being seen as the
very blood of the Mother Goddess. The notion of the inherent
sanctity of water – after all life itself depends on water – was
common to all ancient societies at one level or another. There is
also the fact that, as on mountain tops, such island groups would
be separate from the day-to-day existence of the rest of
contemporary society.

Another version of the Island of Women from the same source
reflects the widespread existence of the motif. This example
comes from the island of Raratonga in Oceania:

In the Raratonga tale there are various dangers to be encountered, chief of them is the island or land of fierce women, all of whom wish to marry a rash intruder. (9 p66)

There is no mention of the women being nine in number but the reference to a rash intruder perhaps echoes those instances already noted in which a single male visits an Island of Women for sexual purposes.

We started this chapter looking at Avalon, the home of Morgan and her sisters. Geoffrey of Monmouth in the *Vita Merlini* relates that these nine sisters took the wounded Arthur off to their island home after the fateful Battle of Camlaan. As I have argued in *The Quest for Arthur*, the Battle of Camlaan is well attested in early sources. We know that each tribal community would tell the matter of their mythological and legendary traditions within the known environment of the tribe and as it has been argued that Camlaan was in fact fought at, or near, modern Camelon, now a suburb of Falkirk on the southern shore of the River Forth, we can perhaps locate a specific local site for Avalon. Most commentators to date have always seen Avalon as being in the west, but as we know that the Lothians on the south of the Forth, and in all probability the lands of Fife on the north of the river, were inhabited by P-Celtic speaking peoples who knew of Arthur, surely there should be a local candidate for Avalon. Out in the Firth of Forth a few miles off Fife Ness there is the Isle of May, which, as noted above, means the Island of the Maiden, or perhaps Maidens. The Isle of May is known to have been a site of early Christian activity and excavations in the 1990s suggest that it had in fact been used as a burial site in the pre-Christian period, supporting the possibility that it had previously been a pagan ritual site. While the idea of Avalon has been generally seen as primarily a mythological concept, it is an intriguing thought that if Geoffrey was relating a specific event after a historical battle, then Arthur, or perhaps the warrior who had taken a powerful name from his people's traditions to bolster his own influence, could have been buried on the Isle of May. We saw that the Isle of May was traditionally visited by Thenew, before she gave birth to St Kentigern, a significant figure in the history of Christianity in Scotland, and Thenew herself was supposedly the niece of Arthur. In this respect is worth recalling that JS Glennie referred to Thenew as perhaps being one of the maidens accompanying St Monenna, whom as we have seen numbered nine. However why would a group of pagan priestesses have taken the dying Christian warrior to a pagan site? Perhaps we are seeing here a tale that survived as part of ongoing pagan belief within an ostensibly Christianised society. Many pagan practices, often designated as superstitions, continued in Scotland, as elsewhere, well into the twentieth century, and, as we have seen, ancient tales likewise survived.

If the author links European beliefs/tradition of the nine to others in other parts of the world, eg Oceania, the he should, probably, produce a theory which links these people to common yet specific cultural or religious concepts. It is not enough to say that the nine are also mentioned in Oceania without offering a link, because the implications of such a link are enormous, ie that they were connected or came from a common source or root. Without such a stated link the legends of Oceania can be dismissed as coincidence.

# CHAPTER 6

# Sagas and Sea Spirits

THE WRITTEN SOURCES on the subject of pre-Christian beliefs from Scandinavia are comparatively late and fragmentary. What we know, as elsewhere, comes to us mainly through the writings of Christian scribes. Scandinavia became completely Christian -ised relatively late in the 12th century though pagan rites and beliefs survived long afterwards there as elsewhere. The problem of the written material is exactly the same as in the Celtic-speaking countries. It isn't just the issue of the influence of Christian beliefs on the texts, it is also that Christian scribes were trained in a strictly classical fashion and were thus heavily influenced by the models from which they had learned. We have to rely on sources such as Snorri Sturlusson's *Heimskringla*, a chronicle of early Norse kings, the collections of poetry and story known as the *Eddas* and various surviving sagas that have survived in literary form. Ultimately though, they derive from the oral tradition. However the use of rhyme, rhythm, alliteration, assonance and all the other mnemonic tricks of the poets and storytellers are virtually absent from these stories which are arranged for presentation on the page, as literature. Just because the scribes were writing the stories down in this way, however, does not mean that the myths and legends were no longer being told, and listened to. In Scotland as we have seen, the storytelling tradition of the travelling peoples has survived into the late 20th century and much of what has been described as 'folklore' or 'superstition' can now be seen to contain useful information about ancient belief and practice, much more than had been previously realised. Sometimes ancient motifs have been transformed and survive as stories, or even jokes, in urban environments. This is true everywhere. It is easy to forget that near universal literacy and the widespread availability of books are relatively recent phenomena, even in the Western world. Just three hundred years ago, books, apart from the Bible were very scarce, and in the scale of human existence that is a short time indeed. It is an especially short time when we are dealing with beliefs and institutions that are thousands of years old.

There are many instances of the importance of the number nine in Norse tradition but perhaps none more intriguing than that of the god Heimdall, watcher of the gates of Asgard, who was said to have been born to nine mothers. In the poem the *Rigspula* which is part of the *Poetic Edda*, one of the great core collections of Norse myth and lore, Heimdall is said to have fathered the ancestors of the thralls, the farmers and the earls, i.e. all of humanity. The tale of a wandering god travelling from house to house and fathering children is also told of the Celtic god of the sea, Manannan. This link with the sea is very significant.

In the ancient text the *Heimdallargaldar* the god is quoted as saying, 'I am the child of nine mothers, I am the son of nine sisters'. This is reinforced by an ancient poem from the *Shorter Voluspa*, quoted by Davidson in *Gods and Myths of Northern Europe*:

One was born in olden days,
of strength surpassing, kin to the Powers.
He, nail-resplendent, was born to nine
giant maids, on the edge of the earth. (p175)

In Norse mythology these nine females were the daughters of the sea-god Aegir and his wife, the sea-goddess Ran. As in so many other instances of Nine Maidens groups, there is the motif of their relationship with a single male. This apparently strange idea of the Nine Maidens being mother to one son is a motif that also occurs in the Irish saga of Ruad, son of Rigdonn. Heimdall is a complex figure. He is the watcher at the gate, the father of the people and, variously, a sun god, a god of the moon, a ram god, the spirit of the rainbow, and as the personification of the spirit of the World Tree itself. Heimdall, as the watcher, sits on guard on the rainbow bridge Bifrost, needing no sleep, seeing as well by night as by day and constantly listening for the slightest sound of threat to Asgard, the home of the Norse gods. It is his great horn Gjallahorn that sounds to waken the gods before the final battle of Ragnarok. Such a diversity of aspects in one figure demonstrates his great importance in Scandinavian mythology.

The nine sisters who are said to be Heimdall's common mother have been interpreted as the personification of the sea. As we discussed earlier the ninth wave is believed in various countries to be the strongest; in Welsh folklore fishermen are said to have called the ninth wave the ram of Gwenhiddy with the other eight waves being her sheep, reminding us that one of Heimdall's aspects is that of a ram god. Another similarity with Welsh tradition concerns Aegir, father of the nine sea maidens. He has a great cauldron in which he brews mead for his feasts, recalling Cerridwen's cauldron of poetry and inspiration, which was tended by Nine Maidens. Mead inspires poetry and it was for the mead of poetry that Odin seduced the giant Suttung's daughter, by reciting her nine poems.

The association of these Nine Maidens with Odin, the chief of the Norse gods is precise. In *The Norsemen*, HA Guerber tells us:

> In the course of a walk along the seashore Odin once beheld nine beautiful giantesses, the wave maidens Gjalp, Greip, Egiea, Augeia, Ulfrun, Argiafa, Sindur, Atla and Iarnsaxa sound asleep on the white sand. The god of the sky was so charmed with these beautiful creatures, the Eddas relate, he wedded all nine of them, and they combined at the same moment, to bring forth a son, who received the name of Heimdall... The nine mothers proceeded to nourish their babe on the strength of the earth, the moisture of the sea, and the heat of the sun, which singular diet proved so strengthening that the new god acquired his full growth in a remarkably short space of time and hastened to Asgard to join his father. (p146)

The mothers of Heimdall seem to be closely related to the Nine Maidens who at the beginning of the world in Norse mythology, ground the body of the great giant Ymir on the great World-Mill. Ymir was the first being, formed from the primeval universe and the world was formed from his body. The Nine Maidens of the Mill appear to be the same as the Daughters of Ran, the sea-goddess who was Aegir's wife. As Donald Mackenzie in *Teutonic Myth and Legend* says:

> The great World-mill of the gods was under the care of Mundilfore. Nine giant maids turned it with much violence, and the grinding of the stones made such fearsome clamour that the loudest tempests could not be heard. The great mill is larger than is the whole world, for out of it the mould of the earth was ground. (p4)

Mackenzie goes on to provide more detail of the creation of the world by the Nine Mill-maids:

> When Ymir was dead, the gods took counsel among themselves, and set forth to frame the world. They laid the body of the clay-giant in the mill, and the maids ground it. The stones were smeared with blood, and the dark flesh came out as mould. Thus was earth produced, and the gods shaped it to their desire. From Ymir's bones were made the rocks and the mountains; his teeth and jaws were broken asunder, and as they went round at their labour, the giant maids flung the fragments hither and thither, and these are the pebbles and boulders. The ice-blood of the giant became the waters of the vast engulfing sea. Nor did the giant maids cease their labours when the body of Ymir was completely ground, and the earth was framed and set in order by the gods. The body of giant after giant was laid upon the mill, which stands beneath the floor of the Ocean, and the flesh-grist is the sand which is ever washed up round the shores of the world. Where the waters are sucked thorough the whirling eye of the millstone is a fearsome maelstrom and the sea ebbs and flows as it is drawn down to Hvergelmer, 'the roaring cauldron', in Nifelheim and thrown forth again. The very heavens are made to

swing by the great World-mill round Veraldar Nagli, 'the world spike', which is the Polar Star. (p5)

The idea of the roaring cauldron, Hvergelmer, echoes the Corryvreckan. Here we have a description not only of the origin of the physical earth but perhaps also an account of the precession of the equinoxes – the circling of the stars over any particular point which takes 25,800 years to come back to its original position. This basic idea is very like that of the well known motif of the Axis Mundi – literally the axis of the world, the fixed centre point round which the heavens revolve. Such ideas were known in ancient Egypt and elsewhere and underpin the notions of astrological 'houses'. In his remarkable book on this phenomenon, *Hamlet's Mill*, Georges de Santillana tells us:

> Medieval writers, and after them Athansius Kircher located the gurgus mirabilis, the wondrous eddy, somewhere off the coast of Norway, or of Great Britain. It was the Maelstrom, plus probably a memory of the Pentland Firth. (p91)

The Pentland Firth, initially Pjettaland Firth, the Firth of the Picts, is off Scotland's north coast and the sea there can be horrendous but this 'wondrous eddy' sounds to me more like a reference to the Corryvreckan though it is on the west, rather than the north, of Scotland. There is though, something similar in the Pentland Firth. Here it described by F Burton in *Wonderful Curios*:

> Between the coast of Caithness and Orkney is a dreadful Frith or Gulf, in the north end of which by reason of the meeting of 9 contrary Tides or Currents is a Male Stream or great Whirlpool. (p22)

Again we come across the number nine. In the *Revue Celtique* of 1885, Whitley Stokes wrote in a similar vein:

> A great whirlpool there is between Ireland and Scotland on the North. It is the meeting of many seas – it resembles an open cauldron

which casts the draught down and up, and its roaring is heard like far-off thunder. (p16)

The idea of Hvergelmer, the roaring cauldron, and Stokes' description of the whirlpool could hardly be better suited as descriptions of the Corryvreckan. One intriguing aspect of this is Santillana's reference to the World Spike. In the Gulf of Corryvreckan there is a great underwater pillar of rock, or spike, round which the waters are forced by the powerful tides to create the whirlpool. The spike is known in tradition as the Cailleach and I have been told by storyteller George MacPherson of Skye that the whirlpool is said to be the breath of the Goddess under the waves.

One of the earliest referents to the maelstrom motif comes from an ancient fragment of poetry attributed to a Norwegian *skald*, or poet, Snæbjörn who wrote:

Men say that the nine maidens of the island-mill are moving the host-fierce mill of the skerries out beyond the skirts of the earth, they who long ago ground Amlodi's meal. (Hansen, p129)

Here Amlodi is the original of Hamlet in Scandinavian mythology. Mackenzie's account of these remarkable mythological beings, in *Teutonic Myth and Legend*, continues:

These giant maids at the beginning ground Ymir's body on the World Mill. And ever do they turn the great mill at the sea bottom. Angeyja and Eyrgjafa grind mould; Jarnsaxa is the crusher of the iron which comes from clay and the sea; Imder, Gjalp, and Greip are fire-maids, for whom the world-mill is fire sparked forth and there is fire in the sea; Eistla, Eyrgjafa, and Ulfrun are also at work like the others. (p99)

Here we have the Nine Maidens at the very start of creation, portrayed as the agency by which the world is brought into being and by which the universe keeps on turning. Jarnsaxa in some tales is said to have been the first wife of the great god Thor.

Other names for the Nine Maidens given by Snorri Sturlusson in the *Skaldasparmal* are Himingglaeva ('the heaven-shining one'), Blodughadda ('bloody hair'), Dufa, Udr, Hronn, Bygla, Bra and Kola ('the cold one'). It is probable that these names were derived from descriptive appellations of waves in the tradition of the Norse poetic technique of kennings. A kenning is metaphor; thus a boat can be a cleaver of the waves, a spade, the sword of the soil or the ladle of the earth, and gold the fire of the serpent or sun of the sea.

Before looking at other Norse and Icelandic Nine Maidens groups we should consider an intriguing tale that links Norse and Irish mythology. This is the story of Ruad, son of Rigdonn. Rigdonn recalls one of the names of Heimdall – Rig – in the the poem *Rigspula*, where he is described as travelling around the countryside fathering the different sectors of Norse society, sleeping in turn with the wives of a thrall, a farmer and an earl. HRE Davidson says of this in *Gods and Myths of Northern Europe*:

> There appears to be Celtic influence behind this poem. First the name Rig is presumably to be derived from the Irish word rig, 'king'. Secondly this story of the travelling god, going from house to house among his subjects and begetting children, shows a striking resemblance to certain Irish traditions connected with Mannanan mac Lir an his son Mongan. Mannanan is a Celtic god of the sea, associated with the Isle of Man and called Son of the Sea. The same name might be given to Heimdall. (p174)

The marine aspect of all of this is very strong, perhaps linking in some way to the motif of Islands of Women. The marine link continues in the tale of Ruad whom we encounter sailing north from Ireland to Norway in a company of three ships. The vessels come to a stop and will go no further despite a favourable wind. Ruad decides to investigate and dives into the sea. He discovers there are three giant maidens hanging from each of his ships, stopping them from going on. The Nine Maidens take him to

their realm below the sea. In *The Metrical Dinshenchas*, a series
of poetic and sometimes mythological explanations of early Irish
place-names, the tale is translated from the Gaelic:

> Nine women of them excellent and strong
> hard it was to approach them;
> He slept nine nights with the women
> without gloom, without fearful lament
> under the sea free from waves
> on nine beds of bronze.
>
> Though a woman of them was with child by him
> it was a disfigurement of a little space
> he separated from them without wrongful offence
> on condition he should come back again. (2, p27)

This is somewhat like the story of Heimdall's birth – again we
have the motif of the Nine Maidens and a single male. Although
Ruad promised to return to the nine women he in fact went
straight back to Ireland after trading in Norway. The women
pursue him and the poem continues:

> Nine of them, fierce, radiant and bright
> to high Inber Ailbine
> an evil deed then wrought;
> a woman of them, with no unconscious burden
> even the slaying of the son of Ruad strong and good
> and her very own son
> [She made] a cast with her son, worse than any crime
> it was a stain on his house for him in earth;
> She hurled [him] out in fair combat
> so that he died the death. (ibid)

Although this is rather obscure, the motif of sacrifice is pretty
clear, though here the reason for the death of the child is because
Ruad has broken his word to return to the Nine Maidens. There

are echoes here of the visits of men to Islands of Women for sexual purposes and though it is never explicit, it seems at least possible that tales like this refer to situations where the role of the man was to father a new member of the community of nine women. Although many of the Nine Maidens groups, like the Maidens of the Mill, do seem to be primarily mythological, we have seen enough references to specific sites and activities for us to be certain there were actual groups of them functioning as priestesses in some way. There is only one other obvious mention of a child among the Nine Maiden groups, in the story of St Monenna. The actual priestess groups would have had to replace their members as they died off, to keep up their numbers. Their separation from day-to-day society would require some sort of process through which sexual intercourse could be arranged with a man for one of them to conceive a child. Other possibilities do exist – there could have been candidates in waiting to replace a lost group member – but the ongoing association with a single man, with overtones of sexual congress, does at least raise such a possibility.

Perhaps in the story of Ruad, with the Nine Maidens no longer presented as the mothers of a god, but as brutal and sadistic semi-supernatural beings, we are seeing the influence of Christianity. However, Mother Goddess figures in many societies are portrayed as capable of brutality, or what seems to us as brutality. This may merely reflect their overall control of both life and death, as giver and taker-away.

The description of Ruad's Nine Maidens as 'fierce, radiant and bright' would also fit the most famous of the female figures in Norse mythology, the Valkyries, the hand-maidens of Odin. They are variously given the capacity to decide victory, select which warriors would die on the battlefield and then choose which warriors were worthy of being taken to partake of the joys of Valhalla, the Norse warriors' Paradise. Their presence on the battlefield is like that of the Morrigan in Irish mythology.

The Valkyries occur in different numbers in Norse mythology but Grimm in his *Teutonic Mythology* makes the following point:

Usually nine valkyjrur ride out together... their lances, helmets and shields glitter.... This nineness is also found in the story of Thidrandi to whom nine disir [sorceresses] appear first in white raiment then nine others in black.... Nine, as the favourite number of the valkyrs, is confirmed by Saemunddredda 228, where one of them speaks of [having] atta systra (eight sisters). To our surprise, a hero Granmar turns valkyra in Asgard, and bears nine wolves to Sinfiotli... (p421)

Asgard is the home of the Gods and Sinfiotli was a member of the heroic family of the Volsungs, who along with his father, the hero Sigmund, became a werewolf for nine nights.

Guerber, in *The Norsemen,* tells of the Valkyries in Valhalla:

These maidens, nine in number according to some authorities, brought the heroes great horns full of delicious mead, and set before them huge portion's of boar's flesh, upon which they feasted heartily... (p19)

And further:

The numbers of the Valkyrs differ greatly according to various mythologists, ranging from three to sixteen, most authorities, however, naming only nine. (p174)

The significance of boar's flesh as the meat of heroes again links us to the Celtic traditions wherein the hunting and eating of the boar is a recurring motif. We should also remember the association of swine with several Goddess figures.

Guerber gives the names of the Valkyries as Skuld, Skaugul, Gunnr, Hildr, Gaundul, Geir-skaugul, Olrun, Alvit and Svanhvit. Geir-skaugul is suggestive of the Scots Gyre-Carlin. The Gyre-Carlin in Scots tradition was often called the Queen of the Witches, and was clearly at one time a Goddess figure. 'Gyre' in this context is usually interpreted as meaning 'biting' but can also mean a ring, spiral or even vortex. Which, in the light of the spiral as a symbol, as well as the living manifestation of the

Corryvreckan whirlpool, perhaps illustrates the complex cross-referencing of ideas in pagan symbolism. Svanhvit suggest another aspect of the Valkyries – their ability to change into swans. This returns us to the theme of shape-shifting so common amongst Nine Maiden groups.

The Valkyries did occasionally appear in the form of swan-maidens, as in the tale in which the Valkyrie Brynhild, heroine of Wagner's musical drama, incurred the wrath of Odin. One day when she and eight of her sisters were flying from Valhalla, they landed on earth and removed their plumage. Unseen by them, King Agnar approached, seized the discarded apparel and hid it under an oak. From then on the nine Valkyries were in his power.

Agnar forced Brynhild to counteract Odin's wishes in battle and as a result she was banished to earth and could only be married to a hero who would ride through flames for her. In time Siegfried appeared as this hero. Here again we have a shape-shifting motif and it is significant that the king hid the swan plumage below an oak tree, a sacred tree in so many cultures. Like other Nine Maidens groups, there is also a relationship with mountain tops.

Grimm in *Teutonic Mythology* tells us:

> ... it is conceivable, why Brynhilde, the valkyr dwelling on her mountain, had lif med laekning (pharmaca cum medela) ascribed to her... she is a wise woman skilled in magic, a pharmaceutria, herberia and moreover understands the binding up of wounds.... At medicinal springs, by mineral waters, appears the white lady with the snake. (p1149)

This medical knowledge is like that of Morgan and her sisters and the Gallicenae of the Isle of Sena, while the association with the well and the snake reminds us specifically of Bride. That these similarities exist between the Germanic and Celtic belief patterns suggests a closer inter-relationship between these different tribal language groups in terms of mythology and culture than has

generally been realised. The similarities in the descriptions of so
many of the Nine Maidens groups and their activities underlines
this.

Grimm links the Valkyrie with other Norse wise-women and
tells us:

> ... Skuld and Heid are, like Hulda and Berhta, purely pagan half-
> Goddesses, round whom gathers the magic ring-dance; they stir
> up storm and tempest, they make invulnerable, they prophesy...
> (p1044)

Again this is remarkably like the Gallicenae and the storm-raising
is reminiscent of the Cailleach as Mother Goddess; the power of
raising the wind was once accredited to witches as well. The ring
dance and the tempest-raising are also suggestive of both
Hvergelmer and the Corryvreckan. The reference to making
invulnerable takes us again to the motif of the teaching and
arming of heroes like Peredur and Cu Chullain.

Grimm comments further that:

> ... sorceresses have at their command, a bird's shape, a feather-
> garment, especially that of the goose, which stands for the more
> ancient swan, and they are like swan-wives, valkyrs, who traverse the
> breezes and troop to the battle. (p1045)

Mazota, the eldest of the Pittempton Nine Maidens group, is
said to have been able to stop geese from eating the corn she and
her sisters had planted. Did she have powers over birds? And
if so, is this power a faded memory of a connection with bird-
priestesses of some kind? Shape-shifting into the form of swans is
also given as an attribute of the Greek Muses, another group of
nine females. Grimm makes an interesting comparison between
the witches in Shakespeare's Macbeth and the wise-women of
Norse tradition.

In Macbeth three witches – but they are weird sisters too... – meet on

Note : Freya, the Vanir Goddess, possessed a feathered
cloak which allowed her to shape-change
and fly, it was once used by Loki.

He believed enough to institute a witch trial from which the 'flutes' were killed.

a heath and in a cave to boil their cauldron. They are not so much enchantresses in league with the Devil, as fate-announcing wise-women or priestesses, who prophesy by their cauldron. (p1046)

As they dance around their cauldron, the weird sisters in the play sing, 'Thrice to thine, And thrice to mine, and thrice again to make up nine'. It is likely that Shakespeare found this chant in contemporary folklore. He would have known that the king, James I of England and VI of Scotland, had a strong interest in witchcraft, believing he had been the subject of a plot by witches to sink his ship by raising a storm in the river Forth in 1590 AD. Hope, in *A Midsummer Eve's Dream*, suggests the existence of a 'fairy cult' in fifteenth century Scotland; this would have been based on ancient pagan belief. It is quite likely that such beliefs continued into the later years of the sixteenth century. As we have seen some such survivals lasted well into the twentieth century. Although there is no mention that the North Berwick witches, led by a single male, were nine in number, they have certain things in common with the Nine Maidens groups. They are involved specifically with weather-working, Devil worship, which probably refers to paganism, and at North Berwick itself there is very prominent hill called North Berwick Law. Many such sites have been the locations for sacral activity in pagan times, and several different groups of Nine Maidens have been associated with prominent hills.

The Valkyries are nine in number and shape-shift, sometimes into swans. Grimm notes that they are also involved in storm-raising and prophecy like so many other Nine Maidens groups. They are also close to the most important of the pagan Norse gods, Odin. All this places them firmly within the Nine Maidens type. They were not the only such groups in Scandinavian lore.

Davidson tells us in *Gods and Myths of Northern Europe*, 'Human princesses are said to become Valkyries, as though they were priestesses of some cult' (p61). She also tells us of wise women prophesying in the *Flateyjarbok*, another compilation of Scandinavian lore, and quotes the use of the term 'spae-wife', a

The witches did not refer to 'paganism', but specifically to the Devil. That in itself is curious when one thinks of it, because they were aware that their cult was pre-Christian, yet they insisted on including the Devil, a very Christian concept.

term that has survived in Scots, meaning a medium, or one who can get in touch with the spirits of the dead. Here again we have a modern remnant of an ancient belief. Davidson describes an act of divination by a wise woman known as a *volva* and says:

> The volva in Greenland was described in detail was said to be the last survivor of a company of nine women and the sagas elsewhere represent the seeresses as going about in groups. (p120)

In the mythology of the Scandinavian peoples there is another particularly interesting group of Nine Maidens associated with the goddess-figure Menglod. Her name means 'necklace-glad', which links her to the goddess Freyja, who had a famous necklace Brisingamen. Freyja is a Norse goddess of fertility and thus akin to the Mother Goddess figures we have already considered. Interestingly she often appears with her brother Frey, a different kind of duality than the one previously considered. In the *Svipdagsmal*, a poem in the *Elder Edda*, we meet Menglod. She is the object of a search by Svipdag whose mother, the seeress Groa, has come from beyond the grave to help him in his quest. She sings nine charms over him. Svipdag then searches through nine worlds before he finds Menglod on a mountain top within her magic hall, Lyr, the Holder of Heat. Lyr had originally been created by Loki, the Norse trickster god, with the help of nine dwarves. These nine dwarves are called Uri, Iri, Bari, Jari, Var, Vegdrasil, Dori, Ori and Delling. Like other nine-name lists, this has something of the sense of a chant about it and may reflect some old ritual. The recurrence of nine in this tale is remarkable.

Menglod's hall is on Lyfiaberg, the Hill of Healing. There Svipdag sees her surrounded by Nine Maidens sitting at her knee, Hlif the Helper, Hlifthrasa, Thjodvara, shining Bjort, Bleik the white, Blid, Frid, kindly Eir and the gold-giving Aurboaa. The names again have a ring of poetry about them. Crossley-Holland says, '... they soon help all those who make offerings on the high altars' (p122), which is reminiscent of supplicants approaching the Gallicenae.

Note i Having read Crossley-Holland's book I would not use or rate him as a worthwhile source.

Svipdag was the greatest warrior in the North, he defeated Thor in the winter War, the worlds Son of Earl O wandered the river of Fresa

*Note: Freyja was renowned as a witch, shapeshifter and seeress.*

Speaking of Freyja, Guerber tells us that:

> Although Goddess of love, Freyja was not soft and pleasure-loving only, for the ancient Northern races believed that she had very martial tastes, and that as Valfreyja she often led the Valkyrs down to the battlefields, choosing and claiming half the heroes slain. She was therefore often represented with corselet and helmet, shield and spear, the lower part of her body only being clad in the usual flowing feminine garb. (p131)

Here Freyja relates to the Valkyries just as Bride, Cerridwen, Monenna and Morgan relate to their different Nine Maidens groups. One of Freyja's other names was Vanabride which leads us to a remarkable comparison. Within Scottish mythology we have the embodiment of vicious winter in the Cailleach, or Carlin. However we also have at least one tale that tells of the Cailleach becoming Bride at Beltane by drinking from a magic well, Bride, the goddess of summer who is beautiful and kindly and clearly a fertility goddess. In this double aspect we can discern an ancient dual goddess. Freyja seems here to contain something of the same duality and as Valfreyja she is clearly linked to the Nine Maidens motif, as is the Cailleach in Scotland. Freyja, like Bride is often referred to as being golden-haired. Menglod herself is a supernatural female being with nine attendants, is associated with healing and to whom prayers are made. The Valkyries and volvas and Menglod's companions are all clearly Nine Maidens groups.

We now return to the Icelandic tale that has already been mentioned. This is the story of *Thidrandi whom the Goddesses Slew*. He was a handsome, brave and intelligent young Icelander but his father's friend Thorhall Seer feared for his future. One night at a harvest-feast held at the start of winter in Thidrandi's father's house, Thorhall told everyone not to go outdoors that night, no matter what happened. Thidrandi had given up his own bed to a guest and slept in the main hall. Late that night when all but Thidrandi were asleep a knock came at the door. Three times the knock came and Thidrandi, forgetting Thorhall's words thought it must be more guests arriving. This is the story from Gwyn Jones' *Erik the Red and other Icelandic sagas*:

> He picked up his sword and went outside, but he could not see a soul. Then it occurred to him that some of the guests must have ridden on ahead to the house and then have turned back to meet those who were coming along more slowly. So he walked under the woodpile and heard the noise of riding from the north into the home-field. He saw that there were nine women there, all in dark raiment, and they held drawn swords in their hands. He heard likewise the noise of riding from the south into the home-field, and there too were nine women all in bright raiment, and on white horses. Thidrandi now wanted to get back indoors and tell them of this sight, but the dark clad women came up with him first and set upon him; and he defended himself well and bravely.
>
> A long while after Thorhall awoke and asked whether Thidrandi was awake too. He got no answer. They had slept too long! Cried Thorhall.
>
> They went outside. It was moonlight and frosty weather. They found Thidrandi lying wounded, he was carried indoors, and when they got word of him he told them all that had appeared to him. He died the same morning at daybreak and was laid in a howe after the old heathen fashion. (p161)

Wanting to understand the events of the previous night Thidrandi's father, Hall, asks his friend, Thorhall the Seer, what it all meant. Thorhall tells him that the two groups of nine women were wraiths of Hall's kinsfolk. He then comes out with what must be one of the most blatant manipulations of traditional lore by a Christian scribe, saying the event must mean that a new faith is coming to Iceland, the dark nine being spirits who followed the old faith and, knowing they would be rejected once the new faith took hold, determined to exact some price for this betrayal by

1'. Then why support the 9 good spirits, they are clearly tardy and cannot forestall the 9 dark maidens?

taking Thidrandi. The white nine were good spirits who had arrived too late to help him. The new faith of course would be a good thing for Hall, his kinfolk and their descendants.

This tale seems to be a Christian attempt to give credence to the new religion by claiming it had been foretold. The idea of the black, bad spirits and the white, good spirits is plainly Christian with the emphasis on the battle between good and evil. The use of the Nine Maidens motif in such would suggest they were widely known in Iceland at the time the story was composed and were perhaps based upon the idea of the volvas or seeresses. The slaying of Thidrandi himself is, as in some other tales of the Nine Maidens, suggestive of some sort of sacrificial rite. The tale also conforms to the motif of the single male and the nine females though here the females appear in two separate, and opposite, groups.

These various stories are evidence of the existence of groups of nine women with some sort of sacred or divinatory function among the Scandinavian and Icelandic peoples, echoing tales of Morgan and her sisters or the Gallicenae, and there are links to North Eurasian shamanistic practices in the references to prophesying and shape-shifting. The point has already been made that the Islands of Women motif is particularly widespread and we should keep in mind that the pagan Norsemen were expert sailors. As Iceland was the last part of Europe to be Christianised there are perhaps stronger clues as to pagan practice in Icelandic traditions than elsewhere.

Although the link between the Nine Maidens and Heimdall is obvious, we should remember that Odin was his father as they were his mother. The motif of the nine women and the one man can therefore perhaps be seen twice here, once with Odin and once with Heimdall. This, and the function of the Nine Maidens of the Mill grinding out the physical universe from the corpses of the Frost Giants, shows them to have been very close to the heart of pagan Norse mythology and this must strengthen the possibility that they have an origin in the very far distant past indeed.

1: It may also signify ~~what with~~ echoes of matriarchy giving way to patriarchy, where matriarchy is too imbedded in the history folk memory of culture to be evoluted entirely. So must be incorporated, clumsily and badly as it happens, into a male dominant world.

# CHAPTER 7

# Muses and Maenads

THE MOTIF OF THE NINE MAIDENS occurs in many different societies and locations. Perhaps the most widely known example in Europe is that of the Nine Muses, attendants on the god Apollo. This arises from the influence of classical learning on the education systems of Europe. The theory which interprets Europe – and eventually the world – being civilised by the spread of influence from the Mediterranean nation states of Greece and Rome borders on racism. The obsession with the classical world has however determined the perspective of teaching at most European universities, particularly since the Renaissance. Even now, as the limitations of such classically-centred ideas are being appreciated, their influence still lingers. Only in the last few years has archaeological investigation in Scotland ceased to focus primarily on Roman sites, despite the fact that the Romans were only in Scotland on a handful of occasions and never for more than for a couple of decades at a time. Despite this, archaeologists and historians have treated the Romans, little more than visitors, as being of more importance than, say, the Picts, the people whose direct ancestors, the Caledonians, had fought off the Romans. The Picts subsequently laid the basis for the creation of Scotland, one of the oldest nation states in Europe. Thankfully the balance is beginning to be slowly redressed. Our museums are still overly full of Roman antiquities, which tell us more about the mindset of the establishment than about our own past. After all, how many times is it necessary to dig up a Roman marching camp when we already know all there is to know about them? Surely we would be better off devoting our limited resources into finding out more about our own ancestors?

Note: This is very true, and also very Scottish. We can't seem to progress towards a national goal without a negative to complain about: 'They held us back' etc. but first Scottish lords have traditionally done us more real harm than any foreigners.

*1! This changed quite some time ago*

The ongoing search into the Nine Maidens is part of my attempt to try and redress this balance by finding out more about my own culture, but I have been taken far beyond Scotland in the search. Several authors have noticed similarities between different groups of Nine Maidens, but the very idea of the pagan peoples of Europe having significant, long-term and highly developed sacred institutions of their own is not one that sits easily with the emphasis on the classical world; the Greeks and Romans, and subsequent classically-dominated scholarship, have seen most other peoples as barbarians – which the *Oxford English Dictionary* defines as:

a. one not Greek;
b. one living outside the pale of the Roman empire and its civilization, applied especially to the northern nations that overthrew them;
c. one outside the pale of Christian civilization.

Out of this essentially imperialist insularity comes the stereotype of the barbarian or outsider peoples as being brutal, ignorant and bent on wilful destruction. It is particularly regrettable that such stereotypes have occurred so often here in the British Isles. Millennia before the Greek cities or the Roman state developed, the inhabitants of Britain were, in a presumably illiterate society, erecting such sophisticated and magnificent structures as Avebury, Calanais, Maes Howe and Stonehenge.

Without hard evidence to the contrary, I see no reason to assume other than that the population of Scotland one or two thousand years ago descended directly from the people who raised the megaliths. There was a continuity of culture and thus belief even if it seems clear the skills of the Maes Howe builders disappeared. It is my contention that the Nine Maidens existed within that continuity of belief in a mythological sense and also as extant groups. There is evidence to suggest the Nine Maidens existed elsewhere while the ice still covered Britain over ten thousand years ago, long before the rise of Greek civilisation.

*So, the author is now going to use the myths of the same Greeks who called us barbarous, to prove his point. The previous polemic to sounds like whinging it could have been stated better.*

Because European literacy developed in Greece before the advent of Christianity we have many more literary sources to draw upon. For the purposes of this study we will concentrate on Robert Graves' *The Greek Myths*, which drew upon his lifetime's study and contemplation of this material. There are many instances of priestess groups in classical mythology and some of them, while not reported as being groups of nine have many aspects in common with Nine Maiden groupings. Classical mythology itself developed directly from pagan ideas and motifs in earlier societies in and around the Mediterranean. In Greek mythology, after the Olympians had defeated the Titans, they asked Zeus to create divinities who were capable of celebrating their victory. Zeus then went to Pieria, where he slept with the nymph Mnemosyne for nine consecutive nights. Mnemosyne gave birth to nine daughters who became the choir of the Muses. According to Graves, the Muses had initially numbered three but developed into nine.

The Muses are clearly significant in their own right but they show many similarities with other Nine Maidens groups. They are the personification of the creative arts and this is a close parallel with the Nine Maidens who tended Cerridwen's cauldron of poetry and inspiration in Welsh tradition. They were the companions of the inspirational god Apollo and were seen as patrons of poetry themselves as well as being the guardians of the oracle at Delphi. They also possessed the gift of prophecy and were known to teach others the arts of divination. This is reminiscent of other Nine Maidens groups like the druidesses of Gallicenae, the sisters of Avalon and the volva of Iceland, who also foretold the future. The Muses were associated with Mount Helicon and also with the mountains of Olympus and Parnassus and various Nine Maidens groups are associated with mountain or hill-tops, including the companions of Menglod in Scandinavia and St Monenna in Scotland. Mount Helicon was the site of fragrant plants which provided an antidote to snake venom, which suggests the Muses had knowledge of healing, another attribute of these groups. We might also remember that snakes

*! In fact Graves points out that Apollo was foisted on the concept of the Muses in order to place their poetic and oracular skills under a male ... the feminine gifts were thereby 125 transferred to the male and deified under a masculine auspices; they, therefore, were subsumed and controlled.*

are a recurrent symbol of the Goddess. Helicon was a site of many springs and the Muses are strongly associated with the spring of Castalia at Parnassus which suggests parallels with the Nine Maidens Wells in Scotland. At Delphi, the officiating priestess was known as the Pythoness, reminiscent of the Goddess Bride and her symbol, the adder, which figures so often on Pictish symbol stones. This is truly ancient symbolism, as noted by Marija Gimbutas, talking of the fourth millennium BC, in *The Goddesses and Gods of Old Europe*:

> The presence of the Bird and Snake Goddess is felt everywhere – on earth, in the skies and beyond the clouds, where primordial waters lie. Her abode is beyond the upper waters, i.e. beyond meandrous labyrinths. She rules over the life-giving force of water, and her image is consequently associated with water containers. The Snake Goddess and the Bird Goddess appear as separate figures and as a single divinity. (p182)

The symbolism of water and the snake are implicit in many of the variants of the Nine Maidens groups; an example already given is the ritual at St Bride's Well at Sanquhar in south-west Scotland, where nine white stones were placed in the well by local lasses into the 20th century.

These similarities between the Muses and other Nine Maiden groups are not a result of classical influence on northern Europe, but derive from a truly ancient source.

The Muses themselves are:

| | |
|---|---|
| **Clio** | who represents History and is associated with the trumpet and clepsydra, a form of lute; |
| **Euterpe** | who is associated with the flute and its music; |
| **Thalia** | who represents Comedy; |
| **Melpomene** | representing Tragedy and who carried the club of Hercules; |
| **Terpsichore** | who represents Lyric Poetry and Dance, and is linked with the cithara, a form of harp; |
| **Erato** | the nymph of Love Poetry; |

1: Apollo became the greatest musician - all others derived their art from him, eventually. The same can be said for the dramatic arts and poetry.

The muses end up under the direction of Apollo. The male associated with this particular Nine ended up as their lord.

*But in the case of Cerridwen's cauldron it was a female who owned it.*

Polyhymnia who initially represented Heroic Hymns, then Mime;

Urania who represents Astronomy and is symbolised by a globe and compass; and

Calliope the leader of the Muses, who represents Epic Poetry and Eloquence, shown by a stylus and tablets.

The wide range of subject matter the Muses are associated with can be seen as similar to the idea of the Nine Maidens who tended Cerridwen's cauldron of poetry and inspiration, while in Irish tradition Bride was seen as a goddess of poetry and poets. Many springs were dedicated to the Muses, which were presumably the locations of rites in their honour. It is possible that these groups performed a role as officiating priestesses at such wells. This perhaps makes sense, in that though we clearly have mythological sources for the Nine Maidens, there do seem to have been many sites where at some point in the distant past they carried out actual rituals as priestesses. This makes them both remote divine beings and humans participating in everyday life.

The Muses are said to have been priestesses of Apollo, who, like the other groups we have looked at, operated in groups of nine. The dramatist Thomas Heywood discusses the number of the Muses in *Gunaikieon*:

> But there are nine received and allowed amongst us, and that for diverse reasons; as first because the number nine is held to be vertuall and perfect; being an even foure, arising from a first odde, and then oddlie to an odde; it is likewise divided into three equal oddes; then it consists of Triangulors etc.; Besides Mnemosine, who is said to be the mother of the muses, her name consists of nine letters. Fulgentius saith, that the nine muses, with their brother Apollo, import nothing else than the tenne modulations of man's voyce, therefore is Apollo's harpe represented with ten strings. (p59)

This is somewhat obscure but the passage shows that within the ideas of his time the number nine was seen as significant, underlined by the use of the word of 'vertuall', meaning 'virtuous'. He gives a list of places associated with the Muses:

> I will onlie speak brieflie from what places they took their generall denominations, and so precede to every particular person. They were called Pierides, of the mountain Pierus, or as some will have it Pierius, who had nine daughters; Likewise, Caameanae, a Canendo of singing; Heliconides, of the fountain called Helicon, that flowed from a mountain in Boetia; Pernasides, of the Pernassus, situate in the region of Phocis; Aonides, of the Aonian mountain; Pegasides, from a spring or well so called, first discovered by the hooffe of Pegasus; Citheirides, of Citheron, a hill near to Thebes; Libethrides, from a mountain in Magnesia; Pimpleades, from a place in Macedonia; Ilissiades, from a flood near Athens; Thespiades, from the Thespians; Ligyae, of a people of Larissina, who ayded Xerxes Against the Greeks; Castalides, of the fountain so called; Corycides, of a hill or rather a cave amongst the Delpheans; Pateides, of a well in Macedonia; Oilimpiades, of the mount Olimpus; Ardalides, of Ardalus, the sonne of Vulcan; (p61)

It is striking that many of the locations given are at wells or on mountains, so often where we find the Nine Maidens groups. This spread of locations, some of which, like Parnassus and Olympus, are particularly important sacred mountains, strongly suggests that the Muses, either originally or at some point in the development of Greek religious experience, existed as separate groups. Their geographical spread is what one would expect if there were diverse groups of nine priestesses originally honouring the Mother Goddess, and later the god Apollo. The links with Parnassus and Olympus suggest, like the locations of St Monenna in Dark Age capitals in Scotland, an important role, close to the heart of contemporary society. The Oracle of Delphi on Parnassus was the most ancient and sacred site in Greece, while Olympus became known subsequently as the home of the gods. Heywood's earlier comments on the relationship to music are fitting for a group that is so associated with the arts, but the location of different groups in such significant locations suggest that they had earlier had a more central role than simply as the inspirers of the Arts. Given that some groups of Nine Maidens, like the Maenads, were involved in bloody and orgiastic rituals, the arts may be more related to ancient and visceral notions of religion than is realised, though it is generally accepted that drama as an art form arose directly from religious ritual. Within the activities of 'orgiastic priestesses' there were perhaps rituals that eventually gave rise to other artistic activities.

Apollo is a fascinating figure in his own right. In *The Greek Myths*, Graves says '[Apollo] ... brought the Muses down from their home on Mount Helicon to Delphi, tamed their wild frenzy, and led them in formal and decorous dances.' The frenzy here seems like that of the Namnetes, who rebuilt their temple every year and tore to pieces any of their own number who dropped thatch during the annual re-roofing of their temple. Graves continues:

> Every ninth year a hut representing a king's dwelling was built on the threshing floor at Delphi and a night attack made on it. The table of first fruits was overturned, the hut set on fire, and the torch-men fled from the sanctuary without looking behind them. (p82)

This ceremony is called the Septerias (veneration) and the hut is said to symbolise 'the dragon's lair'. This takes us back to the dragon at Strathmartine; also it was every nine years that the great Norse pagan festival took place at Uppsala. Apollo and his mother Leto are also associated with Hyperborea – the land beyond the North Wind – and every year at the end of autumn he went away north, beyond the Rhipraei mountains towards the mysterious land of the Hyperboreans. It was also said that Leto herself was a native of this blessed land.

Some commentators have surmised that Apollo originated in Asia and Arabia while, others, because of his close relations with the Hyperboreans, think he was originally a northern divinity, brought to the Greeks from the north in the course of their

1: Oden, Thor and Frey were worshipped at Uppsala, as far as I know no female goddesses were involved

129

migrations. The most obvious northern link, apart from the Nine Maidens, would be with Heimdall who was also a god of light.

Leto, Apollo's mother, was said to have been in labour with him for nine days and nine nights. Apollo has powers of healing and divination, giving us another link to Nine Maidens groups like Morgan and her sisters, and the Gallicenae. A more tentative correlation can be made between the Pythoness, Apollo's priestess at the Oracle of Delphi and the snake (adder) in Scottish mythology; the serpent is an ancient symbol of chthonic power, the regenerative force of the earth itself which allows the annual growth of plant life.

In *The Greek Myths* Graves gives another interesting Apollonian association, with swans:

> When Apollo appears in ancient works of art riding on swanback, or in a chariot drawn by swans on a visit to the Hyperboreans, this is a polite way of depicting his representative's annual death at midsummer. Singing swans then fly north to their breeding grounds in the Arctic Circle, and utter trumpet-like notes as they go; which is why Pausanius says that swans are versed in the Muses' craft. Swans sing before they die: the sacred king's soul departs to the sound of music. (2 p294)

Here Graves is talking of the idea of the sacrifice of the sacred king to ensure fertility – a rite many scholars believe used to take place and which provided the thematic background for James Frazer's seminal *The Golden Bough*. We should keep in mind that the sacrifice may have been symbolic. The association of Muses with swans is an intriguing one as it is very like that between the Valkyries and swans. This is not to suggest that the northern versions of the Nine Maidens are ultimately derived from the Greek ones. The opposite might be worth considering given the references to Apollo as coming from the north. Humans only occupied northern Europe after the retreat of the last Ice Age some 10,000 years ago but the concept of the Nine Maidens predates this, as we shall see. What this relationship with swans

1: Most originally, they used the Real McCoy or his substitute.

does show is that the symbolic associations with different Nine Maidens groups are remarkably similar over great distances and periods of time.

The relationship of the single male with Nine Maidens groups varies considerably – Apollo is presented as being supreme over the Muses, Arthur is nursed by the nine sisters of Avalon, Heimdall is the son of nine maidens, Ruad is effectively wooed by nine sea maidens, Peredur is at first aided by then attacks the nine witches of Caer Lyow, St Monenna is accompanied by nine women and a baby boy and the Strathmartine tale has Martin as the suitor of the eldest of the Nine. There are other Nines that conform to some extent to this pattern. In the story of St Samson of Dol, a representative of the Nine kills a single male, though the Wild Woman, while claiming eight sisters, is herself alone. There are also strong hints of sexual intercourse with a single male in Islands of Women such as Sena, Priory Island and others.

The Muses are not the only group of Nine Maidens in Greek mythology and it seems possible that the different locations they appear at might disguise separate groupings of Nine, just as we see elsewhere. Whether all such groups were priestesses of Apollo like the Muses, or whether the Muses have come to represent a wide variety of different Nine Maidens is probably impossible to adduce. There are however many different names and locales associated with the Muses.

## Pierides

This group of Nine Maidens were said to have been the daughters of Pierus, a king of Macedonia. It is said he had nine daughters whom he named after the Muses. Another version of the tale is that these maidens presumptuously challenged the Muses to a poetry contest and predictably were defeated. Their punishment was to be turned into birds, in some cases magpies, by Apollo, or into other birds by the Muses themselves. The names of the Pierides are given as Acalanthis, Cenchris, Chloris, Cissa, Colymbas, Dracontis, Lynx, Nessa and Pipo, all Greek bird names. The Muses are also sometimes referred to as Peirides after the place where Zeus is supposed to have fathered them. Here we have a clear suggestion of the recurring motif of the Nine Maidens on a hill-top.

## The Sirens

The Sirens in Greek mythology were a group of supernatural beings who lured sailors to their deaths, so entrancing them with the beauty of their song that the ships crashed into rocks and were wrecked. The Sirens were turned into birds with women's faces by Aphrodite because they refused to give up their maidenheads to either gods or men. This might be a reference to the changeover from Goddess worship to a patriarchal religion – other Nine Maidens groups are noted for being free of patriarchal influence. Sometimes as with St Samson of Dol, they actually kill a male; the witches of Caer Lyow are equally aggressive, and as we have seen in our discussion of Islands of Women, Nine Maidens groups in several instances are certainly not submissive in sexual matters. Another version of their origin has the Sirens being deprived of the power of flight after being beaten by the Muses in a musical contest. This strongly suggests that they too, like the Peirides, were nine in number. They are said to have inhabited Cape Pelonus, Capri, the Isle of Anthemusa and the Siren Isles, which further links them to the motif of Islands of Women.

The Sirens eventually lost their power of luring sailors to their deaths when the Argo passed their island with Orpheus on board. His singing was more magical than theirs and they lost their power for ever and were changed into rocks. Orpheus eventually died at the hands of the orgiastic Maenads who were also nine in number. A further possible link is that the Sirens have been presented as daughters of Melpomene, herself one of the Muses.

Graves believed that the Sirens were a pre-Olympian cult inhabiting the island of Paestum off Capri and draws a parallel between their island home and the Island of Avalon. He further thought that the Muses superseded them as part of the new Olympian religion, and that this was the origin of the supposed singing contest between the two groups. All of this suggests great antiquity.

## The Hydra

The Hydra was a mythical serpent with nine heads, which came out from its lair in a marsh, near Lerna in the Pelponnese, to ravage the countryside.

Graves tells us in *The Greek Myths*:

> The number of heads given the Hydra varies; as a college of priestesses it had fifty heads; as the sacred cuttle-fish, a disguise adopted by Thetis – who also had a college of fifty priestesses – it had eight snaky arms, and one head on its trunk, together making nine in honour of the Moon-Goddess. (2 p110)

Here again we have the number nine, Goddess figures and the moon. It is also worth noting here that Geoffrey of Monmouth in the *Vita Merlini* gives one of the names of Morgan's sisters as Thiten which may be a possible reference to Thetis, who is strongly associated with the sea. Graves (1 p27) tells us of an incident in which Thetis was involved in an episode of shape-shifting. She had retreated into a cave on an islet of Thessaly where she was pounced upon by Peleus, chosen by the Gods to be her husband. As she struggled to get away from him, she changed into fire, water, a lion, a serpent and lastly a giant cuttle-fish. Despite her shape-shifting and having been burned, clawed, stung and drenched in ink, Peleus held on to her and at last she succumbed and gave herself to him. At their wedding feast the Apple of Discord was thrown into the company by the goddess Eris. The incident said to have led in time to the Trojan War. Shape-shifting occurs in many different Nine Maidens scenarios and it may be that this is an essential part of their original identity. It might even be a reference to some sort of hallucinogenic-induced trance used in prophecy. The apple reference here is reminiscent of Avalon.

## The Maenads

The Maenads were the followers of the god Dionysus or Bacchus who ordered them to tear Orpheus limb from limb when that hero failed to honour the god as he thought was his due. The Maenads are generally presented as being in an ecstatic fury which some scholars consider was the result of eating hallucinogenic mushrooms, rather than drinking alcohol which is more commonly associated with Dionysus/Bacchus. Graves commented on the possible links between the Muses and the Maenads in *Mammon and the Black Goddess* telling us:

> At some time before the 8th century BC, the god Apollo took over the Muse worship and calling himself 'leader of the Muses', transformed the cult to his own sacred precincts. This meant more than self-identification with the lyre-plucking danced leader of a nine-woman Maenad company; he was asserting his authority over the Muse herself. (pp145-6)

Dionysus is also associated with the Muses who, with the Maenads, helped to educate him. Both are Nine Maidens groups and here, in their teaching of Dionysus, we have yet another correspondence with the role of Morgan as teacher of her sisters, and perhaps even more closely with the role of the nine witches of Caer Lyow teaching Peredur. The many references to shape-shifting might find some support in the concept of inspiration by hallucinogenic substances. The flight of witches may well derive from subjective descriptions of drug-induced experiences which seemed like flying. This has been extensively commented on in writings on shamanism where the shaman's spirit flight is frequently described as being preceded by the ingestion of such substances. Dionysus was said to have passed his childhood on the fabulous mountain Nysa where he was sent by his father Zeus to escape the wrath of his maternal grandfather Cadmus. Dionysus was handed over to the nymphs of Nysa – and given their location on a mountain and their association with Dionysus it is worthy considering whether there were nine of them too.

## Telchines

A strange group of nine that occurs in Greek myth are the Telchines, described by Graves in *The Greek Myths*:

> That the Telchines were Children of the Sea, acted as the hounds of Artemis, created magic mists, and founded the cities named after the three Danaids, Cameira, Ialysa, and Linda suggests that they were originally emanations of the moon Goddess Danaë: each of her three persons in triad. 'Telchin' was derived by Greek grammarians from thelgein, to enchant... They were, it seems, worshipped by an early matriarchal people in Greece, Crete and Lydia and the Aegean Islands, whom the invading patriarchal Hellenes persecuted, absorbed or forced to emigrate westward. Their origin may have been East African. (1 p189)

The Telchines are children of the sea, like the daughters of Ran, and their ability to create magic mists is reminiscent of the tradition of weather-working we have seen with other Nine Maidens groups. The suggestion of an East African origin chimes with the story of the origin of the Kikuyu people of Kenya, as we shall see. Graves also tells us that devotees of the Telchines occupied the nearby Mount Nonacris, meaning nine peaks, which was at one time the chief religious centre of Greece. Nonacris was the origin of the river Styx, the river over which the dead were ferried to the Otherworld by Charon, and which plays such a strong role in Greek mythology. In *The White Goddess* Graves expands on Nonacris as a goddess in the story of Lycaon the Pelasgian, son of the Bear-Goddess Callisto:

His clan used the wolf-totem and Lycaon as wolf-king (or werewolf) reigned until the ninth year. The choice of King was settled at a cannibalistic feast. His wife Nonacris was clearly the Ninefold Goddess, and he is described as the first man to civilise Arcadia.... Above Nonacris are the Aroanian mountains and in them is a cave to which the Daughters of Proteus are said to have run when the madness overtook them. (pp367-8)

Although the madness of the Daughters of Proteus might link them to the Maenads, they are generally presented as having been three, not nine. Proteus himself is both a shape shifter and an oracular prophet – attributes common to the Nine Maidens groups. Graves mentions a depiction of Proteus on a vase as fish-tailed, with a lion, a snake and a stag emerging from his body. He was buried on an island and Graves links this to the Island of the Hesperides and Heracles' quest for the Golden Apples. In *The White Goddess* he specifically compares Proteus' island of Pharos, off Alexandria and home of a legendary lighthouse, with the Isle of Avalon. The serpent, the island location and the Avalon-like Garden of the Hesperides are all motifs suggestive of Nine Maidens groups.

This is not the place to go into an extended analysis of how and when the Mother Goddess was superseded by a masculine-dominated pantheon of gods and goddesses in Greece or elsewhere. However it is highly likely that any god-like figures replacing earlier goddesses would take on some of their attributes, much in the same way as the Christians deliberately took over heathen temples and celebrations.

The reference to the goddess Artemis, the huntress, brings us back to the association of deer with priestess groups. The link between goddess figures and deer is widespread. Many Greek priestess groups were, like Nine Maidens groups, strongly linked to the moon, a motif associated with goddesses in many different societies. Given the recurrence of the theme of divination, the derivation of the name Telchines from a term for enchantment is significant. There are other instances in Greek mythology which

*i' When the originals were burnt, the Senate ordered a new set to be made and the system carried on with the forgeries.*

although not directly concerned with groups of Nine Maidens do seem to carry traces of beliefs that might have been associated with them. These often involve the number nine in magical rites and symbols like the serpent.

## The Cumaen Sibyl

The Cumaean Sibyl, or priestess of Apollo, is said to have offered nine books of prophecy to King Tarquin of Rome in the fifth century. He thought the price too high and refused to pay it. The Sibyl threw three books on the fire and demanded the original price for the six remaining books. Again Tarquin refused and the priestess threw another three volumes on the fire asking the original price for the remaining three books. At this the king gave in and paid the full price for the remaining three books. These Sibylline Books were long kept in the temple on Rome's Capitol. They were said to contain details of how to gain the favours of foreign deity which might mean that they were instructions for particular religious rites. Yet again we have the number nine associated with significant religious knowledge.

Another intriguing story is given by Graves in *The Greek Myths*:

> At Aulis, while Agamemnon was sacrificing to Zeus and Apollo, a blue serpent with blood red markings on its back darted from beneath the altar, and made straight for a fine plane tree which grew nearby. On the highest branch lay a sparrow's nest, containing eight young birds and their mother: the serpent devoured them all and then, still coiled around the branch, was turned to stone by Zeus. Calchis explained this portent as strengthening Aius' prophecy: nine years must pass before Troy can be taken, but taken it would be. (2 pp283-4)

Here we have the serpent, with its associations with the chthonic powers of the Mother Goddess, and nine birds being interpreted as a prophecy concerning Troy. Even in ancient Greece such ideas and symbols had perhaps lost their primary meaning. We should remember that Schliemann the German amateur archaeologist who located the site of Troy was dismissed by contemporary professional archaeologists as a dreamer. They were convinced that Troy was either purely mythological or a literary creation based on originally oral stories, and that there was no factual basis to Homer's *Iliad*. It has been suggested that the story of Troy had originally come to Homer by word of mouth from earlier Greek tradition. The suggestion in this work – that we can learn a great deal about earlier societies from the oral tradition – is not that new!

In *The Greek Myths* Graves also writes of Semele, daughter of Cadmus:

> Semele was worshipped at Athens during the Lenaea, the Festival of the Wild Women, when a yearly bull, representing Dionysus, was cut into nine pieces and sacrificed to her, one piece being burned, the remainder eaten raw by the worshippers. Semele is usually explained as a form of Selene ('moon'), and nine was the traditional number of orgiastic moon-priestesses who took part in such feasts, nine such are shown dancing round the sacred king in a cave painting at Cogul, and nine more killed and devoured St Samson of Dol's acolyte in medieval times. (I p58)

Whether or not cannibalism formed part of such rites, the reference to nine as the traditional number of moon-priestesses is significant. Nine is particularly significant in lunar terms, and in many societies the moon has been associated with the Mother Goddess. The moon's effect on the motion of fluids on the earth, including tides and the menstrual cycle of women, was well known in the ancient world and the moon was thought to influence female fertility. As already noted, worshippers of the Mother Goddess might have seen water itself as analogous to the blood of the Goddess. If, as Graves suggests, nine was the standard number of priestess groups in Greece, this might encompass the priestesses of Artemis, Circe, Diana, Hecate and Selene. Certainly Greek mythology includes a variety of instances

*The earliest forms of megalithic sculpture/monuments is at Göbekli Tepe in Eastern Turkey, C 9600 years B.C.E.*

of Nine Maidens. Until recently the orthodox interpretation of this material would have been that all the Nine Maidens groups we have been looking at must have derived from such classical sources. However, contact between peoples is a two way process and, as we have seen, there are grounds for considering Apollo as originating in the north. Given that we know the culture of megalith-construction spread over the area from North Africa to the British Isles and encompassed parts of the Mediterranean, this is certainly not beyond possibility. The growing acceptance of the relative importance of folklore and the retreat from absolute adherence to the classical interpretations of our history will probably lead to a new and fresh interpretation of this evidence. The notion of the barbarian northerners being enlightened by the more 'civilised' peoples of Greece and Rome is not one that we need accept.

Before the rise of the Greek city states and classical Greek society in the 1st millennium BC the islands of the Aegean were flourishing and their influence on later Greek development was considerable. The people of the Aegean worshipped the Mother Goddess. She was the Great Goddess, the Universal Mother, in whom were united all the attributes and functions of divinity. She symbolised fertility above all else, and her influence extended over plants and animals as well as humans. The entire universe was her domain and as the celestial Goddess she regulated the course of the heavenly bodies and controlled the alternating seasons. Here we have an echo of the Scottish Cailleach with her power over the winter weather. The Aegean Great Goddess caused the products of the soils to flourish, gave men riches, protected them in battle and at sea guided them on their adventurous voyages. She also reigned over the underworld and, as mistress of life, she was also sovereign of death.

This duality is akin to that of the Goddess in Scottish mythology, personified in the Cailleach and Bride. In Greek mythology the Mother Goddess is given as Gaea who coupled with her son Uranus to give birth to the Greek pantheon of gods and goddesses. Even in the supposedly patriarchal pantheon of

1 There were people living in Northern Europe during the last Ice Age.
Soughs Cave in the Cheshire Gorge C 12600 years B.C.E.

the Greek gods, Gaea is central as the mother of all life. Worship
of the dual Goddess figure, even if it did not come with the first
settlers to northern Europe after the retreat of the last Ice Age, is
the oldest human religion known. It has survived, if only faintly,
in folklore and what is called superstition, through the overlay of
later pagan thought and the propaganda and education of
subsequent religions. Such survivals demonstrate the power of
oral transmission as this is the means by which this material has
been transmitted in an increasingly literate world. An example of
the tenacity of this type of belief can perhaps be seen in modern
ecologists adopting the idea of Gaea as an all-encompassing single
system vision of life on planet. At a time when we are facing
widespread environmental destruction and pollution born of the
blinkered pursuit of short-term profit, this idea makes a lot of
sense. It is significant in this light, that the Oracle at Delphi, was
devoted to Gaea before being taken over by worshippers of
Apollo.

Concluding this look at classical sources, here is another quote
from *The White Goddess*:

> At Athens the… Festival called the Lenaea, [Festival of the Wild
> Women] was held at the winter solstice, and the death and rebirth of
> the harvest infant Dionysus were… dramatised. In the original myth
> it was not the Titans but the Wild Women, the nine representatives
> of the Moon-Goddess Hera, who tore the child into pieces and ate
> him. (p399)

This link to the winter solstice, one of the most significant points
of the pagan year, still celebrated as Christmas in many parts of
the world, has already been discussed. The eldest of the Nine
Maidens who were remembered as Pictish saints in Scotland was
Mayota, and her saint's day was 22 December, the winter solstice.

Graves accepted that societal change, in this case from a
matriarchal pre-Hellenic religion to the Greek male-dominated
pantheon, came about because of an invasion. The inference is
that such changes result from the defeat of one people by another,

militarily superior one. How then if people are so totally subjugated do their ideas continue? Do they lie quiet for a period and then resurface later? Or is it that, while ruling elites come and go, the ideas of the common people continue relatively unchanged? Or could it be that this militaristic approach to human history misses the point about human development? The obsession with invasion and conquest was probably quite natural within the British Empire but now that the Empire has fallen we should no longer be restricted by its hidebound attitudes and analyses. Some aspects of older religions continue to be practised, even when they have been replaced in public ritual by new concepts and ideas. There is also the well-attested fact that many religions have adopted what they could not change in their predecessors and made it their own, as was the case with Christianity.

There is evidence from the southern side of the Mediterranean which suggests that groups of nine supernatural beings also existed among the Egyptians. Mackenzie, in *Egyptian Myth and Legend* tells us that:

> Representatives of the groups of Egyptian spirits called the Fathers are found at Memphis, where Ptah, assisted by eight earth gnomes called Khnumu, was believed to have made the universe with his hammer by beating out the copper sky and shaping the hills and valleys... But Ptah never lost his elfin character, even after he was merged with deities of different origins. He was the chief of nine earth spirits (that is eight and himself added) called Khnumu, the modellers. (p80)

He later explains:

> As the theology of the sun worshippers developed at Heliopolis, other gods, which were imported or had their origin in Egypt, were included in the divine family. The number three and its multiple had evidently magical significance. Ra, Kephera, and Tum formed the sun triad. The sun god and his children and descendants: Nut, the

1: And Ptah is / was often represented as a ~~foetal~~ hunchback, at other times a dwarfe.

heavens, Shu, the air, Seb, the earth, with the lioness-headed Tefnut, the spitter, Osiris, the deified king and corn spirit, Isis, the Delta Great Mother, and her sister Nephthys, and the Semitic Set, formed Ennead of Heliopolis. The group of Nine Gods varied at different periods. (p161)

Further south in Africa, a story is told that is even closer to our subject. This version is from the pen of the late President of Kenya, Jomo Kenyatta in his *Facing Mount Kenya, The Traditional Life of the Gikuyu*:

According to tribal legend we are told that in the beginning of things, when mankind started to populate the earth, the man Gikuyu, the founder of the tribe was called by the Mogai (the Divider of the Universe), and was given as his share, the land with ravines, the rivers, the forests, the game and all the gifts that the Lord of Nature (Mogai) had bestowed on mankind. At the same time Mogai made a big mountain which he called Kire-Nyaga (Mount Kenya), as his resting place when on inspection tours, and as a sign of his wonders. He then took the man Gikuyu to the top of the mountain of mystery, and showed him the beauty of the country that Mogai had given him. While still on the top of the mountain, the Mogai pointed out to the Gikuyu, a spot full of fig-trees, right in the centre of the country. After the Mogai had shown the Gikuyu the panorama of the wonderful land he had been given, he commanded him to descend and establish his homestead on the selected place which he named Mokorwe wa Gathanya. Before they parted Mogai told Gikuyu that, whenever he was in need, he should make a sacrifice and raise his hands towards Kire-Nyanga, and the Lord of Nature will come to his assistance. Gikuyu did as he was commanded by the Mogai, and when he reached the spot, he found that Mogai had provided him with a beautiful wife whom Gikuyu named Moombi (creator or moulder). Both lived happily and had nine daughters and no sons. Gikuyu was very disturbed at not having a male heir. In his despair he called upon the Mogai to advise him on the situation. He responded quickly and told Gikuyu not to be perturbed and everything would be done according to his wish, then commanded him saying, 'Go and take one lamb and one kid from your flock. Kill them under the big fig tree near your homestead. Pour the blood and the fat of the animals on the bark of the tree. Then you and your family make a big fire under the tree and burn the meat as a sacrifice to me, your benefactor. When you have done this, take home your wife and daughters. After that go back to the sacred tree, and you will fine nine handsome young men who are willing to marry your daughters under any condition that will please you and your family ... Gikuyu told the young men that if they wished to marry his daughters he could give his consent only if they agreed to live on his homestead under a matriarchal system... (p3)

Though this tale is not a precise match with any of our European material it is striking that the Kikuyu people are said to have descended from nine sisters and that the original system of the tribes was matriarchal. Here we have an idea stemming from a period before the establishment of a patriarchal society, being used to explain that society. Could this be along the same lines as Christianity taking over the pagan temples to maintain some form of continuity? Intriguingly this version of a Nine Maidens tale comes from that part of our planet where human life is believed to have originated.

# CHAPTER 8

# Magic Use of Nine

SEVERAL OF THE MYTHOLOGICAL FIGURES we have looked at illustrate that the number nine itself is of importance within pagan belief, and survives within a wide variety of folkloric beliefs and superstitious practices. Odin hung for nine nights on the World Tree, Yggdrasil; Apollo's mother was in labour for nine days and nights before he was born; the Dagda had a cauldron that fed warriors nine at a time. Other striking instances of the importance of the number nine include the spell of the witches in Macbeth and the placing of nine white stones in Bride's Well at Sanquhar. This latter case is interesting in that it has been said that the nine stones were specifically in honour of the Nine Maidens. The Sanquhar rite also raises the question of whether the groups we are looking at number nine because of the magical/pagan importance of the number or, whether the significance of the number might arise from the Nine Maidens groups themselves. The repetition of actions nine times within folklore magic certainly appears to have descended from earlier pagan practice and belief. In Appendix B there is a further selection of this extremely widespread magical use of nine from a diversity of locales, but some are worth considering here.

The widespread belief in that every ninth wave is stronger than the rest has been noted and could possibly be linked to such Nine Maidens groups as the daughters of the sea goddess Ran, the nine sea maidens encountered by Ruad and the Maidens of The Mill who grind out the physical universe in Norse mythology. The fact that the ninth wave is also named after Goddess figures in different traditions might be seen as a further example of this association. Several commentators have noted that the names of the daughters of Ran are all names that echo the sea itself.

Bessie Smith, on trial for witchcraft before the Presbytery of Lesmahagow in west central Scotland in 1623, admitted that she had been guilty of 'charming the heart fevers' by recommending 'the waybore [plantain] leaf to be eaten nyne mornings' while the patient was kneeling and chanting the following spell or charm, as given in *The Silver Bough*:

For Godes sak
For Sanct Spirit
For Sanct Arkit
For the Nine Maidens that dyed
Into the Bourtrie in the Ladywellbank
This charm to be beuk and bell to me
And that sua [shall] be. (2 p148)

This spell, like so many that survive in folklore, combines a certain amount of Christianity with older belief. The Sanct Spirit might be a reference to the Holy Ghost but the Sanct Arkit is obscure. The reference to the Nine Maidens could be specifically to the group at Abernethy who are said all to have been buried at the foot of an oak tree there. Bourtrie is generally used for the elder, which was used in witchcraft, both black and white. The spell itself suggests some sort of continuity into later practice from a time when the reference to the Nine Maidens would have been clearly understood. On this point the folklorist Eleanor Hull comments in *Folklore of the British Isles*:

... there is no break between the ancient magical formulae chanted by the Druids and the later incantations of the wizard and the wise woman. They both arose in the Veda-like sacred hymns which formed the repository of the learning professed by the body of Druidical teachers and diviners and taught orally in the Druidic schools. Most of them were never written down, and the fragments we possess in writing are probably only the remains of a considerable body of oral literature. In course of time these forms became antiquated and were unintelligible even to the bards themselves. (p173)

The druids are known to have taught by memory and considered it sacrilegious to write down their teachings to be. This type of belief is incredibly tenacious. For instance the mother of James Hogg, the 19th century Scottish novelist and poet, knew a great many stories and ballads and is on record as saying that, if written down, such material would lose its power. Oral transmission was not a haphazard process in pre-literate societies and even today many storytellers have a clear set of ideas of what is and what is not permissible. The role of the storyteller has probably evolved from the sacred educator of the tribe, druid, druidess or whatever else.

Scottish folklore is full of instances of the use of the number nine in magical activity, much of it directly associated with witches. In the great Middle Scots epic *The Flyting betwixt Montgomerie and Polwarth* we have the following:

Thir venerable virgins, whom ye wald call witches
In the time of their triumph tirr'd me the taide,
Some backward rade on brodsowes and some on black bitches,
Some in steid of staig over a stark monk straid.
The how to the hight some hobles, some hitches.
With their mouthes to the moon murgeons they maid
Some be force, in effect the four windes fetches
An nyne time, withershins, about the thorne raid. (Bawcutt and Riddy, 1 p285)

To 'tir the taid' is to strip a toad, a 'staig' is a horse and to go 'widdershins' is to circle something anti-clockwise. Going with the sun or deasail is the positive direction, withershins definitely negative. Flyting was a standard form of poetic combat based on creative insult, and in the quoted section Montgomerie is claiming Polwarth to be witch-born and effectively a practitioner of the Black Arts. As Hope (1970) points out there is evidence for some kind of organised fairy cult in Scotland in the Middle Ages. In the poem Montgomerie describes NicNiven, the Queen of the Witches, perhaps herself a degraded form of the Mother Goddess, her companions and their magical practices. The detail implies he knew what he was talking about, and that his audience did too. The point here is that they went against the sun, nine times to work harm, just as we shall see nine times *with* the sun was used for benefit. Earlier we looked at the witches in *Macbeth*; it seems probable that Shakespeare drew upon contemporary folklore for his portrayal of witch activity in the early years of the 17th century.

In various parts of the British Isles, there are stone circles known as Nine Maidens, four in Cornwall alone at Boskednan, St Buryan, Stithians and Columb Major, though this latter is a row rather than a circle. There are others in Aberdeenshire and Derbyshire with Ninestone circles in Derbyshire and Roxburghshire. This association with standing stones underlines the antiquity of Nine Maidens motif in Britain. Intriguingly some of these circles share the relatively common origin story of Sabbath revellers being turned into the stones, which hints at pagan activity.

In considering the magic use of nine, we should return to the semi-mythical Welsh poet, Taliesin. There is ongoing debate as to when he wrote, some people suggesting the sixth century while others consider the Welsh poetry attributed to him as having been ninth or even twelfth century re-workings of traditional material. There is also the suggestion that there have been several Taliesins, the name being interpreted as some sort of bardic title. MacCulloch in his *Religion of the Ancient Celts*, writes this of him:

> Taliesin was probably an old god of poetic inspiration confused with the sixth century poet of the same name, perhaps because he identified himself, or was identified by other bards, with the god. He speaks of his splendid chair, inspiration of fluent and urgent song in Caer Sidi or Elysium. And, speaking the god's name or identifying himself with him, describes his presence with Llew, Bran, Gwydion, and others, as well as his creation and his enchantment before he became immortal. He was present with Arthur when a cauldron was

stolen from Annwfn, and basing his verses on the mythic transformations and rebirths of the gods, recounts in highly inflated language his own numerous forms and rebirths. His claims resemble those of the Shaman who has the entree of the spirit-world and can transform himself at will. (p117)

The capacity of societies dependent on oral transmission to intermingle god figures with humans has already been commented upon. Caer Sidi is itself clearly an idealised location, which does not however mean that it could not have specific locations identified with it in the physical as well as the metaphysical sense. The poems attributed to Taliesin present ideas and beliefs from a time before Christianity arrived in Britain. If the arguments in this book have merit then we must consider the possibility that some such ideas might have survived for millennia, and that they might even have come into what we now call the British Isles over ten thousand years ago with the first settlers. The magical significance of nine is underlined in the poem the *Cad Godeu*, the Battle of the Trees, taken here from JG Evans' translations of Taliesin:

Twas not of father and mother
whence I was born,
Thus after a new fashion I was created
from the nine constituents:
From the essence of fruits
did God begin;
from Primrose flowers
from the pollen of shrubs
the pollen of Oak and Nettle,
of Meadow-sweet and Broom;
from the Mould of the earth;
from the water of the Ninth wave;
from the fire of Lightning
of these things was I made. (p35f):

Whether this specific combination of plants has some particular effect in combination or whether they are simply used to make up the magic number nine is not something I can comment on, but the possibility exists that we are dealing with some kind of hallucinogenic used in initiatory rites. The reference to the water of the ninth wave clearly refers to beliefs we have looked at and the fire of lightning could be linked with the suggested druidic belief that mistletoe was caused by lightning. In the account of the Taliesin story we saw earlier, he was originally called Gwion Bach and was touched by three magic drops from the cauldron of Cerridwen. After a shape-shifting chase that follows, Cerridwen, in the form of a hen, ate him in the form of a grain of corn. After this she carried him for nine months before he was born as Taliesin. Despite the reference to God in this poem what we have here appears to be a remnant of something pagan and very old. Despite our reliance on written materials derived from earlier oral tradition, it is impossible to discern how old the pagan ideas in the *Cad Godeu* are, or to determine what were the specific practices or rituals associated with them. The linguistic analysis that is used to try and date such works can go no further back than essentially theoretical dates, which even then are late – in the sense that material recorded in the 6th century AD Wales or Ireland might have already been passed orally for thousands of years.

As different writers like Graves and Lethbridge have commented, nine is strongly associated with the moon and this is also true of goddesses from many parts of the world. This association, deriving from the actual physical effect of the moon on all fluids, and thus on female menstruation, has created obvious links with ideas and rituals of fertility. The Nine Maidens motif would seem to incorporate some of these types of association. Further, the use of divination has been thought to derive from attempts to communicate with the spirits of the ancestors to try and ensure the future fertility of crops, and probably to plead for the success of the hunt before that. The rites of magic, like those of religion, stem from this type of early belief. Throughout human existence there have always been rites and rituals to try and ensure future fertility, of crops, of animals and of humans. Perhaps in the Nine Maidens and the single male there is an echo of some such ancient practice.

The extensive use of the number nine in ritual and magic is looked at further in Appendix B.

## Nine

We have seen that the Nine Maidens crop up in many places and in many guises, though always as women of sanctity and/or power. In many instances they appear to be pagan priestess groups who, with their powers of divination and shape shifting, were perhaps involved in similar activities to those of shamanism – healing, divination and the like. Additionally some are said to have had control over the weather – an ability also attributed to later witch figures. This might mean no more than that they had sophisticated meteorological knowledge, though in this respect we should remember the close relationship with Mother Goddess figures, and that such beings are often portrayed as weather creators. This is also a talent, or skill, attributed till relatively recently, in many cultures, to those women called witches. We have seen how, particularly in Scotland, Goddess figures are often associated with mountains known for changeable and dramatic weather. The link to shamanism however, is stronger than just their skill in divination and healing.

Mircea Eliade in his classic work *Shamanism,* refers to the Buryat people of Siberia and their beliefs:

> ... the shaman's career begins with a message from a shaman ancestor, who then takes his soul to the sky to teach him. On the way they stop to visit the gods of the Centre of the World, especially Tekha Shara Matzkala, the god of the danced, fecundity, and wealth, who lives with the nine daughters of Solboni, god of dawn. These divinities are peculiar to shamans, and only shamans make offerings to them. The young candidate's soul enters into amorous relations with Tekha's nine wives. When his shamanic instruction is finished,

his soul meets his future celestial wife in the sky; with her too his soul has sexual relations. (p75)

There are several familiar motifs here – the reference to Tekha as being a god of the dance is reminiscent of Apollo and his Muses and of the dancing women at Cogul. His role as an artist and representation of fertility echoes beliefs concerning Bride, Cerridwen and possibly Menglod, who has also been interpreted as a goddess of fertility. There are obvious links to the nine sisters of Avalon, itself a symbol of fertility. Here again we have the nine as sisters – reminiscent of the Nine Maidens of Abernethy, daughters of a saint, the Maidens of the Mill, daughters of the sea goddess Ran and the nine sisters who founded the tribes of the Kikuyu. The reference to sexual involvement with nine women again is a familiar one from Islands of Women tales and particularly in the story of Ruad, son of Rigdonn. This recurring motif of nine females and one male is perhaps linked with lunar symbolism in the same way as the widespread motif of twelve plus one has been seen as deriving from solar myth, one example being Jesus Christ with his twelve apostles. Other similar groupings are Arthur and his twelve knights, Balder and his twelve judges in Norse tradition, Odysseus and his twelve companions, Romulus and his twelve shepherds, Roland and the twelve peers of France, Jacob and his twelve sons. The single year itself is divided into twelve months and it may be that some ancient belief concerning the visible moon being divided into nine discreet periods underpins some of the ideas linked with groups of nine women. It does appear that the motif of the nine females and one male is a faint echo of some kind of fertility rite. Talking of the Teleut, another Siberian people, Eliade tells us:

> The shaman is assisted in his labours not only by his celestial wife but also by feminine spirits. In the fourteenth heaven dwell the nine daughters of Ülgän. It is they who confer his magical powers on the shaman (swallowing live coals, etc.). When a man dies they come down to earth, take his soul, and carry it to the heavens. (p77)

The carrying of the soul to heaven is very like the concept of the Valkyries convoying dead warriors from the battlefield to the Paradise of Valhalla, of the Morrigan of Irish tradition who haunts the battlefield in the shape of a crow or raven, and of both Morgan and the shape-shifting raven maiden. Here it is specific that the shaman receives his powers from the nine daughters of Ülgän, a motif reminiscent not only of the arming and training of Peredur by the witches of Caer Lyow, but of traditions such as the training of Cu Chulainn by the warrior woman Scathach in Irish tradition, and the teaching and arming of Norse heroes like Sigurd and Regner by Valkyries.

Eliade extensively discusses stories of the Sky God who occurs under many names among the northern Eurasian and Asian peoples. He lives in the highest sky and has several sons or daughters who are subordinate to him and who occupy lower heavens. Their names and numbers vary from tribe to tribe; seven or nine sons or daughters are commonly mentioned, and the shaman maintains special relations with some of them. The fact that some groups of women occur as sevens as well as nines long confused me. Recently I have been told that, within Scottish tradition handed down from original pagan sources in the Gaelic-speaking world, there was a belief that seven represented the colours of the spectrum and nine the spectrum plus black and white. Given the importance of colour in many aspects of traditional lore this seems relevant but how the symbolism of colours might fit our overall picture is beyond the scope of this work. It is worth noting that there are instances of groups of seven sisters in many traditions.

Eliade shows that shamanism is not all of ancient origin and that there have been many developments over the past couple of centuries, showing that, while oral traditions can sustain ideas and beliefs over extraordinary time-scales, there is always the capacity to change and develop in response to contemporary needs.

One creature that links what we know of shamanism with any of the goddess figures we have briefly looked at is the deer. The existence of a deer-goddess cult with female devotees in Scotland was suggested by JG Mackay in *Folklore* (1934). He based this on the extensive stories of hag figures being associated with deer, which were in several instances known as the cattle of the Cailleach. There are perhaps then grounds for suggesting that the deer heads on Pictish symbol stones may represent masks. We know the Pictish artists were adept at representing animals in a true-to-life fashion, and the deer heads do not look like severed heads so much as masks with clearly defined bottom edges. If so, it seems relevant to think of such masks being used in sacred ritual, we can perhaps postulate the existence of both the Nine Maidens groups and deer-priestesses among the P-Celtic speaking peoples of Scotland. In the instance of the Seven Big Women of Jura, the Deer-isle, that feature in the Gaelic story of Mac Iain Direach (Campbell 1994, 2 p90ff) we are perhaps seeing something similar within Q-Celtic tradition. At Abbot's Bromley in Staffordshire, England, there is an annual Horn Dance which includes a bowman who pretends to hunt the dancers who are imitating deer and it has been suggested this ancient ritual might have originated in the Stone Age. Within Gaelic oral tradition in a tale called the *Widow's Son* (Campbell 1994, 1 p62-3), there is a description of what appears to be a woman taking off a deer costume; it seems likely that she is a deer priestess. There are Scottish examples of stories wherein hunters require the blessing of a powerful female, clearly a witch or hag figure, before going out to hunt deer. In the fascinating work *The Deer Goddess of Ancient Siberia*, Jacobson points out a close relationship between females and deer which may link to the Nine Maidens priestess groups and she notes the following:

> The shifting reference from deer to women to deer, found in many archaic Siberian mythic traditions, is vividly reflected in the Ngaanasan belief in a swamp where their animal mothers live as naked women with the hair and antlers of deer. (p242)

The reference to the swamp may also be of some relevance here, given the close links we have seen between the worship of the

Goddess and water, and particularly the idea of the Islands of Women. Swamps are by their nature out-of-the way places and inhabiting a swamp would be as effective a way of living apart from society as inhabiting an island. The doyenne of Pictish studies, Dr Isabel Henderson, has referred recently to Pictish art, with its animal symbols, as being part of a broader concept – that of Eurasian hunter art, which suggests strong links with the peoples and perhaps even the beliefs of areas across northern Eurasia as far as Siberia. The contemporary fascination with shamanism might lead us in time to identifying aspects of pagan belief in different parts of pre-Christian Europe as being fundamentally shamanistic. The possible deer masks on the Pictish symbol stones might be part of that particular jigsaw of ideas. The importance of deer can also be seen in the material concerning Finn Mac Cuill in Irish and Scottish Gaelic tradition: his wife is turned into a deer by a druid and his son is called Oisin, which means 'fawn'; according to Jean Markale, Finn's own original name, Demne, can be interpreted as *dam nijo*, 'little deer'. Dowsers have shown that deer-rutting stands, where the animals mate, show similar patterns to stone circles when dowsed. All of this makes it possible that Mackay was right in presuming the existence of deer-priestesses though I would suggest the deer-goddess cult is just one aspect of the worship of an overall Mother Goddess figure.

The association of the Nine Maidens with Goddess figures, such as Bride, Cerridwen, Menglod, suggests that the form of pagan religion practised by these groups was Mother Goddess-based. The work of Marija Gimbutas shows that Goddess worship permeated the societies of the Balkans in the 4th and 5th millennia BC and there is no reason to suppose things were substantially different elsewhere in Europe. Gimbutas also noted many examples of deer motifs being used as symbols of the Goddess. Recently I have been researching hills and mountains in Scotland that are named after the fact that they resemble the female breast. Several of these locations are associated with the Cailleach, with place-names referring to women, adders, swine and the like, and with wells and a variety of prehistoric monuments either on the mountains/hills or very close by. This, combined with specific tales of hag-type figures suggests that such mountains and hills were locations for ritual activities worshipping a goddess figure and the names and tales survive in both Gaelic and Scots language forms, indicating widespread ritual activity of this type. Apart from Mackenzie's reference to the Cailleach of Ben Nevis and her eight sisters I have not, as yet, come across Nine Maidens material at any of these locations but I am convinced of the reality of these locations as sacred sites associated with the Mother Goddess. And if the Nine Maidens worshipped the Goddess, as I suggest, such a spread of locales in Scotland would be supportive of their survival into recent times. The sites specifically associated with St Monenna are almost all prominent hills in flat landscapes and some can be construed as being breast-shaped.

There is one particular Nine Maidens locale which suggests an extraordinarily long continuum of existence for the motif. This is the painted cave at Cogul, near Lerida in Catalonia. The painting is generally believed to have been created in the Magdelanian period which puts it between 10000 and 15000 BC. It clearly shows nine women dancing around a startlingly obvious male figure. Included within the group is the figure of a deer. Robert Graves interpreted this as a representation of an orgiastic ceremony which culminated in the physical dismemberment of the male by the females in an erotic frenzy. He wrote that the male figure at Cogul was priapic – possessed of an outsize penis, symbolic of fertility – which it is, but the male organ is not erect in the painting, which one might expect if this is direct representation of a basically erotic ritual. Nevertheless the grouping can surely be interpreted as being some kind of fertility rite. However, in the context of this work, the most important point about the cave painting at Cogul is its age. If this group is indeed an example of the Nine Maidens motif (and the association with the single male strengthens this), we are clearly dealing with something extremely ancient, though we cannot be sure that the Stone Age artist in Catalonia thought of his nine women in the same way as the Norse storytellers thought of the Maidens of the Mill or their Welsh counterparts thought of Morgan and her sisters. It is worth reiterating that we have evidence for cultural contact over wide areas, particularly along the eastern littoral of the Atlantic Ocean, the spread of megalithic monuments from north-west Africa to north-west Europe in the fourth millennium being a particular example. One of those particular monuments, Calanais, on the Scottish Isle of Lewis, is said in local tradition to have been originally built by black men.

Repeatedly we find Nine Maidens groups being involved in divination, shape-shifting and weather control, activities also traditionally associated with witch figures. In this respect the spell given by Isobel Gowdie, referred to above, with its reference to 'the Nine Maidens in the Bourtrie bank' is perhaps of particular significance. This spell suggests at least a memory of the Nine Maidens group being active in a particular place, enhancing the possible link with the witches.

We have seen how original Goddess figures have been turned into hag figures and I have suggested that such figures appear, in Scotland at least, to be linked to the winter aspect of an ancient dual goddess. One of the terms used for the Queen of the Witches is the Carlin which is the Scots equivalent of the Cailleach, or Hag, in Gaelic tradition. The term *gwrach* in Welsh meant precisely the same thing. Comparing this again to Donald Mackenzie's portrayal of the Cailleach, riding out from Ben Nevis with eight sister hags, to spread winter over the land, we see a strong association between such hag figures and the later witches who were traditionally represented as old women themselves. As the beliefs and practices of what we think of as witchcraft were undoubtedly passed exclusively through the oral tradition another possibility faces us. It seems at least possible that some of those covens of witches that survived into the 16th and even 17th centuries may in fact have been directly descended from earlier Nine Maidens groups. The regular occurrence of a coven of female witches with one male might be seen as strengthening such a link. I hope I have shown that the association of Nine Maidens groups with goddess figures suggests an origin in Mother Goddess worship. The figure of the Queen of the Witches might also be understood as a remnant of this earlier form of religion. Although covens are generally described as being of 13 members, this is not universal, and it may be that some of these groupings were ten in number, with nine women and a single male. The problem in trying to obtain a clear picture of witchcraft activity is that the relatively extensive written reports of witch trials in most post-Reformation European countries are almost exclusively focused on confessions to crimes which seem to have existed almost solely in the imaginations of the interrogators of these unfortunate women. With singularly few exceptions such interrogators were male and driven by a need to have the women confess to formulaic crimes. In the sense that the witch practices were probably descended from remnants of the Old Religion, such righteous brutality would be perfectly justifiable – to the interrogators.

An ancient pedigree is not the only noteworthy aspect of the Nine Maidens. The ongoing centrality of the motif in various pagan belief systems is illustrated by the wide variety of different mythological and legendary figures with whom they are associated. This is looked at more extensively in Appendix A.

Some of the rituals involved with the existence of the Nine Maidens survived till very late, as at Sanquhar, Pittempton and perhaps in the magic practices involving the number nine. Such rituals and practices were not necessarily genteel or even gentle, the Goddess being both malevolent and beneficent. She is Goddess of both life and death. The recurring possibility of the idea of sacrifice is impossible to ignore but we should remember that some evidence exists to show that in many societies sacrificial victims went willingly to the ritual. We have a different mind-set.

The existence of the motif of the Nine Maidens across so much of the world – in this respect the Kikuyu founding myth is particularly relevant given the theories of human life originating in the East African Rift Valley – suggests the possibility of a very old belief. The similarities between widely separated groups seem to retain some sense of the continuity of that belief. The divergence of detail within the various groups might be because we are looking at a motif of human thought, and a social institution, of vast antiquity, developing independently over many millennia.

We find the Nine Maidens as mythological beings like the attendants of Cerridwen's cauldron in Welsh tradition or the Maidens of the Mill at the heart of Norse mythology, as daughters of Zeus in Greece, yet also as apparently functioning priestess groups in locations such as Mount Olympus, the Isle de Sein and Pittempton. What I suggest this shows is that the motif of the Nine Maidens is so old as to have passed into mythological traditions in many instances, like the nine daughters of Ülgän or the founding sisters of Kikuyu society, while at the same time they continued to exist in different locales as practising religious groups. The material from Iceland suggests they were still in existence close to the arrival of Christianity there, a thousand years ago. Whether they still existed among the tribal peoples of north-west Europe as late as this is moot, but it is certain some such groups still existed in Roman times. The existence of the stone circles in Great Britain called the Nine Maidens, sometimes with the standard Christian explanation that they were humans turned to stone for dancing on the Sabbath, might be proof, not just of their antiquity but of their continued existence during Christian times. In this light it is worth remembering that some witch groups were known to frequent such ancient sacred sites.

In some places these two different aspects of the Nine Maidens motif seem to have survived alongside each other. The Nine Maidens at Pittempton, with the associated dragon story and the holy well, seem to belong to the mythical tradition, while just over the hill from Martin's Stone where the dragon is said to have been slain, we have another group of Nine Maidens, surviving in story as a group of saints, who are said to have gone to Abernethy at a definite, if unspecified, date.

The locations in significant political centres in Scotland, like the sites of the varied Muses groups in classical Greece, suggests that though some such groups found it necessary to live apart from society, others were at the very heart of their own communities. What we see in these different locations, like the differentiation between actual and mythological Nine Maidens groups, is perhaps a result of their antiquity. If they were in existence over the millennia suggested, their survival shows their ongoing social importance, arising from their mythological significance, and it is possible that the actual formation of the groups in sets of nine females, became the norm for a variety of sacral and ritual functions within differing societies. This in itself might help to account for the variety of post-Christian representations of them as healers, witches and seers. Even in Christian times there were substantial presences of priests and monks in all major urban locations while others of their brethren deliberately sought out isolated spots in which to live.

Many of the locations in which we find the Nine Maidens, Iberia, Brittany, Cornwall, Wales, Ireland, Scotland, Norway and Iceland are within relatively easy sea contact of each other it at certain times of the year. We should remember also that people raised Megalithic structures as far south as Africa, thus proving that long-range contacts were taking place even in the Stone Age. The Greek material also can be fitted into this pattern as we know that their earliest geographers had knowledge of the British Isles, Iberia and Gaul – knowledge that could be very ancient indeed. The spread of megalithic structures stresses the importance of sea communication and we should not forget that communication is a two-way process. Our understanding of contact between different societies and peoples in the far past has been coloured by the portrayal of expanding Western influence over the past few centuries. This has been shown as 'advanced' Westerners coming into contact with primitive, usually taken to mean inferior, peoples. Human contact over millennia has not been restricted to colonial expansion on the part of rapacious, technologically superior peoples. The spread of both the Nine Maidens motif and the magical/ritual use of the number nine might suggest a greater degree of commonalty between differing societies in the past than has been realised.

The ability of oral transmission to pass on factual data is only just beginning to be appreciated and material from the various storytelling traditions of all the countries considered, combined with archaeological investigation, is a procedure that could be of great assistance in helping to give us a clearer picture of our common human past.

I have suggested the relationship of the nine women to the single man might be a lunar equivalent to the notion of twelve plus one, which has been interpreted as a basic solar myth – twelve months in one year – that some commentators have seen as underlying the story of Jesus in Judaeo-Christian belief. If this is so we can construe this motif of Nine Maidens and a single male as being an older, matriarchal concept that was superseded by later patriarchal ideas developed subsequent to the replacement of the Old Religion by newer, male dominated belief systems. In this light it is remarkable that male figures such as Apollo, Heimdall and Arthur, all of whom have been interpreted as sun-god figures, are all so closely associated with Nine Maidens.

Throughout much of the world in pre-Christian times there were groups of Nine Maidens who had similar functions and were closely associated with that most ancient of beliefs, the Goddess as mother of us all. They were priestesses who had healing knowledge, practised the arts of divination and had specific meteorological and medical knowledge which appears to have been used for the benefit of the communities in which they existed. As such they had an important role within society and it seems likely that, like shamans, they were believed to have the power to communicate directly with the spirits of the ancestors, the gods, or the Goddess. Their centrality within mythological structures shown by their close connections to such diverse figures as Apollo, Arthur, Heimdall, Odin and Zeus and to Mother Goddess figures such as Bride, the Cailleach, Cerridwen, Menglod and Morgan is reflective of an important societal function. Other instances of nine females, such as within Kikuyu belief in Africa and Kogi belief in South America, show that the basic motif is not restricted to Europe. Likewise the magic use of nine seems to be almost universal, as are some of the symbols we have considered, like the serpent or dragon.

The suggested survival of the Nine Maidens motif from the Magdelanian cave painting at Cogul through to the faded remnants of practice such as the 19th century visits to the Nine Maidens Well at Pittempton or the 20th century rite at St Bride's Well, Sanquhar, reflects a potential continuity of belief and perhaps even practice for over 15 millennia. If this is the case then perhaps the references to the widely differing Nine Maidens groups gathered here is not so surprising, and there may be much more yet to be brought to light. I am not suggesting that the different traditions from so many diverse locations are all remnants of a single cult, though there are obvious grounds for seeing close links within the Celtic and Germanic traditions of Europe. What the chronological and geographical spread of the motif of the Nine Maidens suggests is something more intriguing. Although we know that in the ancient world travel and cultural contact was much more widespread than has often been credited, the idea that all of these locations arose from a single source is highly unlikely. What the recurring use of nine in magic and the particular significance of groups of nine women linked to fertility and magic suggests is that our distant ancestors in many parts of the planet came up with very similar ideas. If this is so then the basis for these must lie in some appreciation of what we know we all share – experience of the planet, the seasons, the sun the moon and the stars. In the Nine Maidens are we in fact seeing a series of essentially localised reactions to common phenomena? As the basis for such a common reaction the component parts could be female fertility and perhaps some time based analysis based on observation of the moon. Just as the number twelve is associated with solar myth so the number nine has strong lunar connotations and in the nine females and a single male we perhaps are seeing the lunar equivalent of the solar myths mentioned. If this is so then, just as the Mother Goddess pre-dates the rise of the patriarchal religions of the modern world, did the idea of the female lunar nine plus one precede the notion of the solar, twelve plus one – a concept that includes no recognition of the female principle? I think TC Lethbridge's suggestion of the creation of nine goddesses from one might be close to the underlying reality of how the Nine Maidens arose. In his book *Witches* he writes:

> In Britain the Great Mother had three aspects and three apparent personalities... if there were three Great Mothers all of one aspect, they must have obviously have each possessed two other aspects or personalities. You then get nine Goddesses out of one. This is probably the origin of the frequent occurrence of Nine Maidens, particularly in connection with the names of sacred springs. In Scotland in particular these maidens are often associated with Brigid. There were probably no other maidens originally, save Brigid alone. It is an interesting to note that the Teutonic Goddess of war became nine Valkyries. ... the Nine Maidens and their association not only with Brigid, but with a dragon are certainly part of our Great Mother picture. The dragon may well be the same old beast who was cast out by Michael and worsted by Indra. (p83)

Here we have the well and the dragon, just as at Pittempton. As we have seen the motif of the casting out of the dragon has been interpreted as a metaphor for the Christian triumph over paganism, though we have also seen that remnants of such paganism survived in many parts of Christian Europe at least till very recently – not least the various traditions concerning the Nine Maidens. His argument as to the development of the Nine from the One is possible. Earlier in the same work (p82) he mentions the link between the concept of the three Mothers, found in many European traditions, and the three phases of the moon – new, full and waxing – and lunar observation through such a process could account for parallel developments of the same idea in widely divergent societies and time periods.

A similar concept of the triple Goddess developing in to nine is discussed by Robert Graves in *The Greek Myths*:

The moon's three phases of new full, and old recalled the matriarch's three phases of maiden, nymph and crone. Then, since the sun's annual course similarly recalled the rise and decline of her physical powers – spring, a maiden, summer a nymph, winter a crone – the Goddess became identified with seasonal changes in animal and plant life: and thus with Mother earth who, at the beginning of the vegetative year, produces only leaves and buds, then flowers and fruits, and at last ceases to bear. She could later be conceived as yet another triad; the maiden of the upper air, the nymph of the earth or sea and the crone of the underworld – typified respectively by Selene, Aphrodite and Hecate. These mystical analogues fostered the sacredness of the number three, and the moon-Goddess became enlarged to nine when each of the three persons – maiden, nymph and crone – appeared in triad to demonstrate her divinity. (1 p14)

Behind this idea, certainly in northern Europe, I would suggest we have the dual Goddess, in her colours of black and yellow, symbolising winter and summer, and at the most fundamental level, life and death. And with her went Nine Maidens.

There is an old cliché that says – how can you know where you're going if you don't know where you have been? At a time of major and ever-increasing global change it is important that we learn as much as we can from the past, and from those who have gone before. Perhaps, in this light, the Nine Maidens can still have a role to play in helping us understand the inter-relatedness, not only of all planetary life, but of the different societies created by human beings in our time on planet Earth.

The wide spread of the Nine Maidens motif both geographically and temporally probably points to common human responses to shared phenomena. Although we know that sea travel in the ancient world was extensive and thus widely separated societies could be in regular contac, it seems unlikely that the different Nine Maidens ideas could all stem from a single common root. For this to be the case, the idea of the Nine, and probably the One, would have to come from a time when humans were still at a very early stage of development. The founding myth of the Kikuyu people of Kenya survives close to where it is thought humanity first came into being but to see this as the source would require us to think of ideas surviving for many hundreds of thousand, if not millions of years. It would appear to be more likely that the motif has arisen in response to common human experience and in this regard the influence of lunar observation may prove to hold the key. The fact is that despite religion, language, colour or class, humans always have more in common than differences that separate us, one from another, and in the Nine Maidens we perhaps see a series of tales and beliefs that arose independently in widely separated branches of the human family.

# Nine

Nine there were then
*anns an innis*
whaur cam nae men

songs were sung there
*ceol na caomradh*
sainin the air

een raisit tae the lift
*rathad an reul*
they tellt seasons' drift

cam there ae braw callant
*snamhiche nan uisge*
manfu, the gallant

intae the auldest dance
*gille is nighean*
new life an oorie chance

spierin the omens then
*naomhichean naoi*
a secret tae men

calmin the ragin flame
*fluich is fuar*
til callant won hame

roun cam the seasons' turn
*dh'eug i aon reul*
a new bairn is born

nine were then
*anns an innis*
whaur bade nae men


www.ninemaidens.org

# Major Figures Associated With Nine Maidens Groups

WE WILL LOOK FIRST at male figures associated with Nine Maidens groups, most of which exemplify the motif of the Nine Maidens and the single male:

## Apollo

The Greek sun god with his Muses. As with the Welsh goddess Cerridwen the link to poetry and inspiration is central to this group. Some scholars have suggested that Apollo originated in northern Europe and there are intriguing grounds for linking him with the great Calanais stone circle on the Isle of Lewis. Tradition tells us the Shining One walks the central avenue of the complex every Midsummer's Day and though this is probably a reference to Lugh, a sun god among the Gaelic-speaking peoples, there is a striking reference from the Roman geographer Diodorus Siculus, writing in the 1st century AD but quoting from an original 4th century BC source. He writes of an island in the ocean beyond the land of the Celts, inhabited by the Hyperboreans. This is the quote as given in Ivimy's *The Sphinx and the Megaliths*:

> ... the following legend is told. Leto [Apollo's mother] was born in this island, and for that reason Apollo is honoured by them above all other gods. And there is also on the island both a magnificent precinct of Apollo and a notable temple which is adorned with many votive offerings and is spherical in shape. (p94)

Diodorus Siculus goes on:

They say also that the moon, as viewed from this island, appears to be but a little distance from the earth and to have upon it prominences like those of the earth, which are visible to the eye. The account is also given that the god visits the island every nineteen years. (p95)

Many scholars have identified Britain as the island of the Hyperboreans and Stonehenge with the round temple but, rather than Stonehenge, I would suggest the Celtic-cross shaped megalithic alignment of Calanais on the Isle of Lewis is more likely location. Investigation over the past couple of decades shows that the Calanais complex was created to monitor the changing position of moon rise which reaches its western-most point every 18.6 years. The hills in which the moon is seen to rise at this time forms the outline of a recumbent human shape in the landscape known locally as *caillich na montich*, translated as the old woman, or hag, of the moors. As we have seen, the Cailleach, here *caillich*, is more than a hag. Whatever the possibilities of linking Apollo with Calanais or elsewhere in the British Isles, it seems at least possible that his association with the Nine Maidens make him a figure from much earlier than classical Greece with perhaps his mother being another faded representation of the Mother Goddess herself. As a sun god, Apollo was of course associated with fertility but he was also strongly linked with mountain tops, healing and prophecy, with many oracles dedicated to him in both Asia Minor and Greece. These are all recurrent motifs in Nine Maidens material. Additionally Apollo's birth took nine days and nine nights. All of this makes Apollo and the Muses a classic case of the single male and the Nine Maidens. Most commentators on Greek mythology accept that he originated outside Greece and as Apollo and the Muses were often portrayed as dancing, it is tempting to see a direct link with the dancing scene at Cogul where nine women danced around a male fertility figure.

## *Arthur*

Arguments still rage as to whether or not there was a historical King Arthur. If he did exist in the 6th century he would have been the leader of a tribal warband rather than a king. There are quite varied views as to where the twelve battles attributed to him in the Middle Ages were actually fought, and Scotland provides likely locations. As I have said before, the mythological and legendary stories told in pre-literate societies would normally have been presented within an environment familiar to their audience. It would be particularly important for children to hear such material set in a landscape they knew. This means that the stories of Arthur in Argyll, Lothian and Strathmore in Scotland are every bit as 'true' as those in Wales or Cornwall. At the heart the Arthurian romance as developed in north-west Europe in the early medieval period, are links to female figures such as the lady of the lake, Guinevere, and Morgan and her sisters. The latter are a classic Nine Maidens group with fertility associations – Avalon is an idealised fertile Paradise – and healing powers. The sisters are presented as beneficent healing figures while the nine witches of Caer Lyow, are presented as inherently vicious and evil female warriors. What this perhaps illustrates is that Morgan and her sisters might preserve a direct memory of one, or more, Nine Maidens groups surviving from pagan times, while the Caer Lyow witches are a Christianised version of the same groups, in which they are portrayed as evil in order to denigrate their pagan aspect and undermine whatever hold they still had over the popular imagination. This could be exactly the same process underlying the story of the killing of St Samson of Dol's assistant by the wild woman of the wood. Within pre-literate societies the presentation of mythological and legendary material incorporated moral, social, political and practical information, making such stories a necessary psychological building block of society. Even when Christianity arrived, people would hear the priests once or twice a week while what we know of the storytelling tradition in such societies suggests it was an everyday, normal occurrence. The spoken word continued for a long time in many societies as the sole means of transmitting necessary information.

The arrival of literacy did not destroy the oral tradition and in the early medieval period various writers developed the Arthurian material from such tales into medieval literary romances designed primarily for an aristocratic audience. The Nine Maidens motif continued to be of considerable significance within Arthurian tradition. Darrah in *Paganism in the Arthurian Romances* makes the point:

> The discussion on Avalon suggests that the place was not necessarily unique but rather one where a group of priestesses offered oracular pronouncements. Just as Delphi was not the only oracle in the classical world, we may expect to find more than one oracular site in Wales. Previous commentators on the Matter of Britain have noted a resemblance between Avalon and the various versions of the Castle of Maidens. (p229)

It has already been noted that the Nine Maidens groups associated with St Monenna were linked with specific important locations in Dark Age Scotland, including Edinburgh Castle, consistently referred to as the Castle of the Maidens In 12th and 13th century annals. There is also an Arthur's Seat in the middle of the modern city of Edinburgh which several commentators have tried to maintain is post-medieval and inspired by early literary sources. The Dark Age name of Mynyd Agned and the association of St Monenna and her maidens with the castle rock in the city indicate a more ancient connection.

Another probable Nine Maidens site nearby is Traprain Law twenty miles to the east of Edinburgh. This was a major site of the Votadini [Gododdin] as far back as Roman times and is mentioned in several Arthurian romances as the site of the capital of King Lot or Loth after whom the surrounding area was said to have got its name. Loth figures as Arthur's brother-in-law and as the father of Gawain and in some cases of Modred, the usurper of Arthur's kingdom and the lover of Queen Guinevere. Given that we are dealing with remnants of the pagan feminine principle it is perhaps worth reiterating that there are many strong female figures in the traditions of the Celtic-speaking peoples. The idea of Irish sovereignty being personified in a female figure and the possibility of some level of matriliny in Pictish succession suggests we should at least consider the possibility that Guinevere was the prime mover in the situation, choosing a new mate in Modred. This would make sense if Arthur was a Christian opposing the old pagan ways with their reliance on matriliny and was trying to impose a new order. This might also help explain why the Arthurian stories have continued to be so popular – he can be seen as the winner in the struggle between Christianity and paganism, and thus a worthwhile hero for Christians, just as he was previously a heroic figure, or perhaps a god among the pagan tribes. His association with the Nine Maidens of Avalon seems to come straight from pagan belief.

Traprain Law as a Nine Maidens and Arthurian location leads us to some other starling possibilities. Lot's daughter Thenew is said in the *Life of St Kentigern* to have converted to Christianity and having become pregnant after being seduced by Prince Ewen of Strathclyde, refused to marry him. Her father, after trying to marry her off to a swine herd, first had her thrown off Traprain Law in a chariot which floated gently to the ground, then cast her adrift in an oarless boat on the Forth. She eventually landed at Culross, considerably up river and a substantial Christian site from early times, where she gave birth to St Kentigern. The child was taken under the care of St Serf, an early Scottish dragon-slaying saint. Kentigern is a major figure who is difficult to authenticate but it is in his life that we have possibly the earliest reference to Merlin. In the *Life* the character is known as Lailoken and in the light of what has gone before it is worth noting that Merlin is associated strongly with deer and falls under the power of a woman, Niniane.

Arthur is a classic case of the single male associated with the Nine Maidens and the idea of his being taken off to Avalon to be healed, and that he is still alive awaiting the call to come to the help of Britain when needed, has been reworked time and again in literature. There are those who see him essentially as a god figure and others as the prime model of the Celtic hero. Whatever his origin, and location, Arthur is closely linked to the Nine Maidens and in the references to him in Celtic-speaking traditions we perhaps are seeing a remnant of a much older figure.

## Heimdall

Like Apollo, Heimdall has been interpreted as a sun god and also as the father of the Norse people in his character Rig. He could hardly have a more central role within Norse mythology. Heimdall is also a limnal god – he is at the edge of things and in tales from cultures all over the world, edges are where magic is often worked. Mentioning Heimdall's nine mothers, HRE Davidson tells us in *Gods and Myths of Northern Europe*:

> These appear to be sea-giantesses, or perhaps waves of the sea. We have already seen that the idea of maidens of mighty strength, dwelling beneath the sea, is familiar in both Scandinavian and Irish tradition, and that they are linked with the giantesses of the underworld who play an important part in Norse mythology. (p175)

Talking of Heimdall she says, '… to him was added the might of earth, of ice-cold sea, and sacred swine-blood'. Davidson draws attention to the fact that swine were associated with Freyr and the Vanir, and that they in turn were closely linked with the giantesses. She suggests there were also links between Heimdall and Menglod, who had her own Nine Maidens and to the fertility goddess Freyja. It seems Heimdall was also involved with the powers of the underworld. We have already seen there are grounds for thinking that prayers to the spirits of the underworld were a means of invoking fertility. Heimdall was also known as the White God and white in many societies has been considered especially sacred. Davidson also refers to the concept of the White Youth among the Yakut peoples of Siberia, a people who practise

1: Bulder was known as the White God, the Shining One. The word Bulder loosely being related to the Slavonic Bielbog, the white god.

shamanism, and this youth was said to have been protected by the spirit of the world-tree and fed on milk. This is reminiscent of the central role of the world tree in so much northern mythology but it is also notable that the Mamas, the priests of the Venezuelan Kogi, are raised on milk and white foods only. Yet again there are resonances between belief patterns in widely spaced locations with links to the magical use of nine. The reference to sacred swine-blood also echoes the associations of the sow with British goddesses and particularly Cerridwen.

Heimdall's mothers appear to be essentially the same as the Maidens of the Mill who are the creators of the physical world from the bodies of the Frost Giants. This is classic foundation mythology and underlines the importance of the group. They are at the foot of the roaring cauldron, Hvergelmer, and it is tempting to compare this to the Corryvreckan between the Hebridean islands of Scarba and Jura. Since humans have gone into space, photographs of the earth have been taken from a considerable distance. This has led to the discovery that there are great eddies, or whirlpools, in the oceans that circulate warm surface water to the layers of cold water far below, thus providing nutrition for deep sea life. As all life originally came from the sea, the idea of the cauldron of the Goddess as the fount of life seems to be based on observable reality!

## Odin

He is the Norse god who is both shaman and poet, linking him with the notions of poetic inspiration common to the Muses and Cerridwen. His Nine Maidens are the Valkyries whose warrior aspect is similar to other Nine Maidens groups like those associated with St Samson of Dol, the nine black spirits in the story of Thidrandi and the witches of Caer Lyow. Odin is magically associated with the number nine as well. His hanging on the World-tree Yggdrasil for nine nights to acquire wisdom after having been pierced by a spear has been compared to the Crucifixion but the use of nine here is purely pagan. One of the problems we face in the modern post-literate world is that we tend to see symbolism as simple. Symbolism in pre-literate societies is generally complex. Just as a circle can refer to a cauldron, the sun, the turning of the seasons and particular figures associated with any of these, so there can be many levels of symbolism associated with one individual. To us some of these might appear as contradictory but it is a general rule of thumb that the more one knows of the thought patterns of any people the more one can understand their symbolism. This would also apply within societies where those with more knowledge than their fellows – the initiated – could read more meanings into visual and linguistic symbols. Thus Odin might represent a series of different things to different groups within Norse society.

These male figures are all of significant importance in the contemporary mythologies of the societies in which they originated. Other figures like Martin, Ochonochar, Peredur, Ruad, son of Rigdonn, Thidrandi, the widow's son accompanying Monenna, while of apparent lesser importance, carry on the motif of a single male associated with Nine Maidens who are in some way sacred. While the specific rituals of the Nine Maidens groups are probably unknowable, their divinatory and healing activities clearly show them as acting within the religious sphere. In this respect it is perhaps worth remembering the nine daughters of Ülgan in shamanic tradition with whom the shaman sleeps. Apart from the obvious links with Ruad son of Rigdonn and the mangled remnants of tales concerning lusty nuns, what we have here is perhaps a reference to a stage on a journey, whether of healing or prophecy. It is part of the role of the male in this situation to deal with these Nine Maidens before he can attain his goal. Of all the single male figures linked to the Nine Maidens groups, only St Samson's acolyte, Ruad's son and perhaps Arthur are said to have been killed and in the latter's case although mortally wounded, the prospect of recovery is strongly attested. Darrah in his book on the pagan aspects of the Arthurian material builds much of his theoretical construct on the idea of the ritual challenge and subsequent rule of the challenger who is successful at the sacred grove of Nemi. This seems to be missing the point of the underlying feminine principle in much of what we know of paganism. However the role of the Nine Maidens and one male might be something like a rite that had to be re-enacted, annually, every full moon or at some period that we can no longer discern. This would account for the survival of the motif over such a wide geographical and geological span and it is tempting to see in the almost universal magic use of nine something of this same idea.

The goddesses who have Nine Maidens associated with them are likewise varied.

## *Bride*

We have looked at the fact that Bride is common to both Scotland and Ireland, and I have suggested that she could date back to a time before Celtic languages were spoken in Britain. Problems of understanding this clearly delineated fertility goddess have arisen from the assumption that the first place we find a written source for anything must be its original source. This has led to the situation where Scottish Gaelic culture is seen as ultimately deriving from Ireland, as if language both defined ethnicity and culture in some specific 'Celtic' fashion. This overstates the importance of language. Recent works such as Professor Simon James' *The Atlantic Celts* points out that the very notion of Celticity is based on a reaction to Britishness. According to Professor Markale the name Briton, and thus Britain and British, actually derives from the name the Britons gave to the P-Celtic speaking Picts – Pretani – which is ironic.

Bride seems to be, in a truly ancient idea, the summer half of a dual Mother Goddess, with the Cailleach as the winter aspect. Such a duality could encompass life and death, cold and warmth, night and day, peace and war. This underlines the capacity of the Mother Goddess concept to incorporate all aspects of human thought and experience. The extent of Bride place-names in

Scotland, Ireland, England and Wales points to her widespread influence and it seems likely the Brigantes, a P-Celtic speaking tribal group from north-eastern England were named directly after her. The wells named for her at Abernethy, Kilbride, Sanquhar and many other locations throughout the British Isles all evince the strong connection between the idea of the Mother Goddess and the inherent sanctity of water. This is practical – no water, no life. Bride is, like water, the source of fertility and thus of the ongoing life. Her dominant role in the Christian beliefs of the Celtic-speaking peoples of western and Hebridean Scotland was remarkable. The notion that she was the birthmaiden of Christ, transported at the hour of need to the Middle East, is a clear exposition of her importance. She might have been superceded to some extent but she could not be replaced.

## Cailleach

I have suggested that the Cailleach is the other, complementary half of an ancient dual Goddess. The story of the Cailleach turning to Bride at Beltane makes this explicit. The suggestion here is that what we are dealing with in this dual Goddess is a concept from so far back in human time we can not even guess at its antiquity. The suggestion that the Cailleach is not an imported idea from Ireland was noted by DA Mackenzie in *Scottish Folk-Lore and Folk Life,* where he quoted Eleanor Hull as saying, 'The Scottish stories about the Cailleach are far more alive and widely spread than in Ireland...' (p169). Mackenzie talks of the Cailleach and Nine Maidens being linked to Ben Nevis and the Corryvreckan. This makes sense as Ben Nevis is Britain's highest mountain and a natural place to locate the winter, or hag, aspect of the Goddess, while the Corryvreckan was, and is, the most dramatic geophysical event in Europe. The association of the Cailleach in many parts of the country with significant local mountains, usually the highest and thus the focal point for changing weather patterns, reminds us of the supposed weather-working powers of Nine Maiden groups, many of whom are also found on hill or mountain tops. This can be interpreted as stressing their link to the Mother Goddess and is perhaps a direct expression of it – they control the weather because they are her representatives among the people. Perhaps like the shamans who intercede with ancestral spirits, they are officiants who can intercede with the source of all life, the Mother Goddess herself. It is noticeable within a Scottish context that several of the mountains with strong links to the Cailleach have names are shaped like the female breast In Gaelic place-names the term is generally *Cioch* and in Scots *Pap*. Several of these hills and mountains have Cailleach place-names, wells and archaeological remains of different kinds. Elsewhere I have commented on the fact that all hilltop sites have been interpreted as essentially military but this would appear to owe more to the interpreters' preconceptions than any archaeological certitude.

Another interesting aspect of the Goddess's association with the mountains arises in the interesting thesis of George Terence Meaden in his book *The Goddess of the Stones*. He suggests that the British stone circles were originally raised on the sites of small whirlwind-induced crop or vegetation circles. He further remarks that such crop circles are often found near the foot of peaked hills – some of which are named for their resemblance to the female breast. A particular example can be found with the stone circles in Aberdeenshire near the foot of Bennachie, its name meaning precisely the hill of the breast, or nipple. Such mountains and even particular hills could have been seen by Mother Goddess worshipping peoples as being an actual marker of the Goddess. If she created all life – and therefore the planet itself – then there is no great imaginative leap in believing that the creation of such obvious female characteristics in the landscape must have been put there to have been noticed. Thus they could become even more important as mythological and thus sacred sites. The habit of mountain top pilgrimages which all commentators have seen as deriving from pagan times is still not dead. This type of idea might help explain mythological references, relevant place-names, wells and possibly other artefacts on hilltops underlining the importance of such sites to a variety of Nine Maiden groups in different locations. It is also worth remarking that the shape of the whirlwind is essentially the same as that of the whirlpool.

## Cerridwen

Cerridwen is a Welsh Mother Goddess figure strongly associated with poetic inspiration and prophecy. She sometimes is represented by the sow, as are many other Mother Goddess figures in different traditions. The location of her magic cauldron and its attendant Nine Maidens at Caer Sidi is said to have been on an island. Many islands have been suggested, most of the potential candidates being off the western coast of Britain. Before seeing them as rival candidates, we should remember not only the commonalty of mythological material but also that the easiest means of communication until only a couple of centuries ago was by water. Darrah talked of the possible locations of Avalon as Sein, and Grassholm but as we have seen there are more candidates for that magic island. Given the widespread provenance of Arthurian material it is possible that there are such locations off the east coasts of both England and Scotland. One candidate here would be the Isle of May, meaning the Maiden, in the Forth estuary.

Darrah realises the continuity with the far past, but in attempting to locate all of the original Arthurian material specifically in Wales he overlooks the wider provenance of Arthurian place-names and traditions. He mentions that Glastonbury, once an island, is a good fit for Avalon but concludes, as I do, that there was no one original location but that all the possibilities were probably early cult sites, and effectively, where you can locate Avalon, you can locate the Nine Maidens.

Cerridwen has been seen by some commentators as being primarily a witch-type figure, but we should remember that the

Hag and the Cailleach are one and the same. Jean Markale in *Women of the Celts* links Cerridwen to the *groa'ch*, a witch figure in a Breton traditional tale. She is connected with the Isle of Lok and entrapped men whom she turned into fish. This association with an island is striking as is the similarity to the term used for the druidesses of Sein, *gra'ch*. It has also been noted that Cerridwen's cauldron boils the magic drops which give inspiration to Taliesin, and thus might be one of the original ideas behind the Holy Grail of medieval romance. Taliesin becomes inspired by drinking from the potion distilled in the cauldron of the goddess Cerridwen, which is kept boiling by the breath of Nine Maidens. This might suggest that Taliesin too is akin to the single male figures mentioned above. In her pursuit of Taliesin mentioned earlier, both of them are said to shape-shift, an attribute of some of the Nine Maidens groups themselves. Taliesin, by effectively being born again after Cerridwen swallows him at the end of the shape-shifting chase is clearly an initiate into the mysteries. All pagan mysteries required initiation ceremonies and such types of ritual are the norm rather than the exception among tribal peoples all over the earth. Although they are not the norm in modern Western societies, even here we find remnants of them in various types of social groupings. This is only to note the general importance of initiation which can end up as little more than acknowledgement of a rite of passage. Taliesin is doing something altogether much more significant when he is reborn by Cerridwen. This is a form of religious or magical initiation through which the individual either develops new powers or at the very least learns a great deal about himself/herself and thus about human psychology and, perhaps, how to use that knowledge. It is worth considering that what we have been seeing in all these various groups where there is a single male and nine women is partially remembered rites of initiation into the mysteries of the Goddess cult.

The links between the Isle de Sein, Grassholm and the mythical Avalon that Darrah points out can be seen as supportive of the idea that their inhabitants, or the inhabitants of communities to which they were linked, were in touch by sea. The significance of islands would perhaps be stronger amongst people living beside the sea and might even account for the importance of islands in lakes in areas that were settled later than the coasts and rivers. Whatever the reality of this, the idea of initiation on islands or hilltops – places apart from the rest of society is not a difficult one.

## Monnena

Although we only know of Monnena in a Christian guise, and under other names such as Modwenna and Darerca, she does seem to correspond to Bride in some ways. Skene and others recognised patterns in the stories of different saints suggesting that in such tales we are seeing Christianised figures based on earlier pagan ideas that occurred in different locales. Her association with wells and caves in the south east of Scotland strengthens the idea that we have a figure derived from pre-Christian times. The fact that churches were dedicated to her at significant Dark Age capital sites suggests these as having particular relevance in the pagan worship. This centrality within different Dark Age tribal groupings as the Britons, Gododdin and Picts is suggestive of a powerful mythological figure. Whether this was accompanied by any political or temporal influence on the part of the Nine Maidens groups in these capitals is impossible to say. It would appear likely that their role would give them some influence, and it is likely that it is this importance that gave rise to the titles of Mynyd Agned and subsequently the Castle of Maidens. This takes us back again to the idea of significant mountains and hills being relevant in paganism. At one time the fire-festivals of Beltane and Samhain took place in most parts of the British Isles, generally on prominent hill-tops. The recent revival of such practices on Edinburgh's Calton Hill and elsewhere certainly seems to strike a strong chord in many people, not only the party-hungry young folk, and it may be that there are deep-seated psychological reasons for the choice of hill or mountain tops for sacred practices and mythological concepts.

## Morgan

Jean Markale in *Women of the Celts* has this to say of Morgan as she appears in the medieval romance called the *Estoire de Merlin*:

> This is undoubtedly a portrait of the ambiguous, original mother Goddess, both good-natured and spiteful, the very image of the divinity who both gives and takes away, warm and sensual like the great Eastern Goddess, but a virgin nevertheless, because unwilling to submit to masculine authority. (p137)

Here he realises that the original concept behind Morgan, like so many of the other examples of figures associated with the Nine Maidens, is that of the all-encompassing Mother Goddess. Within the Arthurian tradition we have both Morgan of Avalon who comes to help the dying Arthur and in various other versions Morgan la Fee who sets out to bring him down. This can be seen as a clear exposition of the dual nature of the Mother Goddess as 'she who gives and she who takes away'. It is not that remarkable that such a duality has survived in the Arthurian material from the Middle Ages when all of Europe was ostensibly Christian. Although the official religion was Christianity, there were many, and not only among the 'common folk', who held on to aspects of much older, pagan beliefs. Some of this might account for practices mentioned in a few witch trials, though most were, as has been stated, opportunities for the persecutors to indulge their own twisted fantasies rather than the persecution of women actively working to the detriment of the society to which they belonged. It might also account for many practices that have been gathered under the general heading of folklore from all over Europe well into this century. Within this material I would include the magical use of nine and the continuing visits to wells even though many were Christianised centuries ago. Hope in *A*

*Midsummer Eve's Dream* suggests an active fairy cult in 15th century Scotland and this must have involved continuity with earlier beliefs.

In the *Vita Merlini*, Morgan is one of the Nine Maidens of Avalon and clearly their leader. This can be contrasted with the figures of Bride, Cerridwen, Menglod and Monenna who all have Nine Maidens as priestesses, acolytes or followers. Perhaps this came about because Morgan entered the literary romance tradition in Christian times and became one of the maidens to make her essentially pagan aspect less blatant to the courtly audience. Much of what we know of these other female figures comes from oral tradition that continued long after Morgan had attained fame within Arthurian literature.

Darrah makes the following point about Morgan and her sisters:

> At Avalon the Goddess and her priestesses are Morgan and her bird-transforming sisters. Morgan is also resident, with many maidens, in the Castle of the Marvel, one of the equivalents of the Castle of the Maidens; and in another Castle of Maidens the Goddess is the Queen of Danemarche who has many attendant maidens in her garden, surrounded by a hedge of air. (p229)

This hedge of air is reminiscent of the hedge around Bride's sacred flame at Kildare into the Christian period. No men were allowed to cross, or look over this hedge, on pain of death. Here Darrah is seeing Morgan as the Goddess and many scholars have seen some resemblance with the Irish Morrigan. It is interesting that Darrah mentions an Arthurian instance of a raven attacking a knight at a ford; the raven, when killed, turned into a maiden whom Darrah clearly sees as one of Morgan's companions (ibid p226). The Morrigan is of course seen on battlefields in the shape of a raven and the idea of the battle attendant finds some further echo in the figures of the Valkyries in Norse tradition. Here we also have the recurring motif of shape shifting among Nine Maidens groups which may be related to the idea of spirit journeying in shamanism. Darrah also notes that there are references to the Nine Maidens of Sein flying through the air and as with the raven-maiden here mentioned this is redolent of the supposed capacity of witches to fly through the air, interpreted in modern times as being descriptive of spirit journeys taken under the influence of drugs of one kind or another.

Morgan is clearly an otherworldly figure and in Breton traditions the term Morgan actually became associated with specific types of fairy. As an Otherworld female her links with the figure of Arthur perhaps suggest he is an initiate into the pagan mysteries – he does after all go into the underworld to seek a magic cauldron in the poem by Taliesin we have looked at RS Loomis tells us that:

> Giraldus Cambrensis speaks of Marganis as… a certain imaginary Goddess; and even late in the fourteenth century the author of Gawain and the Green Knight speaks of her as Morgne the Goddess. (1993 p192):

Whoever she was originally, the Goddess herself or her chief priestess, or both, there is no doubt that the figure of Morgan has continued to inspire generation upon generation of writers and has retained a considerable amount of the ambiguity originally associated with the Mother Goddess herself.

## Ran

As the Norse goddess of the sea, Ran clearly has great importance for the Norsemen who were great seafarers, the dominant image we have of them being of the gold- and battle-hungry vikings. We should remember however that much of the British Isles was actually settled by people from Scandinavia, a fact clearly discernible in a host of place-names in areas now portrayed as essentially Celtic. The fact is that the orally transmitted traditions can and do transcend language shifts, which have themselves too often have been interpreted as a result of mass immigration or invasion and suppression. That there are ideas from Norse mythology inherent in different parts of what has been called the Celtic world and vice versa suggests we might better look to interpret the past in terms of cultural contacts between different groups instead of looking for military explanations. Ran is portrayed as a being who actively welcomes drowned sailors and Davidson tells us of how she was seen in Iceland:

> A folk belief quoted in one of the Icelandic sagas is that when people were drowned they were thought to have gone to Ran, and if they appeared at their own funeral feasts, it was a sign that she had given them a good welcome. In a late saga, Fridjof's Saga, it is said to have been a lucky thing to have gold on one's person if lost at sea. The hero went so far as to distribute small pieces of gold among his men when they were caught in a storm, so that they should not go empty-handed into Ran's hall if they were drowned. The idea of the hospitality of Aegir and Ran, who were so anxious to throng their underwater world with the hosts of the dead, may be compared with that of the god of battle. (1990 p129)

It can also clearly be compared to the goddesses of battle like the Morrigan and therefore directly to the destructive aspect of the Mother Goddess. Ran's daughters are represented as the waves themselves and this is perhaps the agency of her drawing sailors into her net. Sailors throughout the world have a particular attitude towards the sea. In many parts of the world, including Scotland, seamen traditionally refused to learn how to swim. They were entirely at the mercy of the sea, which would spare them if their fate decreed it. Here we are very close to the idea of the giving and taking Goddess in that fishermen or traders might flourish through her agency, or they might drown. Such ideas are ancient indeed. We know that in much of the period since the last Ice Age, some 10,000 years ago, people have been travelling around northern Europe by sea and weather changes at sea can be dramatic at any time of the year. In Norse mythology we have Ran and her husband Aegir while in the Q-Celtic areas we have the male Manannan mac Lir alone, perhaps suggesting an older

*[handwritten note at bottom]* 1: An echo of this belief can be found in the very old custom of sailors carrying a gold ring in their ear; it's payment/gift to the sea goddess.

Not surprising realy, when one remembers that both P and Q Celtic derive from a common root Language.

stratum existing among the Norsemen. Manannan has a counterpart in Welsh literature Manaddwyn, son of Lir who marries the goddess Rhiannon. She had birds who were said to have the ability to bring the dead back to life and send the living to sleep with their singing. This seems to echo the associations that Morgan has with the raven mentioned above and underlines the fact that many of the Goddess figures seen in material derived from the oral tradition in both P- and Q-Celtic speaking areas seem to hark back to much older ideas of the Mother Goddess. This is not to suggest a specific link between Ran and Rhiannon but to show the complexity of, but also the continuity inherent in, much of this material.

In the Irish saga of Ruad son of Rigdonn he comes across the daughters of Ran and it is worth noting that Heimdall, of the nine mothers, was known in some sagas as Rig, which most commentators have seen as link to Celtic ideas. The name Rigdonn has the component Donn here which is reminiscent of the goddess Danu from Irish tradition.

## Menglod

We saw in the story of Svipdag, son of the witch Groa that Menglod lived on a mountain of healing surrounded by her Nine Maidens. She was said to have been the daughter of a giant of the underworld, who might be linked to Heimdall as both are referred to in different locales as being 'nail-resplendent'. Menglod's name – 'necklace-glad' – seems to link her directly with the Norse goddess Freyja, who owned the famed necklace, Brisingamen. Freyja is clearly a fertility goddess and Davidson in *Roles of the Northern Goddess* writes of the goddesses Frigg and Freyja:

> Both are associated with fertility, and while Frigg is presented as the divine mother, queen of heaven, Freyja is apparently of a younger generation, the daughter of Njord and Skadi, and is said to hold the title 'Bride of the Vanir'. (p86)

This is somewhat like the duality of the Cailleach and Bride in that we have two generations of goddesses though it is not an exact match and Davidson also tells us that Freyja was associated with the sow – redolent of the Welsh goddess Cerridwen among others. So we have Menglod linked to healing, a mountain site and the sow, as well as fertility. All of these are recurrent themes in the motif of the Nine Maidens. Svipdag who woos her, has help from beyond the grave, again taking us into the realms of Life and Death. All of this, like the turning of the seasons seems very much the realm of the Mother Goddess.

# Further Magic Use of Nine

IN POLSON'S SCOTTISH WITCHCRAFT LORE there are several mentions of the use of the number nine. He tells us of Thomas Greave who, in 1623, cured a child by wrapping it nine times in an unguent-covered cloth, while repeating prayers (p103). From Aberdeen he tells us:

> Another method of cure was to put the patient nine times through a hasp of unwatered yarn, and then a cat as many times backwards through the same hasp, and thus the sickness was transferred to the cat. (p122)

Davidson's analysis of folklore practices in *Rowan Tree and Red Threid* includes the spell used by the North Berwick witches who tried to drown James VI and I early in the 17th century:

> Cummer ye afore, cummer gae ye
> Gin ye wanna gae afore
> Ring o ring widdershins
> Loupin, lichtly, widdershins
> Kilted coats and fleein hair
> Three times three. (p18)

Again this is an example of going widdershins nine times to effect black magic. It is also reminiscent of the activities of the three witches in Shakespeare's *Macbeth*. Davidson mentions a coven, in which the men, 'turned nine times widdershins about and the women six times,' (p62) and quotes this from the trial of Marion Rickhart in 1633. In treating sick cattle she gave the following instructions:

Go thy way to the sea and tell nyne boares of the sea come in. that is to say nyne waves of the sea, and let the hindmost of the go back again and the nixt thereafter take thrie loofullis [handfuls] of the water and put within stoupe [jug] and quhan thou comes home put it within thy kine [cattle] and thow will get thy profeit gane [again]. (p28)

This connects with beliefs about the ninth wave being of particular significance. Another manifestation of this magic use of nine comes from Shetland. *The County Folklore Series for Shetland* tells of the cure for a child rescued from trows or trolls (1903 p146). The mother had to collect the 'nine mithers' mait' for her child. 'Mait' in Scots means food. She would solicit nine mothers whose first born were sons for three articles of food each, to be used during the convalescence of the child. The cure was also used in the case of the wasting diseases known locally as trowie, probably connected with the belief in trolls.

This is reminiscent of the Nine Herbs Charm used amongst the early Anglo-Saxon inhabitants of Britain, given in the Everyman edition of *Anglo-Saxon Poetry* edited by Bradley. Though superficially Christian, it does refer to Woden as the originator of the charm:

This is the herb which is called Wergelu;
The seal sent this over the back of the ocean
to heal the hurt of other poison
These nine sprouts against nine poison

A snake came crawling, it bit a man.
Then Woden took nine glory-twigs,
Smote the serpent so that it flew into nine parts
There apple brought this to pass against poison,
That she never more would enter her house.

Thyme and Fennel, a pair great in power,
The Wise Lord holy in heaven

Wrought these herbs while He hung on the cross;
He placed and put them in seven worlds
To aid all, poor and rich.
It stands against pain, resists the venom,
It has power against three and against thirty,
Against a fiend's hand and against sudden trick,
Against witchcraft of vile creatures.

Now these nine herbs avail against nine evil spirits
Against nine poisons and against nine infectious diseases,
Against the red poison, against the running poison,
Against the white poison, against the blue poison,
Against the yellow poison, against the green poison,
Against the black poison, against the blue poison,
Against the brown poison, against the crimson poison,
Against snake blister, against water- blister,
Against thorn-blister, against thistle-blister,
Against ice-blister, against poison blister;
If any poison comes flying from the east
Or any comes from the north
Or any from the west upon the people.

Christ stood over disease of every kind.
I alone know running water, and the nine serpents heed it;
May all pastures now spring up with herbs,
The seas, all salt water, be destroyed,
When I blow this poison from thee. (p93)

This is some kind of charm! There are some very interesting
aspects to this mish-mash of the pagan and the Christian. We
have of course come across serpents associated with Bride and the
apple is the fruit after which Avalon is supposedly named. The
reference to Christ on the cross could be interpreted in different
ways as anyone who was bought up a pagan among the
Germanic-speaking peoples would know that Odin hung for nine

nights on the World-Tree, Yggdrasil, in order to attain inspiration. Are we seeing here yet another example of the Christian world overlaying the beliefs of an earlier time? This charm also is reminiscent of Taliesin's claim that he was born of the 'nine-form faculties'.

At Beltane even in the 19th century, it was the custom to raise the neid-fire in many countries. This is the practice as known from Scotland. All fires in the parish were put out and people congregated a traditional hill-top spot for the ceremony. The point of the ritual was to create fire by friction, without the use of metal or chemicals, a tradition probably harking back beyond datable time. After the fire was created the Beltane bonfires were lit, cattle were driven through the smoke, special food and drink were consumed and there are hints that in earlier times there was a great deal of sexual activity. Each family would light a torch from the sacred fire, at dawn and after walking around their own fields and houses with the holy fire, would go into their home and ceremonially light the hearth fire – and the fire would be kept going continuously till the next Beltane. The process of driving the cattle through the smoke (which perhaps had an antiseptic component as the fire tended to include such pungent woods as juniper) and carrying fire round holdings and homes was to sain, or sanctify, home and hearth against all evil influence and to guarantee fertility. The guarantee of fertility is the older concept as we see the idea of defence against evil becoming more dominant in the 17th and 18th centuries.

Specifically protection was sought against witches – an idea that seems to have taken hold after the Reformation. Frazer gives us a good account of fire festivals in *The Golden Bough*: 'In some places three times three persons, in others three times nine, were required for turning round by turns the axle tree or wimble' (p803). This describes large equipment to create fire by the friction of wood on wood – a public, ritual development of the universal fire-drill technology for creating fire.

Another interesting ritual at 1 May is reported by Pennant:

The rites begin with spilling some of the caudle [a custard of eggs and milk, cooked in the open air] on the ground by way of libation: on that, everyone takes a cake of oatmeal, upon which are raised nine square knobs, each dedicated to some particular being, the supposed preserver of their flocks and herds, or to some particular animal, the real destroyer of them. Each person then turns his face to the fire, breaks off a knob, and flinging it over his shoulders, says, 'This I give to thee, preserve thou my horses, This to thee, preserve thou my sheep, and so on. After that they use the same ceremony to the noxious animals. This I give to thee, O fox! Spare thou my lambs! This I give to thee, O hooded crow.' (1 p90)

This would appear to be an 18th-century remnant of a very ancient ceremony indeed, possibly preserved because it was thought to have been efficacious. The pre-Reformation Catholic Church turned a blind eye to such practices but in many areas the Presbyterian Church was also unable to eradicate the remnants and practices of ancient belief. Clearly the number nine had a deep significance over many areas. The following excerpt is from Ramsay's *Scotland and Scotsmen in the 18th Century*. Talking of Highland practice he tells us that:

After kindling the bonfire with the tein-eigin (neid-fire) the company prepared their rituals. As soon as they had finished their meal they amused themselves a while in singing and dancing round the fire. Towards the close of the entertainment, the person who officiated as master of the feast produced a large cake baked with eggs and scalloped round the edge, and called am bonnach beal-tine – the Beltane cake. It was divided into a number of pieces and distributed to the company. There was one particular piece which whoever got was called cailleach beal-tine – the Beltane carline, a term of great reproach. Upon his being known, part of the company laid hold of him and made a show of putting him into the fire; but the majority interposing, he was rescued. And in some places they laid him on the ground, making as if they would quarter him. Afterwards he was pelted with egg-shell, and retained the odious appellation during the whole year. And while the feast was fresh in people's memory, they affected to speak of the cailleach beal-tine as dead. (2 pp242-3)

It seems this passage describes a remnant of what was once a sacrificial act. The notion of the scapegoat is quite clear, probably the result of Christian influence. Similarly the cry of 'burn the witches' at such Beltane ceremonies was a distortion of earlier belief where the 'wise woman' was the repository of knowledge and healing within the community. Sacrifice in many societies was seen as a method of sending a messenger to the gods on behalf of the community. The name of the chosen one in this excerpt, the *cailleach beal-tine*, takes us back to the idea of the Cailleach as the Winter Hag aspect of the Mother Goddess. It was at Beltane that she went to the sacred well just before dawn, and drinking from it, was transformed into the beautiful golden Bride, Goddess of Summer and Fertility. This might be describing a rite that had begun in the far past and was truly pagan. The types of women singled out for persecution in the witch trials were generally old and therefore full of a lifetime's learning and experience, particularly in herbalism and healing. It is also likely that some of their spells preserved some sort of continuity with ideas from much earlier.

In Banks' *Calendar Customs* we are told of this Scottish belief associated with Halloween:

> ... if, on Halloween, any person should go round one of these (fairy) hillocks nine times, contrary to the course of the sun, a door would open, by which he would be admitted to the fairy realms. (p165)

The belief in fairies inhabiting hillocks, which were in fact often ancient burial mounds, is very reminiscent of the supposed rituals that took place at Stone Age chambered cairns. It has been suggested that 'priests' tried to communicate with the spirits of the ancestors through ritual, to bring fertility in the future. This is also undoubtedly linked to the common Scottish motif of musicians being lured into fairy hills where they spend a night playing for the fairies to dance, which then turns out to have been many years, an idea of course that is not restricted to Scotland. In Wales the people also lit the Beltane fires and Frazer tells us:

> The fire was done in this way. Nine men would turn their pockets inside out, and see that every piece of money and all metals were off their persons. Then the men went into the nearest woods, and collected sticks of nine different kinds of trees. (p155)

These 'nine woods' were then used to create a large fire which was started by the friction of two pieces of oak rubbed together. In the 19th century a well at Tullybelton in Strathtay was visited on Beltane morning and after drinking from the well the visitor would walk round it nine times in a clockwise direction, and then round the standing stones beside it. At Oystermouth Castle in West Glamorgan it was the custom to wish on the Wishing Post, a stone in the dungeon. It was part of the ritual to walk round it nine times. The Garrack Zans at Sennen in Cornwall was the site of a good-luck ritual where old people used to go nine times daily round a large flat stone. The Stone of Odin at Stenness in Orkney was highly venerated until its destruction in 1814. Anyone who wished to gain magical powers visited it at the full moon in nine consecutive months and went round the stone on bare knees nine times, then made his wish while looking through the hole in the stone.

There is also evidence of the ritual use of nine far beyond the British Isles. Talking of the St John's fires in Scandinavia, Frazer tells of the practice in Norrland:

> The fuel consists of nine different sorts of wood and the spectators cast into the flames a kind of toadstool (Bäran) in order to counteract the power of the Trolls and other evil spirits, who are believed to be about that night. (p172)

This is Midsummer, a date for fire festivals in many parts of Europe including Britain. The trolls and evil spirits were traditionally believed to have come forth from inside mountains, which opened up on this night. This is very much like the old ideas associated with Samhain or Halloween in Scotland and elsewhere and is perhaps another faint echo of ancient practices at chambered tombs when the spirits of the ancestors were contacted.

Frazer recounts numerous similar activities. At Midsummer in Moravia, now part of the Czech Republic:

> ... on the same mystic evening Moravian girls gather flowers of nine sorts and lay them under their pillow when they go to sleep; then they dream every one of him who is to be their partner for life. (p175)

In Brittany Midsummer bonfires were also lit, and Frazer tells us it was believed that 'every girl who danced round nine of the bonfires would marry within the year'. This particular belief is also noted in Berry, central France while in the Pyrenees leaping over nine of the Midsummer bonfires would assure prosperity for the coming year. A slight variation is recorded in Flanders where women were said to leap over the fires to ensure easy childbirth.

As each village or community would have its own St John's Fire, the act of dancing round or jumping over nine different fires would involve some travelling outwith the individual's immediate community. This would in turn lead to greater romantic possibilities, thus actually helping in the search for a suitable husband.

In Wales, St John's fires were common and according to Frazer:

> Three or nine different kinds of wood and charred faggots carefully preserved from the last midsummer were deemed necessary to build the bonfire, which was generally done on rising ground. Various herbs were thrown into the blaze; and girls with bunches of three or nine different kinds of flowers would take the hands of boys, who

wore flowers in their buttonholes and hats, and together the young couples would leap over the fires. (p210)

The preservation of charred wood from one fire till the next is also a feature of the Scottish Midwinter fire festivals, and I have been blessed on several occasions by having been given shards of the Clavie, the great fire bucket traditionally burnt at Hogmanay (New Year's Eve) at Burghhead in Morayshire. Some continuities remain unbroken.

The use of the number nine in ritual also occurred at Halloween, the Christianised version of the earlier Feast of the Dead. At this time of the year it was believed the boundaries between the worlds of the living and the dead were at their weakest and it was possible to move from one realm to the other. Halloween ceremonies were probably derived from rituals designed to get in touch with the ancestors who had returned to the earth and ask them to use their magic on the seed that had been buried in the ground, to ensure the growth of crops in the coming season. In later times however much of the ritual associated with Halloween seems primarily concerned with affairs of the heart. Constant references to the activities of young people at the significant feast days of the traditional year emphasises what was general practice – these were times of sexual initiation and of heightened sexual activity. In societies not affected by the Christian concept of sin, the act of making love at these specific times was seen as a form of sympathetic magic, even worship.

Again referring to the neid-fire ceremony, but this time in Germany's Wassgaw mountains at Halloween, Frazer tells us (p271), 'Others use a thick rope, collect nine kinds of wood, and keep them in violent motion until fire leaps forth.' On the lower Rhine he informs us, 'The bonfires so kindled were composed of wood of nine different sorts...' (p278), which is echoed in eighteenth century Swedish practice:

... the neid-fire was kindled, as in Germany, by the violent rubbing of

two pieces of wood against each other; sometimes nine different
kinds of wood were used for the purpose. (p280)

Frazer documents Halloween divination practices in County
Leitrim in Ireland at Halloween which were designed to help
young girls to find their husband to be. It is likely that the
divination in ancient times was more to do with trying to foresee
the success of planting and what the future held for the tribe or
family in general. Frazer goes on to mention another method of
such divination:

> Another way was to take a rake, go to a rick and walk round it nine
> times, saying, 'I take this rick in the devil's name.' At the ninth time
> the wraith of your destined partner would come and take the rake
> out of your hand. (ibid)

The appeal in the Devil's name suggests that here, as in so in
many rural areas of Europe, the Devil was not seen as the
embodiment of absolute evil.

Martin Martin writing in A *Description of the Western Islands
of Scotland* gives a graphic account of the neid-fire being raised
as an antidote against the plague, or murrain, in cattle:

> All the fires in the parish were extinguished, and then eighty-one
> married men, being thought the necessary number for effecting this
> design, took two great planks of wood, and nine of them were
> employed by turns, who by their repeated efforts rubbed one of the
> planks against the other until the heat thereof produced fire; and
> from this forced fire each family is supplied with new fire, which is
> no sooner kindled than a pot full of water is quickly set on it, and
> afterwards sprinkled upon the people infected with the plague, or
> upon the cattle that have the murrain. (p113)

Martin observed this pagan practice in the late 17th century on
both Lewis and Skye. These fertility and saining rites were used
to affect a cure for diseases. This is a clear example of how pagan

traditions carried on for hundreds of years after people were supposedly Christianised, perhaps because such rituals had the reputation of having worked before, and so should work again.

LC Wimberley in *Folklore in the English and Scottish Ballads* describes magical instructions from a witch in the ballad, *Broomfield Hill,* which:

> ... tells how a maiden, under instructions from a witch woman retains her honour by using sleep charms. She puts her lover to sleep by means of a combination of herbal and circle magic.

> But when ye gang to Broomfield Hill
> Walk nine times round and round
> Down below a bonny bank
> Ye'll find your lover sleeping sound. (p300)

The magical use of nine also crops up in the ballad *Willie's Lady*:

> Willie had loosed the nine witch knots
> That was ain o that ladie's locks. (p356)

So Willie lifts the evil spell from his household. Banks in *Calendar Customs* tells of a song used in north-east Scotland while scattering the ashes of the Halloween fires. This was sung by farm servants, hired on a half-yearly basis, who wished to find new positions:

> This is Hallaeven
> The morn is Halladay;
> Nine free nichts till Martinmas
> An soon they all wear away. (p110)

In a pass through the Ochil Hills behind Newburgh on the south bank of the river Tay is the site of Macduff's Cross. Only the base now remains this ancient monument which has strong associations with the number nine. Nearby there are the Nine

Wells, and we are only a few miles here from Abernethy with its Nine Maidens associations. As late as the 16th century, MacDuff's Cross was a sanctuary for those who had committed murder. Andrew Laing in *The History of Lindores Abbey and the Burgh of Newburgh* tells us that the right of sanctuary extended only to those who were within nine degrees of kinship of the Earl of Fife, which would probably have covered most of his relatives. He then continues:

> The fine of nine kye [cattle] and a colpindach [a young cow or ox] payable by the manslayer is the same as that which was payable to the king when his rights were infringed. This similarity shows that the privilege was guarded by the highest sanction which law afforded. The fine of nine kye, and the traditionary necessity of washing nine times in the Nine Wells [which rise on the lands of the town of Newburgh, in a field next to Cross Macduff], tends to show that there was a mystical property connected with the number nine, and that the tradition had its origin in some principle which is lost in the mists of antiquity. (p329)

The fine of nine cows and a young ox, as part of the sanctuary process at MacDuff's Cross, is reminiscent of the recurring feature of nine females and a single male and this excerpt shows just how central the number nine seems to have been to magic ritual in Scotland.

Dalyell quotes a further few instances of the magical/ritual use of nine in Scottish folklore in *Darker Superstitions of Scotland*:

> Nine enchanted stones were cast or laid in a field for the destruction of the crop. A skein of yarn through which a patient had been transmitted nine times was cut into nine parts and buried in three Lairds' lands for a cure. On the 11 August 1623, a mother hired a woman to go silent to the well of Ruthven, to wash her bairn for the restoration of its health; the woman, the mother averred before the Kirk Session of Perth, put her bairn through ane cake made of nine curnes of meal gotten from women married maidens, and that it is a

common practice used for curing bairns. A draught repeated nine times from the horn of a living ox was prescribed for hooping cough, together with putting the patient nine several times in the happer of a grinding mill. Numerous other instances might be adduced of superstitious reverence for the number nine. One of the very latest that has come under our notice, shows that the superstition is widespread, and stills bear sway over the minds of men. In 1869 the Emir of Bokhara, to propitiate the favour of the Emperor of Russia who suing for peace, sent a costly present by an embassy to the monarch, consisting of nine valuable gifts, the number nine, it was stated, being strictly adhered to, in accordance with the custom of the Turko-Tartaric races. (p395)

He also notes an instance of, 'a distempered cow taken backwards into the sea until washed by nine surges,' which is reminiscent of the belief that the ninth wave was always the strongest. He goes on:

It has been remarked already that, at Beltane, an oaten cake was prepared in the Highlands with nine square knobs, each dedicated to the protector or destroyer of the crops. In the seventeenth century, three cakes were prepared of nine portions of meal, contributed by nine maidens and nine married women... (p394)

There are many instances of the magical use of nine in Scotland and here is one final one. In *Witch, Warlock and Magician*, WH Davenport Adams quotes the following:

James Og is indicted to have passed on Rudday, five years since, through Alexander Cobain's corn, and have taken nine stones from his avine rig [corn rick], and cast them on the said Alexander's rig and to have taken nine lokis [handfuls] of meal from the said Alexander's rig and cast it on his own. He is indicted to have bewitched a cow belonging to the said Alexander, which he bought from Kristane Burnet, of Cloak; this cow, though his wife had received milk from her the first night, and the morning thereafter, gave no milk from that time forth, but died within a half year. He is indicted to have passed, five years since, on Lammas Day, through the said Alexander's corn, and having gained nyne span to have struck the corn with nine strokes of a white wand so that nothing grew that year but fichakis [weeds], (p363)

The link Butler made between the Ninewells and the Nine Maidens suggests there could be a link between the efficacy of the number nine and the Nine Maidens themselves. Where there are Nine Maidens groups we would therefore expect to see the use of nine in magic and ritual. We have already seen there are various Nine Maiden groups in Norse mythology and that nine is a significant magical number. This is how Crossley-Holland describes the significance of nine in *The Norse Myths*:

> ... the number nine recurs again and again in Norse mythology. Odin learns nine magic songs from a giant that enables him to win the mead of poetry for the gods; Heimdall has nine mothers; Hermod, Odin's son, journeys for nine nights in his attempt to win back Balder from Hel; the great religious ceremony at the temple of Uppsala lasted for nine days every in every ninth year, and required the sacrifice of nine humans and nine animals of every kind. Why nine was the most significant number in Norse mythology, has not been satisfactorily explained, but belief in the magical properties of the number is not restricted to Scandinavia. In The Golden Bough, Frazer records ceremonies involving the number nine in... Wales, Lithuania, Siam and the island of Nias in the Mentawai chain. Nine is, of course, the end of a series of single numbers, and this may be the reason why it symbolises death and rebirth in a number of mythologies; hence it also stands for the whole. (pxxiv)

The nine separate levels of existence in Norse mythology are all located on the World-tree Yggdrasil. At Ragnarok, the final battle of the gods, Thor staggers back nine steps before he dies from the venom of the serpent Jormangard and as noted earlier, when the seeress Groa sends her son Svipdag to win the hand of Menglod, she sings nine charms over him. In Norse as in Scottish mythology the use of the number nine is widespread and central to magical practice. Another Norse tale, *The Master Smith*, tells of the making of locks and bolts of the nine gates of Hel, a cold goddess ruling over nine worlds.

However it is not just in Britain and Scandinavia that the number is significant. Just as there are nine worlds in Norse mythology, so in Chinese mythology there are nine levels of heaven and the nine cauldrons of the semi-mythological emperor Yu represented control over the nine provinces of the country. Once again here we have link between the number nine and a cauldron or cauldrons. Other peoples with a belief in Nine Worlds include some of the northern Amerindian tribes and the Kogi of Venezuela. The Kogi are an indigenous tribe who, after beating off the invading Spaniards back in the 16th century, retreated into isolation in the high mountains, only recently coming down to speak with the people they call the Younger Brothers – which seems to represent all of humanity except themselves. Their priests who control the tribe are called Mamas after a goddess who had nine daughters and they believe there are nine different stages of the world. Here we have a link between a Mother Goddess figure and nine daughters – very like Cerridwen and her cauldron maidens or Menglod and her companions. An example from North America is given by Vitaliano in his *Legends of the Earth*, where he tells us:

> The Apaches believe that the hole leading down into Mother earth is located in this range [Superstition Mountains, Arizona], its entrance guarded by a nine-headed snake which allows no mortals to pass.
> (p170)

Here we have the number nine and the serpent figure combined in a way that strongly suggests the chthonic powers of various goddess figures. Nine, as a significant number can be found in many parts of the world. Lyall Watson noted several examples in the 1970s on the Indonesian island he called Nus Tarian in his book *Gifts of Unknown Things*. There the people believe that there were nine families of mankind, corresponding to the nine clans in their village. They hold a traditional danced in the place called the Nine Dance Grounds where the men danced in a nine-fold spiral figure round women grouped in the centre. Each clan has its own 'viewing stone', a talisman handed down through the generations round which important clan business is carried out. At all other times these nine stones are kept hidden. There are similar traditions in New Guinea, particularly on the island of West Ceram. Here the belief is that the nine families of mankind came originally from Mount Nunusaka, again bringing in the motif of mountains and reminding us of the founding myth of the Kikuyu in East Africa.

The number nine has been seen in some esoteric traditions as representing perfection and truth. One of the strange things about the number nine is that it always reproduces itself, e.g.:

$$2 \times 9 = 18: 1 + 8 = 9;$$

$$32 \times 9 = 288: 2 + 8 + 8 = 18: 1 + 8 = 9;$$

$$65 \times 9 = 585: 5 + 8 + 5 = 18: 1 + 8 = 9$$

And so on. This can be interpreted as the number reproducing itself so it is therefore the optimum number to represent regeneration and fertility. Mathematically, I have been told, this capacity to reproduce itself would happen with the number 5 if we counted to base 6, or the number 12 if we counted to base 13, but humans count to base 10, because of the fact that we have 10 digits on our hands.

# Bibliography

The Aberdeen Breviary 1854

Adams, WHD          *Witch, Warlock and Magician*, Chatto & Windus, London, 1889.

Anderson, AO        *Early Sources of Scottish History*, Paul Watkins, Stamford, 1990.

*Anglo-Saxon Poetry* Everyman, London.

Anson, PF           *Fisher Folk Lore*, Faith Press, London, 1965.

Banks, MM           *British Calendar Customs: Scotland*, Folklore Society, London, 1937-41.

Baring-Gould, S     *Lives of the British Saints*, Llanerch, Felinfach, 1990.

Barrow, GWS         Religion in Scotland on the eve of Christianity in

Herde, P            *Gesammelte Abhandlungen and Aufsatze*, 1997.

Barrett, M          *Footprints of the Ancient Scottish Church*, Sands & Co, London, 1914.

Bawcutt, P          Longer Scottish Poems, Aberdeen University Press,
 & Riddy, F         Aberdeen, 1987.

Bede                *A History of the English Church and People* trans. L Shelley-Price, Penguin, London, 1955.

Bellenden, J        *Translation of Boece's History and Chronicles of Scotland*, (ed) W Seton, RW Chambers, EC Batho, Scottish Text Society, Edinburgh, 1821.

*The Black Book of Carmarthen*    reproduced and edited by JG Evans, Pwlhelli, Wales, 1906.

*The Black Book of Taymouth*       by W Bowie, (ed) C Innnes, Bannatyne Club, Edinburgh, 1855.

Boece               see Turnbull, W

Bonwick             *Irish Druids and Old Irish Religions*, Dorset, USA, 1986.

Bord, J, & Bord, C  *The Secret Country*, Paladin, London, 1976.

Bradley, SAJ        (ed) *Anglo-Saxon Poetry*, Everyman, London, 1982.

Brown, GB           *The Art of the Cave Dweller*, John Murray, London, 1932.

Brown, J           *The History of Sanquhar*, Anderson & Sons,
                   Dumfries, 1891.
Burt, E            *Burt's letters form the north of Scotland*
                   (ed) A Simmons, Birlinn, Edinburgh 1998.
Burton             *Wonderful Curios*
Butler, D          *The Ancient Church and Parish of Abernethy*,
                   Blackwood & Sons, Edinburgh, 1897.
Campbell, D        *The Book of Garth and Fortingall*, Inverness,
                   1888.
Campbell, JG       *Popular Tales of the Western Islands*, Birlinn,
                   Edinburgh, 1994.
Carmichael, A      *Carmina Gadelica* (ed) CJ Moore, Birlinn,
                   Edinburgh, 1994.
Chadwick, HM       *Early Scotland*, Cambridge University Press,
                   Cambridge, 1949.
Christie, J        *The Lairds and Lands of Tayside*, Cameron & Sons,
                   Aberfeldy, 1892.
Cockburn, JH       *The Celtic Church in Dunblane*, Society of the
                   Friends of Dunblane Cathedral, Dunblane, 1954.
County Folklore Series     *Shetland*
Crawford, OGS      *The Eye Goddess*, Phoenix House, London, 1957.
Crossley-Holland, K *The Norse Myths*, Deutsch, London, 1982.
Dalyell, JG        *Darker Superstitions of Scotland*, Griffin,
                   Glasgow, 1835.
Dames, M           *The Silbury Treasure*, Thames & Hudson, London,
                   1976.
Darrah, J          *Paganism in Arthurian Romance*, Boydell,
                   Woodbridge, 1994.
Davidson, HRE      *Gods and Myths of Northern Europe*, Penguin,
                   London, 1990.
Davidson, HRE      *Myths and Symbols in Pagan Europe*, Manchester
                   University Press, 1988.
Davidson, HRE      *The Lost Beliefs of Northern Europe*, Routledge,
                   London & NY, 1993.
Davidson, HRE      *Roles of the Northern Goddess*, Routledge, London
                   & NY 1998.

Davidson, T — *Rowan Tree and Red Thread*, Oliver & Boyd, Edinburgh, 1949.

De Santillana, G & von Dechend, H — *Hamlet's Mill*, Macmillan, London, 1970.

Dillon, M & Chadwick, N — *The Celtic Realms*, Weidenfield & Nicolson, London, 1972.

Douglas, S — *The King of the Black Art and other stories*, Aberdeen University Press, 1987.

Dumezil, G — *Gods of the Ancient Northmen*, University of California Press, Berkeley, 1973.

Eliade, M — *Shamanism*, Arkana, London, 1989.

Forbes, AP — *Kalendars of Scottish Saints*, Edmonston & Douglas, Edinburgh, 1872.

Frazer, J — *The Golden Bough*, MacMillan, London, 1922.

Gimbutas, M — *The Goddesses and Gods of Ancient Europe*, Thames & Hudson, London, 1982.

Glennie, JS — *Arthurian Localities in Scotland*, Llanerch, Felinfach, Wales 1994.

Gollancz, I — *Hamlet in Iceland*, Nutt, London, 1898.

Grant, J — *Old and New Edinburgh*, Cassell's, London, 1885-7.

Graves, R — *The Greek Myths* 2 vols, Harmondsworth, London, 1960.

Graves, R — *Mammon and the Black Goddess*, Cassell, London, 1965.

Graves, R — *The White Goddess*, Faber & Faber, London, 1961.

Gray, J — (ed) *Mythology of All Races* 13 vols, Marshall Jones, Boston, 1916-1964.

Gregor, W — *Notes on the Folklore of the North East of Scotland*, London 1881.

Grimm, J — *Teutonic Mythology* 4 vols, Swan, Sonnenschein & Allen, London, 1880-88.

Guerber, HA — *The Norsemen*, Senate, London, 1994.

Guthrie, JC — *The Vale of Strathmore, Its Scenes and Legends*, Edinburgh, 1875.

Gwynn, E — (ed) *The Metrical Dinshenchas*, Royal Irish Academy, Dublin, 1903-35.

| | |
|---|---|
| Hansen, W | *Saxo Grammaticus and the Life of Hamlet*, University of Nebraska Press, Lincoln and London 1983. |
| Heywood, T | *Gunaikieon*, printed by Adam Islip, London, 1624. |
| Hollander, L | *The Poetic Eddas*, University of Texas Press, Austin, 1924. |
| Hope, AD | *A Midsummer Eve's Dream*, Oliver & Boyd, Edinburgh, 1971. |
| Hull, E | *Folklore of the British Isles*, Methuen, London, 1928. |
| Hutton, R | *Pagan Religions of the Ancient British Isles*, Blackwell, Oxford, 1991. |
| Isaacs, J | *Australian Dreaming; 40,000 years of Aboriginal History*, Lansdowne Press, Willoughby, NSW 1980. |
| Ivimy, J | *The Sphinx and the Megaliths*, Abacus, London, 1976. |
| Jacobson, E | *The Deer Goddess of Ancient Siberia*, EJ Brill, NY 1993. |
| James, S | *The Atlantic Celts*, British Museum Press, London, 1999. |
| Jervise, A | *Epitaphs and Inscriptions*, Edmonston & Douglas, Edinburgh, 1875. |
| Jervise, A | *The History and Traditions of the Land of the Lindsays*, David Douglas, Edinburgh, 1882. |
| Joceline | *Life of St Kentigern in The Historians of Scotland* 10 vols, Edinburgh, 1871-80. |
| Jones, G & Jones,T | *The Mabinogion*, Everyman, London, 1994. |
| Jones, G | *Erik the Red and other Icelandic Tales,* Oxford University Press, London, 1961. |
| Kenyatta, J | *Facing Mount Kenya*, Heinemann, London, 1979. |
| Knight, GAF | *Archaeological Light on The Early Christianising of Scotland*, J Clarke & Co, London 1933. |
| Koch, JT | *The Gododdin of Aneurin*, University of Wales Press, Cardiff, 1997. |
| Laing, A | *Lindores Abbey and the Burgh of Newburgh*, Edinburgh, 1876. |
| Leslie, F | *The Early Races of Scotland,* Edmonston & Douglas, Edinburgh, 1866. |

Leslie, Jhone — *Historie of Scotland* 8 vols, Blackwood, Edinburgh, 1888-95.

Lethbridge, TC — *Witches: investigating an ancient religion*, Routledge & Kegan Paul, London, 1962.

Loomis, RS — *Arthurian Literature in the Middle Ages*, Clarendon Press, Oxford, 1959.

Loomis, RS — *Arthurian Tradition and Chretien de Troyes*, Columbia University Press, NY, 1949.

Loomis, RS — *Celtic Myth and Arthurian Romance*, Constable, London, 1995.

MacCulloch, JA — *The Celtic and Scandinavian religions*, Constable, London, 1994.

MacCulloch, JA — *The Religion of the Ancient Celts*, Constable, London, 1992.

McHardy, SA — *The Folklore of the Picts in Stones, Symbols and Stories; Aspects of Pictish Studies*, Pictish Arts Society, Edinburgh, 1994.

McHardy, SA — *The Quest for Arthur*, Luath Press, Edinburgh, 2001.

McHardy, SA — *The wee dark fowk o Scotland, in The Worm, the Germ and the Thorn, Essays presented to Isabel Henderson*, Pinkfoot Press, Forfar, 1997.

Mackay, JG — *The Deer-goddess and the Deer-Goddess Cult in Scotland in Folklore* vol 51(1934.

Mackenzie, DA — *Crete, Myths and Legends*, Senate, London, 1995.

Mackenzie, DA — *Egyptian Myth and Legend*, Gresham, London, 1913.

Mackenzie, DA — *Pre-Hellenic Myths and Legends*, Senate, London, 1995.

Mackenzie, DA — *Scottish Folklore and Folklife*, Blackie, London & Glasgow, 1935.

Mackenzie, DA — *Teutonic Myth and Legend*, Senate, London, 1995.

Mackinlay, JM — *Ancient Church Dedications in Scotland* 2 vols, David Douglas, Edinburgh, 1910-14.

Mackinlay, J — *Folklore of Scottish Lochs and Springs*, W Hodge & Co, Glasgow, 1893.

Mackinlay, JF — *Traces of the Cultus of the Nine Maidens in*

1: This book was actually published ( originally ) in c 1917. Is the one cited above a reprint?

|  | *Proceedings of the Society of Antiquaries of Scotland* vol 1910 |
| Maclean, J | *Translations of names of places on the Breadalbane Estates*, Edinburgh, 1887. |
| McNeill, M | *The Silver Bough* 4 vols, Wm McLellan, Glasgow 1953-61. |
| Malory, T | *Morte d'Arthur,* Penguin, London, 1969. |
| Markale, J | *The Celts,* Inner Traditions International, Vermont 1993. |
| Markale, J | *The Women of the Celts,* Inner Traditions International, Vermont 1986. |
| Martin, M | *A Description of the Western Isles of Scotland 1697,* J Thin, Edinburgh, 1970. |
| *The Metrical Dinshenchas* | see Gwynn, E |
| Morris, K | *Sorceress or Witch,* University Press of America, Lanham and London, 1991. |
| *New Larousse Encyclopaedia of Mythology,* London, 1968. | |
| Newall, V | *The Witch Figure,* Routledge & Kegan Paul, London, 1973. |
| Newman, P | *The Hill of the Dragon,* Kingsmead, Bath, 1979. |
| Parry, JJ | *The Vita Merlini* in *University of Illinois Studies in Language and Literature,* Uni Illinois Press, 1925. |
| Paton, LA | *Studies on the Fairy Mythology of Arthurian Romance,* Burt Franklin, NY, 1960. |
| Pennant, T | *A Tour in Scotland,* Printed for Benj White, London, 1774. |
| Polson A | *Scottish Witchcraft Lore,* W Alexander & Son, Inverness, 1932. |
| Pratt, J | *Buchan,* Lewis Smith, Aberdeen, 1870. |
| Ramsay, J | *Scotland and Scotsmen in the 18th Century,* Wm Blackwood & Sons, Edinburgh, 1888. |
| Rees, A & Rees, B | *Celtic Heritage,* Thames & Hudson, London, 1990. |
| Rolleston, TW | *Celtic Myths and Legends,* Bracken Books, London, 1995. |
| Ross, A | *Pagan Celtic Britain,* Constable, London, 1992. |
| Rufus, A & Lawson, K | *Goddess Sites in Europe,* HarperSanfrancisco NY, 1990. |

get it

| | |
|---|---|
| Rydberg, V | *Teutonic Mythology* trans. Anderson, RB; Swan, Sonnenschein & Co, London, 1889. |
| Santillana, G, de | See De Santillana |
| Sebillot, P | *Le Folk-lore de France*, Maisonneuve et Larose, Paris, 1968. |
| Sinclair, D | *Satan's Invisible World Discovered*, Glasgow, 1840. |
| Skene, WF | *Celtic Scotland* 4 vols, David Douglas, Edinburgh, 1886-90. |
| Skene, WF | *Arthur and the Britons in Wales and Scotland*, Llanerch, Felinfach, Wales 1988. |
| Small, A | *Some Interesting Roman Antiquities recently discovered in Fife*, Anderson, Edinburgh, 1823. |
| Smyth, ALF | *Warlords and Holy Men*, Edward Arnold, London, 1984. |
| Spalding Club | *Collections on the shires of Aberdeen and Banff*, Aberdeen, 1863. |
| Spence, L | *The History of Druidism*, Newcastle Publishing, California 1995. |
| Spence, L | *Legends and Romance of Brittany*, Constable, London, 1977. |
| Spence, L | *The Magic Arts in Celtic Britain*, Constable, London, 1995. |
| Spence, L | *Minor Traditions of British Mythology*, Rider & Co, London, 1948. |
| Spence, L | *The Mysteries of Britain*, Newcastle Publishing, California, 1993. |
| Spence, L | *Shetland Folk Lore*, 1899. |
| Swire, O | *The Inner Hebrides and Their Legends*, Collins, London, 1964. |
| Swire, O | *The Outer Hebrides and Their Legends*, Oliver & Boyd, Edinburgh, 1966. |
| Taliesin | *The Book of Taliesin*, ed JG Evans, Llanbedrog, 1910. |
| Thompson, DP | *On the Slopes of the Sidlaws*, Munro Press, Perth, 1953. |

*Third Statistical Account of Scotland; Perth and Kinross*, Edinburgh, 1979.

| | |
|---|---|
| Tranter, N | *Argyll and Bute*, Hodder & Stoughton, London, 1977. |
| Turnbull, W, ed | *Stewart's Metrical translation of Boece*, London, 1858. |
| Vitaliano, DB | *Legends of the Earth, their geologic origin*, Indiana University Press, Bloomington, 1973. |
| Walters, D | *Chinese Mythology*, Aquarian, London, 1992. |
| Warden, AJ | *Angus or Forfarshire* 5 vols, C Alexander & Co, Dundee, 1880-85. |
| Watson, L | *Gifts of Unknown Things*, Coronet, Sevenoaks, 1977. |
| Watson, WJ | *The Celtic Placenames of Scotland*, Birlinn, Edinburgh, 1993. |
| Wheater, H | *A Guide in hand to Kenmore and Loch Tay*, Keltneyburn, Perthshire, 1980. |
| Wilson, D | *Memorials of Edinburgh in the Olden Time*, A&C, Black, Edinburgh, 1891. |
| Wimberley, LC | *Folklore of the English and Scottish Ballads*, Chicago, 1928. |

# Index

# Some other books published by **LUATH** PRESS

## THE QUEST FOR

### The Quest for Arthur
Stuart McHardy
ISBN 1 84282 012 5 HBK £16.99

King Arthur of Camelot and the Knights of the Round Table are enduring romantic figures. A national hero for the Bretons, the Welsh and the English alike Arthur is a potent figure for many.

This quest leads to a radical new interpretation of the ancient myth.

Historian, storyteller and folklorist Stuart McHardy believes he has uncovered the origins of this inspirational figure, the true Arthur. He incorporates knowledge of folklore and placename studies with an archaeological understanding of the 6th century.

Combining knowledge of the earliest records and histories of Arthur with an awareness of the importance of oral traditions, this quest leads to the discovery that the enigmatic origins of Arthur lie not in Brittany or England or Wales. Instead they lie in that magic land the ancient Welsh called Y Gogledd, the North; the North of Britain which we now call Scotland.

### The Quest for the Celtic Key
Karen Ralls-MacLeod and
Ian Robertson
ISBN 0 946487 73 1 HB £18.99

Who were the Picts? The Druids? The Celtic saints?

Was the famous 'murdered Apprentice' carving at Rosslyn Chapel deliberately altered in the past? If so, why?

Why has Rossslyn Chapel been a worldwide mecca for churchmen, Freemasons, Knights Templar, and Rosicrucians?

Why are there so many Scottish connections to King Arthur and Merlin?

What was the famous 'Blue Blanket' of the medieval Guilds of Edinburgh?

Did Prince Henry Sinclair get to North America before Columbus?

*'The reader who travels with Karen Ralls-MacLeod and Ian Robertson...will find a travelogue which enriches the mythologies and histories so beautifully told, with many newly wrought connections to places, buildings, stones and other remains which may still be viewed in the landscape and historic monuments of modern Scotland....'*

Rev. Dr. Michael Northcott, FACULTY OF DIVINITY, UNIVERSITY OF EDINBURGH

*'Karen Ralls-MacLeod is endowed with that rare jewel of academia: a sharp and inquisitive mind blessed with a refreshing openness. Her stimulating work has the gift of making the academic accessible, and brings a clear and sound basis to the experiential... from 'Idylls of the King' to 'Indiana Jones', the search for the Holy Grail will never be the same again. This is a 'must read' book for all who sense the mystery and magic of our distant past....'*

Robert Bauval, BESTSELLING AUTHOR OF 'THE SECRET CHAMBER', 'KEEPER OF GENESIS'

## FOLKLORE

### Scotland: Myth, Legend and Folklore
Stuart McHardy
ISBN 0 946487 69 3 PBK 7.99

Who were the people who built the megaliths?

What great warriors sleep beneath the Hollow Hills?

Were the early Scottish saints just pagans in disguise?

Was King Arthur really Scottish?

When was Nessie first sighted?

This is a book about Scotland drawn from hundreds, if not thousands of years of storytelling. From the oral traditions of the Scots, Gaelic and Norse speakers of the past, it presents a new picture of who the Scottish are and where they come from. The stories that McHardy recounts may be hilarious, tragic, heroic, frightening or just plain bizzare, but they all provide an insight into a unique tradition of myth, legend and folklore that has marked both the language and landscape of Scotland.

## The Supernatural Highlands

Francis Thompson
ISBN 0 946487 31 6  PBK  £8.99

An authoritative exploration of the otherworld of the Highlander, happenings and beings hitherto thought to be outwith the ordinary forces of nature. A simple introduction to the way of life of rural Highland and Island communities, this new edition weaves a path through second sight, the evil eye, witchcraft, ghosts, fairies and other supernatural beings, offering new sight-lines on areas of belief once dismissed as folklore and superstition.

## Luath Storyteller: Highland Myths & Legends

George W. Macpherson
ISBN 1 84282 003 6 PBK £5.00

The mythical, the legendary, the true… This is the stuff of stories and storytellers, the stuff of an age-old tradition in almost every country in the world, and none more so than Scotland. Celtic heroes, Fairies, Druids, Selkies, Sea horses, Magicians, Giants, Viking invaders; all feature in this collection of traditional Scottish tales, the like of which were told round camp fires centuries ago, and are still told today.

George W. Macpherson has dipped into his phenomenal repertoire of tales to compile this diverse collection of traditional stories,

designed to be read aloud. Each has been passed from generation to generation, some are two and a half thousand years old.

From the Celtic legends of Cuchullin and Fionn to the mythical tales of seal-people and magicians these stories have a timeless quality. Often, strands of the stories will interweave and cross over, building a delicate tapestry of Scotland as a mystical, enchanted land. *'The result is vivid and impressive, conveying the tragic dignity of the ancient warrior, or the devoted love of the seal woman and her fisher mate. The personalities and circumstances of people long gone are brought fully to life by the power of the story-teller's words. The ancestors take form before us in the visual imagination.'*
DR DONALD SMITH, THE SCOTTISH STORYTELLING CENTRE

*'one of Scotland's best storytellers'*
WESTDEUTSCHER RUNDFUNK KOHN

*'I loved all your stories, some were sad and some were great. We all hope to see you another day'*
SARAH BOCCACCIO, ECOLE PRIMAIRE INTERNATIONALE

*'This is your genuine article'*
MARK FISHER, THE LIST

*'Legend and myth join with humour and gentle wit to create a special magic'*
JOY HENDRY, SCOTSMAN

## Tales from the North Coast

Alan Temperley
ISBN 0 946487 18 9  PBK  £8.99

Seals and shipwrecks, witches and fairies, curses and clearances, fact and fantasy – the authentic tales in this collection come straight from the heart of a small Highland community. Children and adults alike responsd to their timeless appeal. These *Tales of the North Coast* were collected in the early 1970s by Alan Temperley and young people at Farr Secondary School in Sutherland. All the stories were gathered from the area between the Kyle of Tongue and Strath Halladale, in scattered communities wonderfully rich in lore that had been passed on by word of mouth down the generations. This wide-ranging selection provides a satisying balance between intriguing tales of the supernatural and more everyday occurrences. The book also includes chilling eye-witness accounts of the notorious Strathnaver Clearances when tenants were given a few hours to pack up and get out of their homes, which were then burned to the ground.

Underlying the continuity through the generations, this new edition has a foreward by Jim Johnston, the head teacher at Farr, and includes the vigorous linocut images produced by the young people under the guidance of their art teacher, Elliot Rudie.

Since the original publication of this book, Alan Temperley has gone on to become a highly regarded writer for children.

'The general reader will find this book's spontaneity, its pictures by the children and its fun utterly charming.'
SCOTTISH REVIEW

'An admirable book which should serve as an encouragement to other districts to gather what remains of their heritage of folk-tales.'
SCOTTISH EDUCATION JOURNAL

# POETRY

### Scots Poems to be Read Aloud

Collectit an wi an innin by
Stuart McHardy

ISBN 0 946487 81 2  PBK  £5.00

This personal collection of well-known and not-so-well-known Scots poems to read aloud includes great works of art and simple pieces of questionable 'literary merit'.

'Scots Poems to be Read Aloud is pure entertainment – at home, on a stag or a hen night, Hogmanay, Burns Night, in fact any party night.'
SUNDAY POST

# POLITICS & CURRENT ISSUES

### Scotlands of the Mind

Angus Calder
ISBN 1 84282 008 7  PB  £9.99

### Trident on Trial: the case for people's disarmament

Angie Zelter
ISBN 1 84282 004 4  PB  £9.99

### Uncomfortably Numb: A Prison Requiem

Maureen Maguire
ISBN 1 84282 001 X  PB  £8.99

### Scotland: Land & Power – Agenda for Land Reform

Andy Wightman
ISBN 0 946487 70 7  PB  £5.00

### Old Scotland New Scotland

Jeff Fallow
ISBN 0 946487 40 5  PB  £6.99

### Some Assembly Required: Scottish Parliament

David Shepherd
ISBN 0 946487 84 7  PB  £7.99

### Notes from the North

Emma Wood
ISBN 0 946487 46 4  PB  £8.99

# NATURAL WORLD

### The Hydro Boys: pioneers of renewable energy

Emma Wood
ISBN 1 84282 016 8  HB  £16.99

### Wild Scotland

James McCarthy
ISBN 0 946487 37 5  PB  £7.50

### Wild Lives: Otters – On the Swirl of the Tide

Bridget MacCaskill
ISBN 0 946487 67 7  PB  £9.99

**Wild Lives: Foxes – The Blood is Wild**
Bridget MacCaskill
ISBN 0 946487 71 5  PB  £9.99

**Scotland – Land & People: An Inhabited Solitude**
James McCarthy
ISBN 0 946487 57 X  PB  £7.99

**The Highland Geology Trail**
John L Roberts
ISBN 0 946487 36 7  PB  £4.99

**'Nothing but Heather!'**
Gerry Cambridge
ISBN 0 946487 49 9  PB  £15.00

**Red Sky at Night**
John Barrington
ISBN 0 946487 60 X  PB  £8.99

**Listen to the Trees**
Don MacCaskill
ISBN 0 946487 65 0  PB  £9.99

## ISLANDS

**The Islands that Roofed the World: Easdale, Belnahua, Luing & Seil:**
Mary Withall
ISBN 0 946487 76 6  PB  £4.99

**Rum: Nature's Island**
Magnus Magnusson
ISBN 0 946487 32 4  PB  £7.95

## LUATH GUIDES TO SCOTLAND

**The North West Highlands: Roads to the Isles**
Tom Atkinson
ISBN 0 946487 54 5  PB  £4.95

**Mull and Iona: Highways and Byways**
Peter Macnab
ISBN 0 946487 58 8  PB  £4.95

**The Northern Highlands: The Empty Lands**
Tom Atkinson
ISBN 0 946487 55 3  PB  £4.95

**The West Highlands: The Lonely Lands**
Tom Atkinson
ISBN 0 946487 56 1  PB  £4.95

**South West Scotland**
Tom Atkinson
ISBN 0 946487 04 9  PB  £4.95

## TRAVEL & LEISURE

**Die Kleine Schottlandfibel [Scotland Guide in German]**
Hans-Walter Arends
ISBN 0 946487 89 8  PB  £8.99

**Let's Explore Edinburgh Old Town**
Anne Bruce English
ISBN 0 946487 98 7  PB  £4.99

**Edinburgh's Historic Mile**
Duncan Priddle
ISBN 0 946487 97 9  PB  £2.99

**Pilgrims in the Rough: St Andrews beyond the 19th hole**
Michael Tobert
ISBN 0 946487 74 X  PB  £7.99

## FOOD & DRINK

**The Whisky Muse: Scotch whisky in poem & song**
various, ed. Robin Laing
ISBN 0 946487 95 2  PB  £12.99

**First Foods Fast: how to prepare good simple meals for your baby**
Lara Boyd
ISBN 1 84282 002 8 PB £4.99

**Edinburgh and Leith Pub Guide**
Stuart McHardy
ISBN 0 946487 80 4 PB £4.95

## WALK WITH LUATH

**Skye 360: walking the coastline of Skye**
Andrew Dempster
ISBN 0 946487 85 5 PB £8.99

**Walks in the Cairngorms**
Ernest Cross
ISBN 0 946487 09 X PB £4.95

**Short Walks in the Cairngorms**
Ernest Cross
ISBN 0 946487 23 5 PB £4.95

**The Joy of Hillwalking**
Ralph Storer
ISBN 0 946487 28 6 PB £7.50

**Scotland's Mountains before the Mountaineers**
Ian R Mitchell
ISBN 0 946487 39 1 PB £9.99

**Mountain Days and Bothy Nights**
Dave Brown and Ian R Mitchell
ISBN 0 946487 15 4 PB £7.50

## SPORT

**Ski & Snowboard Scotland**
Hilary Parke
ISBN 0 946487 35 9 PB £6.99

**Over the Top with the Tartan Army**
Andy McArthur
ISBN 0 946487 45 6 PB £7.99

## BIOGRAPHY

**The Last Lighthouse**
Sharma Krauskopf
ISBN 0 946487 96 0 PB £7.99

**Tobermory Teuchter**
Peter Macnab
ISBN 0 946487 41 3 PB £7.99

**Bare Feet and Tackety Boots**
Archie Cameron
ISBN 0 946487 17 0 PB £7.95

**Come Dungeons Dark**
John Taylor Caldwell
ISBN 0 946487 19 7 PB £6.95

## HISTORY

**Civil Warrior**
Robin Bell
ISBN 1 84282 013 3 HB £10.99

**A Passion for Scotland**
David R Ross
ISBN 1 84282 019 2 PB £5.99

**Reportage Scotland**
Louise Yeoman
ISBN 0 946487 61 8 PB £9.99

**Blind Harry's Wallace**
Hamilton of Gilbert-
ISBN 0 946487 33 2 PB £8.99

**Blind Harry's Wallace**
field [intro/ed Elspeth King]
ISBN 0 946487 43 X HB £15.00

**Plaids and Bandanas: from Highland Drover to Wild West Cowboy**
Rob Gibson
ISBN 0 946487 88 X HB £7.99

## SOCIAL HISTORY

### Pumpherston: the story of a shale oil village
Sybil Cavanagh
ISBN 1 84282 011 7 HB £17.99
ISBN 1 84282 015 X PB £7.99

### Shale Voices
Alistair Findlay
ISBN 0 946487 78 2 HB £17.99
ISBN 0 946487 63 4 PB £10.99

### A Word for Scotland
Jack Campbell
ISBN 0 946487 48 0 PB £12.99

## ON THE TRAIL OF

### On the Trail of William Wallace
David R Ross
ISBN 0 946487 47 2 PB £7.99

### On the Trail of Robert the Bruce
David R Ross
ISBN 0 946487 52 9 PB £7.99

### On the Trail of Mary Queen of Scots
J Keith Cheetham
ISBN 0 946487 50 2 PB £7.99

### On the Trail of Bonnie Prince Charlie
David R Ross
ISBN 0 946487 68 5 PB £7.99

### On the Trail of Robert Burns
John Cairney
ISBN 0 946487 51 0 PB £7.99

### On the Trail of John Muir
Cherry Good
ISBN 0 946487 62 6 PB £7.99

### On the Trail of Queen Victoria in the Highlands
Ian R Mitchell
ISBN 0 946487 79 0 PB £7.99

### On the Trail of Robert Service
G Wallace Lockhart
ISBN 0 946487 24 3 PB £7.99

### On the Trail of the Pilgrim Fathers
J Keith Cheetham
ISBN 0 946487 83 9 PB £7.99

## GENEALOGY

### Scottish Roots: step-by-step guide for ancestor hunters
Alwyn James
ISBN 1 84282 007 9 PB £9.99

## WEDDINGS, MUSIC AND DANCE

### The Scottish Wedding Book
G Wallace Lockhart
ISBN 1 94282 010 9 PB £12.99

### Fiddles and Folk
G Wallace Lockhart
ISBN 0 946487 38 3 PB £7.95

### Highland Balls and Village Halls
G Wallace Lockhart
ISBN 0 946487 12 X PB £6.95

## POETRY

### Bad Ass Raindrop
Kokumo Rocks
ISBN 1 84282 018 4 PB £6.99

### Caledonian Cramboclink: the Poetry of
William Neill
ISBN 0 946487 53 7 PB £8.99

### Men and Beasts: wild men & tame animals
Val Gillies & Rebecca Marr
ISBN 0 946487 92 8 PB £15.00

**Luath Burns Companion**
John Cairney
ISBN 1 84282 000 1  PB  £10.00

**Poems to be read aloud**
Collected and introduced by Tom Atkinson
ISBN 0 946487 00 6  PB  £5.00

**Madame Fife's Farewell and Other Poems**
Gerry Cambridge
ISBN 1 84282 005 2  PB  £8.99

**Picking Brambles and Other Poems**
Des Dillon
ISBN 1 84282 021 4  PB  £6.99

**Kate o Shanter's Tale and Other Poems**
Matthew Fitt
ISBN 1 84282 025 1  PB  £6.99

**Immortal Memories**
Selected and edited by John Cairney
ISBN 1 84282 009 5  HB  £20.00

## CARTOONS

**Broomie Law**
Cinders McLeod
ISBN 0 946487 99 5  PB  £4.00

## FICTION

**The Road Dance**
John MacKay
ISBN 1 84282 024 9  PB  £9.99

**Milk Treading**
Nick Smith
ISBN 0 946487 75 8  PB  £9.99

**The Strange Case of RL Stevenson**
Richard Woodhead
ISBN 0 946487 86 3  HB  £16.99

**But n Ben A-Go-Go**
Matthew Fitt
ISBN 1 84282 014 1  PB  £6.99

**But n Ben A-Go-Go**
Matthew Fitt
ISBN 0 946487 82 0  HB  £10.99

**Grave Robbers**
Robin Mitchell
ISBN 0 946487 72 3  PB  £7.99

**The Bannockburn Years**
William Scott
ISBN 0 946487 34 0  PB  £7.95

**The Great Melnikov**
Hugh MacLachlan
ISBN 0 946487 42 1  PB  £7.95

## LANGUAGE

**Luath Scots Language Learner [Book]**
L Colin Wilson
ISBN 0 946487 91 X  PB  £9.99

**Luath Scots Language Learner [Double Audio CD Set]**
L Colin Wilson
ISBN 1 84282 026 5  CD  £16.99

## **Luath** Press Limited
*committed to publishing well written books worth reading*

LUATH PRESS takes its name from Robert Burns, whose little collie Luath (*Gael.*, swift or nimble) tripped up Jean Armour at a wedding and gave him the chance to speak to the woman who was to be his wife and the abiding love of his life. Burns called one of *The Twa Dogs* Luath after Cuchullin's hunting dog in *Ossian's Fingal*. Luath Press grew up in the heart of Burns country, and now resides a few steps up the road from Burns' first lodgings in Edinburgh's Royal Mile.

Luath offers you distinctive writing with a hint of unexpected pleasures.

Most UK and US bookshops either carry our books in stock or can order them for you. To order direct from us, please send a £sterling cheque, postal order, international money order or your credit card details (number, address of cardholder and expiry date) to us at the address below. Please add post and packing as follows: UK – £1.00 per delivery address; overseas surface mail – £2.50 per delivery address; overseas airmail – £3.50 for the first book to each delivery address, plus £1.00 for each additional book by airmail to the same address. If your order is a gift, we will happily enclose your card or message at no extra charge.

**Luath** Press Limited
543/2 Castlehill
The Royal Mile
Edinburgh EH1 2ND
Scotland
Telephone: 0131 225 4326 (24 hours)
Fax: 0131 225 4324
email: gavin.macdougall@luath.co.uk
Website: www.luath.co.uk